PALEOINDIAN OCCUPATION

Of the Central Rio Grande Valley in New Mexico

W. James Judge

UNIVERSITY OF NEW MEXICO PRESS
Albuquerque

PREFACE

The following study is in essence a verbatim reproduction of my doctoral dissertation. Only very minor changes were made in the original draft prior to publication. As with any dissertation, mine was written for review by university faculty members sympathetic to the fact that graduate students are not necessarily good writers. In my case, elements of style generally considered unpalatable for popular consumption were allowed to pass. For this situation, I offer my sincere apologies and genuine sympathy to the general reader.

On the other hand, I do not apologize for errors of content in theory, methodology, or analyses which follow. None were committed deliberately. I have often discussed the problems of writing and publishing dissertation research with other members of my profession, students and faculty alike, and many have expressed reservations about the idea of publication in the absence of extensive revision of content. I do not necessarily agree with this position, which seems to view graduate research as a compromise between a true commitment to science on the one hand and the irrational demands of a doctoral committee on the other. I feel that if doctoral research is worth undertaking, then it certainly merits the review and scrutiny of one's colleagues. After all, one learns through mistakes. Hopefully others can profit by mine.

iii

I am indebted to a great many people for their advice, encouragement, and assistance throughout my period of graduate study. W. W. Hill provided the initial stimulus toward a career in anthropology, a stimulus which was maintained by the other members of the Anthropology department at the University of New Mexico. I am extremely grateful to all of them.

My most sincere thanks go to Ele and Jewel Baker and Jerry Dawson, who initiated this survey on their own many years before I met them. They not only encouraged and assisted me but also made available to me their own personal collections, the analysis of which constitutes a major portion of this study. I also thank Dennis Stanford for his help in the survey and analytic phases and also for his enthusiasm for dirt archeology, which I found to be contagious. Most of the ideas presented herein are not original with me, but are instead a synthesis of extensive discussion with all of these people.

Many others assisted me in this effort. Among those in the Albuquerque area who were particularly helpful were Terry Booth, Cynthia Irwin-Williams, Bill Jacoby, Ted Reinhart, Bill Roosa, and Frank Vernon. Elsewhere others graciously made available their collections for comparative analysis. George Agogino, Keith Classock, J. P. Mathieson, Jim Warnica, and Bob Weber were particularly helpful in this regard. I am deeply indebted to them, and to the many others in the area who were concerned enough about archeology to bring their discoveries to the attention of the University of New Mexico.

Collections and analytic facilities of the Maxwell Museum of Anthropology were made available to me by Jerry Brody and Ron Switzer, who went out of their way to offer assistance whenever it was needed. Computing facilities, as well as computer time, were granted by the University of New Mexico Computing Center. My own graduate work was supported first by a graduate assistantship and later by a National Science Foundation Graduate Traineeship. The survey was supported in part by a grant from the American Philosophical Society. This research and financial assistance is greatly appreciated.

Finally, my most deeply-felt debt of gratitude goes to my wife and children, whose patience, endurance, and understanding are alone responsible for the completion of this study.

TABLE OF CONTENTS

LIST OF FIGURES

List of Figures (Continued)

viii

LIST OF TABLES

Table of Contents (Continued)

CHAPTER I

The Archeological Survey: An Analytical Model

General Theoretical Framework

An underlying assumption of the present study is that within any geographical region selected for archeological investigation, an adequate knowledge of the archeology of the area is a prerequisite to problem-oriented excavation of sites found therein. By "adequate knowledge" I am implying more than an elementary descriptive acquaintance with the archeological manifestations in the region. Such an assumption, I believe, falls within the framework of recent developments in archeological theory.

Within the past few years, American archeology has experienced a pronounced shift in theoretical perspective (Binford and Binford 1968). As a result, archeologists have become more acutely aware of the potential contribution to the total discipline of anthropology afforded them by the application of modern theory and method in archeology. As Streuver has illustrated, the emphasis on the exploration of cultural process is now "an operational problem for archeologists" (1968:131). It is within this framework that the following study is presented.

To an archeologist, especially one dealing with early hunting groups, culture is best viewed as a component of an ecosystem, in

which the relationship that exists between the cultural system and the
environment is emphasized. This relationship is manifest materially
by both the artifact assemblage itself and its context within the ecosystem, and thus the analysis of these variables becomes critical to
the success of problem-oriented archeological research. Such an
analysis can be termed technological in nature, and the primary focus
of the ensuing study is on the technology of cultural systems.

Technology is considered herein in its broadest scope, not simply
in its mechanical or scientific context. It is fundamentally cultural in
nature, and to the extent that culture is primarily an adaptive mechanism
(White 1959, Cohen 1968), technology is that key component through
which the cultural system achieves adaptive success. Binford has
defined technology as "those tools and social relationships which articulate the organism with the physical environment" (1962:218), and
assuming the word "tool" can be considered in its broadest sense, this
will be the definition accepted here. The primary task of the archeologist thus becomes one of identifying the components of past technologies as manifest materially, examining the nature in which these components articulate with the environment, and explaining the cultural
processes responsible for these patterns of articulation.

In any cultural system, extinct or extant, there are a number of
different types of technological components which can be isolated and
defined by the researcher. I would suggest that the one most important

to archeological research is that which I will label "technology of settlement." Viewed from a broad rather than limited perspective, technology of settlement can be defined as the selection by a cultural system of certain key components of the physical and natural environment for the enactment of specific cultural activities. It involves the interaction of social organization, material culture, and subsistence strategy with both the physical, natural, and social environments. Settlement technology is therefore intimately related to cultural process and as such is of primary importance to archeological investigation.

Assuming this is a valid concept, I maintain that at the regional level of analysis an adequate knowledge of settlement technology is not only essential, but critical, to the definition of problems and the generation of hypotheses for intensive archeological research. It is toward the attainment of such knowledge that this study was directed, and it was felt that only through the implementation of an analytic archeological survey could this goal be attained.

The utility of the regional survey is not a new concept in archeology. In fact, one of the earlier surveys in the Southwest was undertaken by Reginald Fisher (1930), in the same general area dealt with by this study. However, I do not believe that an archeological survey in the traditional sense is necessarily compatible with recent advances in archeological theory, nor does it provide the kinds of data which are

necessary to the formulation of problems relevant to modern anthropological inquiry. I feel that at the regional level, the minimal purpose
of the survey should be the initial formulation of a taxonomy of settlement strategies, and to achieve this, the survey must be analytic, not
just descriptive.

As noted previously, settlement technology involves the interaction
of cultural and environmental variables. Such interaction is patterned,
and the material manifestation of this patterning will upon analysis
reveal an initial taxonomy of settlement strategy. I use the term
"initial" in the sense that the taxonomy must later be verified empirically through actual excavation of sites in the survey region. Prior
to this, however, all the components, cultural and environmental, must
be analyzed to the fullest extent permitted by the nature and quantity of
the data available to the researcher. Only then can the results of the
survey be considered valid enough for further testing by actual site
excavation.

In the past, archeological surveys have been primarily descriptive
in nature. Concentration has been on recording the number of sites in
a given geographical region, with a breakdown of the types of sites and
their location by township, county and section. Since this type of report
is of only limited utility, it is perhaps justifiable that many archeologists
have either ignored or perhaps lost interest in the analytic potential
afforded by an archeological survey. Ruppe noted this in his defense
of the survey, and his statement is worth quoting in full:

There appears to be a widespread feeling that the survey alone
can elucidate only a small amount of the total attributes of an
archeological site. It is probable that many data available on
the surface have been ignored and consequently lost. It is equally
probable that many investigators have failed to extract as much
information from a survey as they could have, had they not held
a preconceived notion about the limited utility of a survey (Ruppe
1966:313).

There is, then, little doubt about the need for updating survey techni-

ques to make them compatible with existing advances in theory and

analytic methods. Recently, there seems to have been an increasing

awareness on the part of archeologists of the key role the survey can

take. Hole and Heizer, for instance, note that "regional studies are

the firmest ground work for future excavation. In fact, serious archeo-

logy is predicated on such surveys" (1969:128). Binford (1964) and

Streuver (1968) are among those who have emphasized the importance

of the survey in the over-all research design.

In addition, there have been a number of attempts to carry this

beyond the stage of rhetoric to field application. Foremost among these

is the work of Plog (1968), who has dealt specifically with the role of

the archeological survey in terms of the most recent advances in

theory.[1] Another example is that of Ruppe, who has presented a classi-

fication of surveys, including one which involves "an intensive study of

a local area designed to extract all possible information from the surface

---

[1]Plog's excellent thesis came to my attention after the theoretical
foundation of this study had been formulated, and after most of the
fieldwork and initial analysis had been completed. He has generously
permitted me the opportunity to quote parts of his work.

6

of every site that can be found" (1966:315). Ruppe's concept of the
survey indicates an awareness of the degree to which an intensive survey can stand by itself as an important contribution to the discipline in
addition to supplying the basic descriptive information.

As an example of a survey which does not quite meet these stand-
ards, I would mention the work of Prufer and Baby (1963) which deals
with the PaleoIndians of Ohio. This is an excellent survey in the traditional sense, and a genuine contribution to the field of PaleoIndian
studies. It goes somewhat beyond the descriptive state, and provides
an interpretative analysis of the early occupation of the region. Its
shortcomings should nevertheless be pointed out. Although selected
portions of the data are examined, there is no complete, exhaustive
analysis of all the data available. For instance, most of the quantitative treatment deals only with projectile point length, thus limiting the
sample to complete points. There is in addition a general neglect of
the environmental components and the manner in which the lithic variables interact with them. I mention this only to illustrate that while
interpretations were offered, a great deal of information was neglected
to the detriment of future problem-oriented studies of the PaleoIndian
in Ohio. While it is true that future investigators presumably could
reanalyze the data themselves to determine the nature of the problems
and the manner in which to solve them, I feel that the original survey
researcher is obligated to provide a complete analysis since it is he
who is most familiar with the data and its sources.

I would suggest that the nature of the archeological information
which will eventually be derived from any particular geographical region will in large part be a function of the quality of the initial survey
of the area. The primary purpose of the survey should be one of problem definition based on an intensive and exhaustive analysis of the
empirical material derived. Furthermore, the problems defined should
be relevant to the explanation of cultural process, and their solutions
should lie within reach of further research within the survey region.
A secondary purpose of the survey might well go beyond problem definition and involve the explanation of cultural process based on the survey data itself. The extent to which this goal can be achieved will be
a function of both the qualitative and quantitative aspects of the data,
and for this reason I do not consider it the primary purpose of the survey. It is extremely important, however, that the researcher attempt
to carry out this type of interpretation wherever possible, since any
success realized will advance considerably the degree to which the
survey will contribute to future research.

Plog has offered a review and redefinition of the survey in terms
of site location: "Survey archeology is the discovery and use of variation in the location of sites of prehistoric activity to test hypotheses
concerning the cultural processes which produced the sites" (1968:6).
Since his emphasis is on the geographical components, Plog demonstrates his research strategy by applying various statistical techniques

of locational analysis to test a specific hypothesis. This is certainly a significant advance in the exploitation of the survey potential. The problem with this strategy, as I see it, is that it is predicated upon the formulation of a testable hypothesis prior to the initiation of the survey. This assumes that sufficient research has been done on the cultures involved to permit the formulation of relevant hypotheses. I doubt that this is always the case, though, and since I feel that the survey should be the first step in the implementation of problem-oriented research in a region, it is the survey itself which must supply the problems from which testable hypotheses can be deduced.

Problem definition can result only from an intensive analysis of all the components which comprise the data, and not just those which serve to test a given hypothesis. For this reason I would suggest that the orientation of survey methods toward the derivation of a settlement technology will maximize the amount of interpretative information which can be derived from the survey data. I do not feel that this viewpoint is incompatible with that presented by Plog, since the analysis of settlement technology will involve the testing of hypotheses wherever possible. Instead I believe that the difference lies in the viewpoint of the priority of objectives which the archeological survey should undertake.

I would define an archeological survey as the collection and intensive analysis of those cultural and natural variables attainable through the investigation and observation of surface assemblages in their environmental context. Its purpose is to formulate hypotheses relevant to settlement technology which are testable by actual excavation, or if possible, by further analysis of the survey data. Such a survey, when carried out successfully, will describe the various archeological assemblages encountered, analyze the component attributes responsible for the articulation of cultural and natural variables, explain cultural process whenever possible, and direct the course of future work in the field by isolating the critical problems to be tested through excavation. As an incidental benefit, such an approach would also be helpful in extablishing relative priorities should urgent archeology become necessary in the survey area.

There is one factor limiting the implementation of this type of survey. In undertaking an intensive analysis of this nature, the investigator must necessarily restrict his research to one specific stage of cultural development (e.g., PaleoIndian, Archaic, Formative, etc.). Such a limitation will perhaps be beneficial in the long run, since sacrificing intensity for extensiveness would in effect defeat the stated purpose of the survey.

Given the definition and purpose outlined above, I would like to offer here an archeological survey model which is hopefully consistent with modern archeological theory. David L. Clarke, who has authored a comprehensive and stimulating presentation of modern archeological theory, has defined three primary spheres of archeological inquiry.

His first deals with contextual analysis (environmental attributes),

the second with specific analysis (artifact attributes), and the third

with synthesis and the formulation of generalizations (Clarke 1968:32-40).

He presents the integration of these three spheres as a generalized

procedural model for archeological research. In addition to the pro-

cedural model, he offers another basic model for the analysis of archeo-

logical entities (taxonomic structure), and finally, a model based on

general systems theory for archeological processes. The model pro-

posed herein is basically procedural, although it combines certain

elements of taxonomic and processural analysis considered minimal

to the success of an archeological survey.

An Analytical Survey Model

Models can be defined as "conceptual tools made of structured

systems of hypotheses which offer a partially accurate predictive frame-

work for the organization of data . . . These structures depend upon

the deliberate and arbitrary rejection of some elements of the data

whilst retaining other elements, which may then be arranged in a speci-

fic manner in order to obtain marked regularity" (Clarke 1968:441).

The survey model offered here is based on the assumption that an

analysis of settlement technology will result in the maximization of the

analytic potential of the empirical material derived in the survey. Al-

though this may involve the rejection of some of the data, it is compen-

sated by the explanatory potential inherent in the derivation of a

settlement technology as the concept is treated herein. In other words,
in formulating the model I have tried to strike a balance between the
necessity to exclude certain data, and the interpretative potential of
those data selected.

Certain key concepts utilized in the model have their basis in
general systems theory, and since this is a relatively new approach to
archeological research design, I will briefly define the relevant terminology.[2]

The level of inquiry here will be that of the system, in this case a
cultural system. There will be no implication that the term culture,
as defined archeologically, approaches the reality of a culture as
understood ethnographically. An archeological culture can be analyzed
as a system without the necessity of defining a social equivalent. David
L. Clarke has presented a statement regarding this enduring problem
in archeological theory which is worth extensive quoting:

> An archeological culture is not a racial group, nor a historical
> tribe, nor a linguistic unit, it is simply an archeological
> culture. Given great care, a large quantity of first class
> archeological data, rigorous use and precise definition of
> terms, and a good archeological model, then we may with a
> margin of error be able to identify an archeological entity in
> approximate social and historical terms. But this is the best
> we can do and it is in any case only one of the aims of archeolo-
> gical activity (Clarke (1968:13).

---

[2]For a basic introduction to systems theory, see Ross Ashby
(1963) and Weiner (1948). Open systems are discussed extensively by
Miller (1965), and the volume edited by Buckley (1968) deals with systems analysis in the behavioral sciences. Clarke (1968) presents a
definitive work on systems theory and archeology.

Since a cultural system is an open system, it interacts with an environment. Both the system and the environment are composed of constituent elements which include components, attributes, and subsystems. These terms are defined as follows:

1. System:

Ross Ashby (1963:227) has emphasized the difficulty of defining a system by equating it with a real entity, thus for purposes of illustrating the analytic model, a system will here be considered coeval with the term "archeological culture" as defined above (e.g., a Folsom cultural system). It is difficult to avoid a rather circular definition of a system and thus it is generally described in terms of its own elements; "a system is a set of objects together with relationships between the objects and between their attributes" (Hall and Fagen 1968:81). These "objects" will here be termed components.

2. Components:

The components of a system are its structural elements. These can be either material or non-material, and of virtually unlimited variety. Components exhibit measurable properties or attributes, and are therefore recognized as variables of the system. Components interact with each other and with the environment in differing configurations as the system is maintained in any of a number of states of equilibria or homeostasis. The system is controlled by a regulatory mechanism or "decider" (itself a component), which monitors the system output through feedback channels. The regulatory mechanism either contains or is coupled with a memory store (sometimes referred to as a template or program), thus permitting the cultural system to act '"in light of' its previous history" (Clarke 1968:65) as the regulator articulates the memory with the feedback channels. The process of the system through time is referred to as its trajectory, and is recorded in terms of successive states of the system.

We can thus speak of a Folsom cultural system comprised of a number of components (human beings, tools, ideas, social relationships, lithic debitage, etc.), occupying a number of successive states of equilibria through time, the trajectory of which is governed by a an interaction of systems components and environmental input, as monitored by feedback information channeled to regulatory mechanisms. It is analytically convenient to group various articulations or couplings of components into functionally relevant configurations which will be termed subsystems.

3. Subsystem:

A subsystem is a particular configuration of components oriented toward a specific function relevant to the maintenance of system equilibrium. It is important to point out that systems themselves are in fact subsystems of larger systems (suprasystems), while at the same time, any subsystem can be analyzed as a separate system itself. Functionally, subsystems are activated to reduce stress imposed upon the system as a whole. Thus a subsystem may function in terms of subsistence procurement (Flannery 1968), or in terms of artifact production, enactment of ritual, defense from invasion, etc. Any one component may be a part of a number of different subsystems contemporaneously.

Cultural systems are very complex systems, and therefore include a large variety of components. The system cannot efficiently respond to environmental stress (adapt) without ignoring some component attributes and maximizing other component attributes. Clarke (1968:71) has analyzed this phenomenon by defining three types of attributes: inessential, essential, and key. Inessential component attributes are those which are not relevant to the structure of the particular subsystem under analysis. Essential attributes are those by which the subsystem is defined. Key attributes are those attributes which covary in a specific manner, that is, the range of variation between attribute states of the key attributes is minimal for the subsystem as defined. When a subsystem is oriented toward a specific function its trajectory is constrained by the limitation of component attributes. Such constraint results in regularity or patterning, and thus permits the formulation of a taxonomy. It can be seen, then, that the identification of key attributes is critical to the formulation of a taxonomy. It should be emphasized that key attributes are defined by a minimal range of variation between covarying attribute states, rather than any single specific value of a given attribute. This permits the emerging taxonomy to be polythetic, rather than monothetic, a distinction which Clarke stresses as being very important to modern typological theory. In a polythetic group, "each attribute is shared by large numbers of entities and no single attribute is both sufficient and necessary to the group membership" (Clarke 1968:37).

4. Environment:

The environment is the contextual setting of the system under analysis. It has been concisely defined by Miller as "the suprasystem minus the system itself" (1965:226). Consideration of the environment thus depends on the analytic level undertaken. At the subsystem level, other cultural subsystems must be considered as part of the environment in addition to the natural and physical surroundings. The environment of a cultural system can also be considered a system itself, with its own components, attributes, and subsystems, all susceptible to analysis similar to that described above. Environmental systems and cultural systems are themselves subsystems of a larger unit, sometimes referred to as an ecosystem.

Given these brief definitions of the characteristics of systems, two things relevant to an analysis of settlement technology become apparent. First, in order to achieve a settlement taxonomy it is essential to determine the system constraints responsible for regularities. In other words, the so-called key variables must be isolated. Second, in order to achieve the first objective a thorough understanding

of the variables themselves--their nature and ranges of variation--
must be attained. In short, settlement technology cannot be understood
in the absence of an attempt to understand thoroughly the relevant cultural variables (lithic, ceramic, architectural, etc.) which articulate
with the environmental components in the settlement subsystem.

For the purpose of constructing a survey model, the settlement
technology of an archeological culture will be considered a subsystem
comprised of a number of cultural and environmental components; the
former includes social, economic, and material culture components,
while the latter includes physical, biotic, and socio-cultural components.

With respect to the elements of the cultural aspect of settlement
technology, the social component is that social unit whose activities
were responsible for the deposition of the artifacts recovered. It is
an unknown component; indeed, one of the aims of archeology is the
cautious elucidation of the nature of this variable (cf. Freeman 1968:
266).

The economic component refers to the subsistence strategy of the
cultural system. This component is usually known in general terms
(e.g., hunting/gathering, horticultural, pastoralism, etc.) prior to the
initiation of the survey, or is derived from analysis of the survey data.
The more specific nature of this component can be derived only through
excavation, however.

The material culture component consists of the artifacts re-covered in their environmental context. In an archeological survey, this generally consists of surface collections of lithic and ceramic assemblages, and observations regarding the architectural remains should these be present. One of the fundamental assumptions in arch-eology is that the contextual attributes of the material culture com-ponent (derived either through survey or excavation) suggest something reliable about the conduct of past cultural behavior.

Of the three cultural components of settlement technology, it is the latter--that of material culture--which offers the most potential of becoming known in detail. It is imperative, therefore, that an arch-eological survey encompass an intensive analysis of this factor.

Regarding the environmental aspect, I have arbitrarily segmented it into three major components relevant to settlement technology. The physical component refers to the geography of the site situation, in-cluding the topographical and climatological attributes. The biotic component involves the floral and faunal attributes of the environment at the time the site was occupied, to the extent that these can be de-rived. The socio-cultural component of the environment refers to those social units which are not themselves elements of the system under analysis (e.g., neighboring cultural systems). This component may be very difficult to derive, since contemporaneity with the princi-ple system must be demonstrated. Nevertheless its importance to the settlement technology of the system analyzed must not be overlooked.

Of the three environmental components, the derivation of the physical component attributes offers the most potential at the survey level, and therefore must be most intensively analyzed.

The following procedural model for the derivation of settlement technology through archeological survey is based on the articulation of the cultural and environmental components within the analytic frame-work of general systems theory. The model acknowledges the differences in the nature of the component attributes involved, and attempts to maximize the interpretative potential in the material culture and physical environmental components.

1. Collection of the Data:

This model does not deal with the actual techniques involved in the collection of survey data.[3] The selection of a survey technique will be in large part a function of the nature and size of the area to be surveyed, and the amount of time and money available to the researcher. Regardless of the actual survey method employed, two important considerations should be mentioned. First, it is essential that proper attention be paid to the sampling procedure utilized to insure that the sample obtained is both reliable and adequate (Binford 1964, Plog 1968).

Secondly, it is important to insure that adequate data are collected on the attributes of all the components involved. The numerous

---

[3]For extensive bibliographies of survey techniques, see Hole and Heizer (1969:142-3), and Heizer and Graham (1967:15). In addition, a new approach to the utilization of aerial photographs in site location is presented in Chatper 3 of this study.

standardized site survey forms available are generally deficient in one or more aspects, and the researcher should, after adequate study of the amount and nature of data derivable in his survey area, prepare his own survey form adjusted specifically to the conditions in his area.

2. Analysis of the Data:

The analytic phase of the survey consists of a basic procedural model comprising four analytic steps which are successively reiterated at increasingly inclusive systemic levels. The first step involves the definition of the basic enities. Implicit in this process is the separation of the essential from the inessential variables comprising the systemic unit under analysis. The second step involves the analysis of the articulation of the essential variables to determine the range of covariation existing between them. Third, those essential variables which exhibit minimal ranges of covariation within the system unit are isolated and defined as the key variables critical to the definition of the particular system trajectory. Finally, based on the isolation of the key variables, the system trajectory is made explicit through the formulation of a functional taxonomy.

This basic procedure is applicable to any and all of the analytic levels involved in the derivation of settlement technology. It is convenient to divide these into the component level, subsystem level, system level, and suprasystem level. The application of the basic procedural model at each of these levels will be considered briefly:

a. Component Level: Here, the component itself is analyzed as a system. For example, a projectile point can be considered a distinct component of the subsystem of lithic technology, along with a number of other components such as scrapers, drills, manos, metates, abraders, etc. At this level of analysis, the component category "projectile point" is systemically analyzed in terms of its own constituent units. Among these might be its morphology, production techniques, and various functions, each of which can itself be considered a component of the category "projectile point" viewed as a system. Invoking the basic procedural model, each of these components is defined by separating the essential from the non-essential variables and determining their covariation either by statistical or other adequate means. It should then be possible to isolate certain key variables critical to the component configuration, and a taxonomy can be formulated on this basis. This procedure is then repeated for other lithic categories (scrapers, knives, milling stones, etc.) until an analysis of the lithic data at the component level is complete.

b. Subsystem Level: The next step is to treat each one of the taxons derived from the previous analysis as a component of the subsystem of lithic technology. Again, the four analytic steps of the basic model are invoked, and the taxons formulated. When completed, this process will result in the most thorough understanding of the subsystem of lithic technology permitted by the lithic data available in the survey.

Following completion of the analysis of the lithic data, other available components (ceramic, architectural, etc.) would be analyzed in a similar fashion. This procedure results in the maximization of the interpretative potential inherent in the artifact assemblages collected in the survey.

c. System Level: Here, taxons derived from subsystem analysis are treated as cultural components of the system of settlement technology. It is at this point that the articulation of these cultural components with the environmental components is analyzed. Again, the basic model is invoked; essential cultural and environmental attributes are defined, key components isolated, and a taxonomy of settlement strategies is formulated. Since the components analyzed are within the sphere of the cultural system as a whole, taxonomic formulation here is termed intracultural in nature, and variations in settlement taxons can be considered subcultural variations.

d. Suprasystem Level: At the suprasystem level, analysis becomes intercultural in scope. Here, the relationship between the settlement technology of a specific archeological culture and that of other cultures identified in the survey can be explored either synchronically (if contemporaneity can be demonstrated), or diachronically. In either case, systems constraints by known or postulated environmental variables can be defined and regularities established.

22

3. Interpretations and Conclusions:

As a final step in his procedural model for archeological analysis,

Clarke includes a recycling stage, basic to scientific procedure. In

his words,

> a feedback route compares the newly devised model or hypothesis
> with the latest state of the observational data and agreements
> and discrepancies are filtered back into the system again, to
> provide fresh modifications or new models. The continuous
> cycle ultimately producing a distillate of synthesizing propo-
> sitions, principles, or hypotheses (Clarke 1968:35).

Certainly during this procedure, problems will emerge which are rele-

vant to cultural process and which will bear testing by formal excava-

tion. In a systems analysis, different ranges of variation of component

attributes are brought into play in the various configurations of varia-

bles to produce different taxonomic structures. Some variables will

be known, others unknown. During each cycling process, data derived

from outside the survey itself (e.g., from the literature) can be utilized

to aid in the construction of hypotheses which can be tested with refer-

ence to the survey data. If some of the unknown variables can be in-

ductively derived and deductively tested, then they can be used as

known variables at the ensuing level of analysis, assuming system

integrity is maintained. The model thus becomes not only analytic,

but somewhat generative in nature.

The conclusions of the survey should, then, yield two types of

results. There should first be explanations of certain cultural pro-

cesses; explanations attainable through analysis of the survey data itself, supplemented by existing archeological knowledge. Secondly, and perhaps most importantly, there should be a formulation of relevant problems from which hypotheses can be deduced and tested through future excavation in the survey area.

The survey model offered here has been presented in very general terms. Theoretically, it should be applicable to any regional survey with minimal adaptation to the local archeological situation. Its purpose is quite simple; to derive the maximum information possible from the data obtained by the survey, and present this in a fashion that will be most beneficial to the advancement of the fundamental goal of archeology--the study of culture as a temporal process. The particular sutdy that follows is devoted to the implementation of this analytical survey model to an acutal archeological situation.

Statement of Objectives

The fundamental operational framework underlying the orientation of the present study can now be stated in more explicit terms:

1. Purpose:

The primary purpose of survey archeology is to provide a framework of hypotheses relevant to the explanation of cultural process, which will guide the direction of more intensive research in the future.

2. Method:

It is suggested here that the archeological survey should focus on the analysis of the technology of settlement, since this is viewed as the primary medium of articulation between a culture and its environment.

3. Propositions:

Consistent with the method stated above, the following proposals are submitted as fundamental to satisfying the purpose of an archeological survey:

a. Intensive analysis of the survey data will permit the generation of hypotheses relevant to the explanation of variation in the subsystem of settlement technology of each culture represented.

b. The systemic orientation of the research techniques will permit the structuring of hypotheses at three different analytic levels: 1) the component level (including both environmental and cultural components); 2) the subsystem (intracultural) level; and 3) the system (intercultural) level. Relevant hypotheses will test variation at all of these levels.

c. The nature of the hypotheses structured will be of two different orders: 1) hypotheses testable with reference to the survey data itself; and 2) hypotheses testable through the employment of future problem-oriented research in the field. In this manner, the interpretive potential of the survey data is maximized.

The following study investigates these propositions with respect to an analysis of the PaleoIndian occupation of the central Rio Grande valley in New Mexico.

CHAPTER II

The Survey Area

Introduction

The remaining part of the present study is devoted to the application of the analytic survey model to the central Rio Grande valley in
the vicinity of Albuquerque, New Mexico. This region offers excellent
research potential to students of anthropology in that it exhibits a cultural continuum of a minimum of 12, 000 years and possibly more.
Some of the most ancient manifestations of culture, represented by
the Clovis occupation, are found near modern Pueblo Indian reservations. Given the nature of this opportunity, it is somewhat surprising
that more intensive work has not already been carried out.

The most extensively analyzed archeological manifestation of the
region is that of the Anasazi. Sites such as Pottery Mound (Hibben
1966), Kuaua Pueblo (Bliss 1948), and the Artificial Leg sites (Frisbie
1967) have been excavated, and other work has been done as salvage
archeology by the Museum of Anthropology in Sante Fe. In addition,
extensive work has been carried out on the Archaic stage (Irwin-
Williams 1967, Reinhart 1968). Relative to this research, however,
only limited investigation of the PaleoIndian occupation of the region has
been undertaken. Over the years a significant number of PaleoIndian

projectile points and other lithic evidence have been recovered from
the region by amateur archeologists, indicating the potential contribution of the area to early man studies. In addition, the geomorphology
of the region resembles both that of the Llano Estacado to the east, and
the plains of northeastern Colorado. Both of these areas have yielded
large amounts of PaleoIndian material, suggesting that the Rio Grande
region might also be a significant source. It was decided therefore,
to focus the analytic survey on the PaleoIndian stage of development.

Preliminary work in the region revealed that the possibilities of
locating stratified sites were quite limited, thus reducing the chance
of finding perishable materials. Lack of stratification also indicated
that there would be little temporal control within the survey region.
Comparative analysis would have to be based on cultural sequences
established by previous PaleoIndian studies elsewhere. Offsetting
these disadvantages to surveying the region were initial indications that
quite a few surface sites could be found, and that evidently there had
been little disturbance by uninformed point collectors, at least with regard to the PaleoIndian sites. It became apparent, however, that in
terms of analytic potential, the two primary sources of interpretative
data would be lithic material and observations on the physical environment. Given the potential importance of the region to PaleoIndian research, and the fact that the data would be somewhat restricted in
nature, the implementation of an analytic survey which maximized the
interpretative potential of the data became essential.

It was decided at this time to utilize a systems approach in which the lithic and environmental components would be analyzed as coupled, component subsystems of PaleoIndian settlement technology. It should be noted at the outset that there was no assurance that a settlement taxonomy could be derived from the study. It was felt, though, that even if success was not attained in this respect, the study would yield valuable information on the relationship between lithic technology and the cultural treatment of the environmental variables. In addition, by the very analytic and possibly generative nature of the model employed, it was probable that a number of relevant problems would be identified which could be approached through continued work in the survey area, or perhaps elsewhere in those areas where PaleoIndian cultural evidence is represented.

Geography

The region encompassed by the survey is termed the central Rio Grande Valley (Figure 1). Although somewhat amorphous in outline, it is roughly 85 miles long (north-south) and 35 miles wide (east-west). The major drainage pattern is from north to south. The Rio Grande river enters the area through a relatively pronounced cut at the northeast corner, and exits at the south end in the same fashion. Two minor rivers also flow within the region. The Rio Puerco enters from the northwest in an area of highly broken topography, and joins the Rio Grande at the southern end of the region. The San Jose river enters in

28

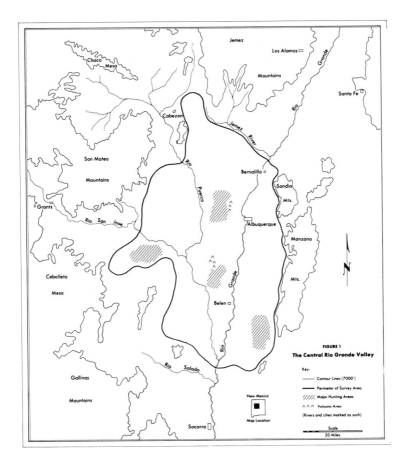

Jemez

Los Alamos ▢

Chaco
Mesa

Mountains

Santa Fe ▢

Rio Grande

Cabezon

Jemez River

San Mateo

Rio Puerco

Bernalillo ▢

Mountains

Sandia
Mts.

Grants

Albuquerque

Rio San Jose

Manzano

Cebolleta

Mesa

Mts.

Rio Grande

Belen ▢

N

FIGURE 1
The Central Rio Grande Valley

Rio Salado

Key:

_____ Contour Lines (7000')

━━━━━━ Perimeter of Survey Area

//// Major Hunting Areas

∧ ∧ ∧ Volcano Area

(Rivers and cities marked as such)

New Mexico

Gallinas

Mountains

Map Location

Scale
━━━━━━
20 Miles

Socorro ▢

a narrow cut from the western edge, and joins the Rio Puerco in the
central part of the region.

The survey area consists of approximately 3,000 square miles
of relatively unbroken plains and plateau type terrain. Its boundaries
are defined by major mountain ranges, high mesas, or other sharply-
defined topography. On the northern edge, the area is bordered by the
Jemez Mountains; on the east and southeast by the Sandia and Manzano
Mountains; and on the southwest and west by the Gallinas mountains,
the high Gallinas Mesa country, and the San Mateo mountains. Access
to the region is afforded primarily by the three rivers, and by Tijeras
Canyon near Albuquerque and Abo Canyon near Mountainair. Thus
except for six passages, all of which exhibit rather sharply defined
topography, the central Rio Grande valley can be considered a closed
interior plateau. On a very gross scale, the elevations of the area
average around 6000 feet above sea level at the northern end and 5000
feet at the southern end.

Looking more closely at the topography within the region itself,
three major types of terrain are revealed: river bottoms, transverse
arroyos, and broad, relatively flat plains. The Rio Grande has formed
a broad river basin, up to two miles wide in places. The Rio Puerco
and San Jose, both of which are spring-fed intermittently, flow throughout the year and have cut very deep, vertically-faced arroyos at the
present. Formerly they too formed relatively wide river bottoms,

though not as extensive as the Rio Grande. There is some evidence
that the deep arroyo cutting of the two minor rivers has taken place
in the 20th century, perhaps as a result of overgrazing.

As shown in Figure 1, there are four major areas within the
region which exhibit a plains-like topography. These are all bordered
by transverse arroyos with a predominant east-west drainage pattern.
The arroyos vary considerably in size and extent; some are quite prominent, others are not well-defined.

There is one other topographic feature which should be mentioned,
although it is not generalized throughout the region. This is the chain
of volcanoes which bisects the area west of the Rio Grande for a distance of about thirty miles, from Albuquerque south to Los Lunas.
There are two main clusters of cones, one directly west of Albuquerque,
the other west-southwest of Isleta Pueblo. These are fairly recent
volcanoes, possibly early Pleistocene in age.

Geomorphology

The survey region had its genesis in early Tertiary times, when
the Jemez, Cabezon, and Mt. Taylor vulcanism took place to the north
and west, and the Sandia and Manzano fault blocks uplifted to the east.
Concurrent with this was the development of a massive structural de-
pression, resulting in the formation of the Rio Grande graben. Late
Tertiary and early Quaternary times were characterized by graben
filling and continued vulcanism in the central Rio Grande area

(Kottlowski, et. al. 1965:292). Beds of the Santa Fe group, which were a source of lithic material for the aboriginal occupants of the area, are both pre-Pleistocene and early Pleistocene deposits.

The relatively flat, open features mentioned above are the result of thick paleosol development on mid-Pleistocene sediments. It is through these sediments that the Rio Grande and its tributaries cut during the middle Pleistocene. Also exposed at this time were beds of the Galisteo formation, another deposit of early Tertiary times which contains a great deal of silicified wood (Kottlowski 1967:36).

Thus most of the gross morphological features of the survey region had attained their present character prior to the beginning of the Wisconsin glaciation. Aside from terracing along the Rio Grande, which continued as late as 2600 B.C. (Kottlowski, et. al. 1965:293), the Wisconsin period consisted of relatively minor alluviation, compared to the developments which had taken place previously. Haynes (1966) has defined the terminal Wisconsin and recent alluvial sequence in some detail.

Prior to or during the late Wisconsin, the middle Pleistocene surfaces in the region saw the development of numerous playas, or shallow basin-like depressions. These playas were formed most extensively in the four major plains-like areas mentioned previously. Some playas could have been formed through seepage action in structural depressions, others through eolian and alluvial ponding of shallow arroyos. Perhaps most frequently, however, the playas were formed through a combination of deflation and duning, such as that which occurred in the Llano Estacado (Wendorf 1961:14, Green 1961). An inspection of aerial photographs of the survey region reveals rather extensive dune formation in a number of areas indicating a prevailing wind from the southwest. On this basis, I would suggest that this was the direction of the prevailing wind during the Wisconsin period. This view is supported by the presence of small, rounded ridges in a general northeasterly direction from existing playas, indicating also that many of the playa depressions may be wind-scoured in origin. As will be seen, these playas play a key role in PaleoIndian settlement technology. Most of them probably contained water during the late Wisconsin period.

Recently, perhaps as a result of poor range management, the entire region has undergone extensive eroding. Because of the low annual rainfall this erosion has taken the form of extensive eolian deflation, accompanied by severe arroyo cutting. Virtually every ridge has a "blowout", and in some areas, such as the confluence of the Rio Puerco and the San Jose, very large flats have been completely denuded.

Ecology

1. Flora:

To my knowledge, there have been no pollen samples taken in the survey region which would reliably reflect the nature of the flora during

late Wisconsin times.[1] Thus the floral assemblage for this period
will have to be reconstructed on the basis of palynological evidence
from elsewhere, and interpretations correlated with faunal remains.
In 1955, and again in 1958-1959, extensive drilling was carried out in
the San Augustine Plains, an extinct Pleistocene lake in southwestern
New Mexico approximately 100 miles from the survey region. This
drilling resulted in an almost continuous 2000-foot core which has
been interpreted geologically and palynologically (Clisby and Sears
1956). Pollen studies indicated that the last 70 feet of the core represents Wisconsin and modern times. The profile showed a gradual
increase of spruce and pine pollen, indicating that during the Wisconsin
the San Augustine Plains were invaded by a spruce-pine forest. Independently, Martin and Mehringer (1965:Figure 4) have interpreted this
area in a similar manner, but do not consider the spruce coverage to
have extended into the central Rio Grande valley. Instead, they reconstruct the latter region as a yellow pine parkland. It should be
remembered that these interpretations are for the full-glacial vegetation of 20,000 B.P. It is unlikely that the survey region was occupied
by humans at that time, almost certainly not by any of the cultures dealt
with in the survey.

---

[1] A possible exception to this is the work of King (1964), but as
Martin and Mehringer (1965:437) have pointed out, King's samples
may represent a mixture of pollen of varying ages.

On the basis of intensive investigations by a number of author-
ities (cf. Wendorf 1961), Wendorf and Hester have interpreted the paleo-
ecology of the Llano Estacado as of 8000 B.C. What are now grasslands
were at that time grass and sage savannas bordered by escarpments
with pine and some spruce. Juniper and oak were found in the shallow
valleys of the savanna (Wendorf and Hester 1962:164). One should not
generalize without appropriate caution between the Llano Estacado and
the central Rio Grande, but there is some supporting evidence that the
two areas may have exhibited similar environments. Martin and
Mehringer (1965:Figure 4) have depicted the two areas as vegetatively
similar, based on intensive pollen studies of the entire southwest. In
addition, Harris and Findley (1964:119) have suggested that the late
Pleistocene environment in the vicinity of the Isleta Caves (in the south-
central part of the survey region) was a sagebrush grassland with few
trees; quite similar, in fact, to the conditions present today in southeastern Wyoming. This interpretation was based primarily on the
species of extinct fauna recovered from the caves (see below), but it
does suggest that late Pleistocene conditions were similar to those
known for the Llano Estacado. Until more palynological studies are
attempted within the region itself, however, the detailed nature of the
floral environment at the time of PaleoIndian occupation will remain
unknown. For the present, we can only assume a grass and sage
savanna.

2. Fauna:

Regarding the terminal Pleistocene faunal assemblage of the survey region, the evidence is somewhat better than that for the flora, but nevertheless still very sparse. This is in part due to the general absence of stratified sites in the area which include PaleoIndian material, and perhaps in part due to the lack of conditions conducive to preservation of faunal remains.

An interpretive report has been published on the fauna recovered by the University of New Mexico from the Isleta Caves (Harris and Findley 1964). More than 3000 specimens were recovered, and the initial analysis grouped them into three categories including recent forms, extant but extralimital forms, and extinct forms. Taxa from the latter two categories are as follows:

Extralimital forms:

Eastern Cottontail	Vole (Microtus sp.)
Yellow-bellied Marmot	Red Fox
Bushy-tailed Wood Rat	Kit Fox
Sagebrush Vole	

Extinct forms:

Cave Bear	Elephant
Camel (2 species)	Horse

I have included the extralimital forms, because it is largely on this basis that the authors interpreted late-Pleistocene Isleta environments as similar to that of modern southeastern Wyoming where these taxa are now found (Harris and Findley 1964:118).

Hibben (1941) has listed the fauna derived from the excavations of Sandia Cave. In the Folsom level were found remains of horse, camel, bison, mammoth, ground sloth, and wolf. The Sandia level included horse, bison, camel, mastodon, and mammoth. These species, all now extinct, are typical of the forms found in many PaleoIndian sites in the Plains and Southwest (Wendorf and Hester 1962:Table 2), and almost certainly occupied the survey area during the terminal Wisconsin times. As noted by Haynes (1966:11, 19), however, there is evidence for a considerable difference in the faunal assemblages between the Clovis and Folsom periods. By Folsom times, the horse, mammoth, and camel had become increasingly rare, if not extinct. Haynes cites the Lindenmeier camel (Roberts 1937) as the only representative of these three species in post-Clovis horizons, although he omitted evidence of horse at the Midland site (Wendorf, et. al. 1955). It is highly probable that these three species were no longer available in large numbers for post-Clovis hunters, who, as the record indicates, concentrated on bison as a major subsistence source. In the case of Folsom, this was generally Bison antiquus.

In view of this, it seems rather anomalous that extinct forms of bison are conspicuously absent from the Isleta Cave faunal assemblage. I would consider it unreasonable to conclude from this that there were no bison in the central Rio Grande valley during the time of PaleoIndian occupation. In the first place, bison does occur in the Folsom level at Sandia Cave. Secondly, extinct bison have been reported from elsewhere in the area, at Comanche Springs (Hibben 1951a:44) and at the Albuquerque Gravel Pit site, where they were associated with other Pleistocene megafauna (ibid.). Third, evidence of bison was reported from Isleta Cave, but was listed as extant (Harris and Findley 1964:115). Since much of the material was identified generically only, it is possible that further analysis could reveal the presence of extinct forms of bison. Finally, given the knowledge we presently have about PaleoIndian hunters, it is difficult to envision them occupying an open grassland area devoid of bison. In their survey of 35 PaleoIndian sites, Wendorf and Hester (1962:Table 2) list 27 sites as having revealed bison remains. Four of the sites in which bison were absent were Clovis mammoth-kill sites. In the post-Clovis horizons, 86.1% of the sites yielded bison remains.

Unfortunately, there has been no documented evidence of the association of early man and extinct faunal forms at any of the sites in the survey area. I would suggest, however, that given the presence of bison in association with Folsom in Sandia Cave, the possibility of the presence of extinct bison in Isleta Cave, the interpreted presence of extensive sage-grasslands during the terminal Wisconsin, and the overwhelming evidence of the association of extinct bison and early man in adjacent Plains and Southwestern areas, that it is highly probable that the PaleoIndian hunters preyed on the extinct Pleistocene megafauna here in the central Rio Grande valley as they did elsewhere.

The position will be adopted here that their subsistence strategy emphasized the hunting of such fauna, in all probability an extinct form of
bison. This is not to imply that bison were hunted to the exclusion of
everything else. In dealing with the PaleoIndian cultural stage, fish,
birds, and insects are all to frequently overlooked as supplementary
sources of subsistence, as well as numerous plant foods which were
undoubtedly available at the time. The following statement by Gordon
Willey presents concisely the position accepted in the present study:

> Certainly their entire livelihood did not depend on the big
> Pleistocene animals of the hunt; there are, in fact, indications
> that smaller game and other edibles were taken or collected as
> opportunities arose. Still, the big-game pursuit is the most
> characteristic and diagnostic feature of the culture shared by
> these particular early Americans. There can be no question that
> it was an activity of great and, probably, primary importance.
> Viewed in the perspective of all of pre-Columbian New World
> history, it imparted a design, a style to their lives (Willey 1966:38).

3. Paleoclimatic Conditions:

Regardless of the views about the severity of Pleistocene climates
which have been suggested in the past, there is increasing agreement
among specialists that in southwestern North America the difference
between late Wisconsin and present climates is relatively minor, and
then primarily in terms of summer, rather than winter, temperatures.
The work of Leopold (1951) is perhaps most pertinent to the present
study in that it deals with paleoclimatic conditions in the area of Santa
Fe and the Estancia Basin, both quite near the survey area. He has
reasoned quite logically that as far south as New Mexico, the climatic

effect of the Wisconsin ice sheet in Canada would be little different from the effect of permanent winter snow cover which exists in Canada in modern times. He then concentrates on defining the degree of difference in summer temperatures, and based on an interpretive analysis of snowline elevations (which are controlled by summer temperatures), he suggests that at Santa Fe, the summer temperature would have been reduced by about 16.2 degrees fahreinheit during the late Pleistocene (Leopold 1951:161). Richmond (1965:228) agrees with this conclusion.

Leopold also applies his data to the question of moisture during the late Pleistocene. He has calculated the mean annual evaporation rate in an attempt to determine the rainfall necessary to maintain Lake Estancia under various climatic conditions. He concludes that increased rainfall was necessary during the terminal Pleistocene, but not in the absence of decreased temperatures (Leopold 1951:167). Earlier Antevs (1949) had suggested that Lake Estancia existed under conditions of both increased moisture and temperature. At the present, it would seem that Leopold's conclusions are more acceptable. Weber (1967: 57-58) concurs that conditions of lower summer temperatures and increased rainfall seem likely for the period.

Wendorf's analysis of the Llano Estacado led him to conclude that during the Tahoka Pluvial (Wisconsin maximum) both January and July mean temperatures were 15°-20° F. cooler than present. During the ensuing San Jon Pluvial, which is the period relevant to PaleoIndian studies, he notes that temperatures were slightly warmer, but the degree to which warming took place is not indicated (Wendorf 1961:130).

It may be beneficial to summarize briefly at this point the late Pleistocene ecology of the central Rio Grande valley as interpreted and accepted herein on the basis of the existing literature: At the time of occupation of the area by the PaleoIndians, the winters were not much colder than those of today. The summers were cooler, however, by about 16 degrees. The mean annual rainfall was somewhat higher than present, but it is not known by how much. As a result of increased moisture and decreased temperature, the small ponds and playas of the area contained water, as did the rivers and some of the major arroyos. Vegetation consisted primarily of a sage grassland, with pine and possibly some spruce along the higher mesas and escarpments. During the early part of the human occupation, now extinct forms of megafauna (mammoth, horse, camel, bison) were present, but as extinction progressed perhaps only bison remained during the later (post-Clovis) PaleoIndian periods. More modern fauna, such as deer and antelope, were probably present throughout the period. In addition, of course, there were numerous other smaller mammilian forms, as well as avifauna, fish and insects.

In view of the recent debate over the causes of the Pleistocene megafaunal extinction, and the role that man may have had in it (Martin and Wright 1967), it should be recalled that the central Rio Grande

valley is a closed basin with only a limited number of access routes,

each of which exhibits fairly broken, rough topography. Given these

circumstances, I would consider it feasible that the PaleoIndian occu-

pants of the region could quite easily induce overkill on a microscale

within the region. Should this have happened, it might have been some

time before the area would again be abundant with megafauna. This is

speculative, but it should be kept in mind if adequate data on the quan-

titative nature of faunal assemblages in the region should even come

to light.

Archeology

As noted earlier, a considerable amount of work has been done on

the Pueblo and Archaic periods in the central Rio Grande valley, but

relatively little research concerning the occupation of the area by early

man has been published. Certainly the most extensive reports presen-

ted deal with the excavation and interpretation of the Sandia material

(Hibben 1937, 1941, 1943, 1955, Roosa 1956a, 1956b, 1968). Aside

from this, no extensive work was done on the PaleoIndian occupation

of the area until recently. A chronological summary of the earlier

published material includes the following:

An early survey which included parts of the central Rio Grande

valley was that by Reginald Fisher (1930). This was followed later by

a reconnaisance of the middle Rio Puerco area by Dorothy Luhrs, summarized in Luhrs (1937). In 1940, according to Dick (1943), a camp site near Isleta Cave was discovered by William McConnell. According to the descriptions given by Dick, this campsite was of an occupation which we know now as "Jay" or Bajada, an early Archaic manifestation which will be discussed briefly in Chapter 5. The Isleta Cave material itself was discussed initially by Hibben (1941), and later by Harris and Findley (1964) following further excavations by the University of New Mexico in the mid-1940's. Herbert Dick (1943) reported on a personal survey he had made in the area east of the Rio Grande. He included information on sites at Coyote Springs, Ojo de Las Huertas, and in lower Tijeras Canyon. The only artifact which could definitely be attributed to PaleoIndian was a Yuma (i.e., Cody Complex) projectile tip found near Tijeras Canyon (Dick 1943:21).

Frank C. Hibben (1951a, 1951b) reported on the association of Pleistocene megafauna with crude implements at two sites east of the Rio Grande. The first was uncovered by gravel quarrying operations, the nature of which precluded positive in situ correlation of the artifacts with the rather extensive inventory of extinct fauna. The second involved the erosional exposure of a bone bed near Comanche Springs, in which a number of crude cutting implements were found. The bones revealed were all of Bison sp. and one horn core indicated the possibility of B. antiquus.

Agogino and Hibben (1958) reported on PaleoIndian and later sites in central New Mexico. Of the sites discussed by them, those which lie within the present region surveyed were not PaleoIndian, but Archaic (ibid:Figure 1).

Hibben and Agogino continued their investigations, aided by William Womsley, and in the late 1950's and early 1960's the full potential of the region in terms of PaleoIndian occupation was becoming apparent. Its importance was demonstrated conclusively by the fieldwork of two people, Gerald Dawson and Ele Baker, under the encouragement of the Department of Anthropology at the University of New Mexico. Preliminary surface collections assembled by these men indicated that PaleoIndian artifacts were much more common than previously thought, and that the evidence came from campsites rather than kill sites.[2]

More recently, interested amateurs in the Albuquerque-Belen area, such as Frank Vernon, Wayne Stell, and William Jacoby, have contributed their own information regarding PaleoIndian sites, and have made their collections available for study to interested students. At the time the present study was initiated, then, a good deal of background information was available, although little of it was published.

---

[2]It should be pointed out that at this time, only a small percentage of the known PaleoIndian sites in North America were campsites. Of Wendorf and Hester's (1962) sample of 35 published plains and southwestern early man sites, only 8 were known to be campsites and the remainder were kill sites.

Mention should be made of the recent excavations which have been initiated in the survey area, specifically those relevant to PaleoIndian research. The Rio Rancho Folsom site (Dawson 1967, Dawson and Judge 1969) was excavated in 1966 and 1967 under the field direction of Gerald Dawson, then a graduate student at the University of New Mexico. One component of this site was excavated in 1967 by members of the Albuquerque Archeological Society. Now completed, this work has resulted in the only completely excavated Folsom campsite in North America.

The Anasazi Origins Project, under the direction of Cynthia Irwin-Williams, has been undertaking research in the Arroyo Cuervo Region northwest of Albuquerque for the past six years. Two aspects of this research are especially relevant to PaleoIndian investigations (Irwin-Williams, personal communication). First, at a locality called Dunas Altas, materials from a Cody Complex occupation were found stratigraphically in place beneath a "Jay" component, thus indicating the lack of contemporaneity between the two manifestations. This had been assumed prior to this discovery, but had not been documented. Secondly, a Folsom component near Ojito Springs was partially excavated by the Anasazi Origins Project, but the recovered material cannot be considered in situ due to prior deflation.

Preliminary testing at Alamo Muerto, a site east of the Rio Grande in the survey area, was carried out in 1967 by Dennis Stanford,

Ele Baker, the author, and a number of interested University of New Mexico students in the hope of revealing stratification sufficient to warrant further excavation. Although the very complex stratigraphy of this site has not yet been fully interpreted, it is doubtful that many of the artifacts and debitage recovered were in place since both eolian and alluvial mixing are evident.

Finally, I would like to mention the excellent work done by Robert Weber of the New Mexico Institute of Mining and Technology at Socorro. Dr. Weber has made surface collections for a number of years in a large region adjacent to and south of the present study area. The quality of Weber's survey work is unsurpassed by amateur and professional alike, and it has led to the identification of the Mockingbird site, a Clovis campsite southeast of Socorro. Under the sponsorship of Eastern New Mexico University, excavations have been carried out at Mockingbird during the 1967, 1968, and 1969 seasons (Weber 1968).

CHAPTER III

Survey Techniques

Sampling

There is little doubt that in the past archeology has suffered considerably from a lack of adequate sampling procedures. All too frequently the most attractive sites have been excavated and the most productive strata screened, with the results labeled "typical". Though not justifiable, the lack of objective sampling is nevertheless partially explicable due to the very nature of archeological research. For analytic purposes it is necessary to obtain as many diagnostic artifacts as possible. Objective sampling procedures often result in much hard work with little to show for it, thus the emphasis has been on the excavation and/or collection of the most productive areas. Yet there seems now to be a definite trend toward the application of adequate sampling, as manifest in the more recent publications concerning archeological research design. Binford (1964:434-36), Clarke (1968:549-51), Plog (1968:13-17), and Streuver (1968:141-43) are among those who emphasize the importance of eliminating hidden biases by the application of objective sampling techniques in archeological research.

Sampling was a definite problem in the present study and hopefully the techniques adopted have eliminated biases to the extent that the derived data can be considered a reliable sample. Undoubtedly the same problem has been encountered before in other surveys and will be encountered again in the future. It is simply a problem of coordinating the need for attaining an objective, unbiased sample with a number of other variables; specifically, the time available, the financial support available, the size of the survey area, and the amount of cultural material needed to carry out intensive quantitative analyses. Perhaps part of the problem in this case is a function of the nature of Paleo-Indian cultural assemblages themselves. Such sites are not too common in North America, and a site which yields a large number of surface artifacts is rare. In contrast, Plog (1968:16) reports that in one area in northeastern Arizona only eight miles square, 250 Pueblo sites were found. PaleoIndian sites simply do not occur in such numbers and the sampling procedure must take these differences into account.

It became apparent at the beginning of the present survey that PaleoIndian sites in the region were of such low yield in terms of artifacts that an effort would have to be made to locate as many sites as possible in order to attain an adequate analytic sample. This led to the development of a new survey technique which is here labeled "site pattern recognition." This technique will now be described, the inherent biases in sampling noted, and the techniques applied to correct these biases explained.

Site pattern recognition is a survey technique developed specifically for the location of PaleoIndian sites in the region analyzed herein (cf. Dawson and Judge 1969:149). The technique was developed over a period of time by Ele Baker and Jerry Dawson, and formalized by the author. Basically, it involves the recognition of the basic criteria used by the PaleoIndian cultures in their selection of site location, and applying these criteria to the interpretation of aerial photographs and maps of the survey area. It consists of three basic steps:

1. Site pattern recognition:

This consists of attempting to approximate as closely as possible the topographic criteria utilized by the early hunters in their site selection. It is accomplished by carefully analyzing the topographic variables of the known sites in the area in an effort to isolate consistencies. In this case, it was noted that the PaleoIndian sites were generally located on ridges near playas (frequently to the northeast of the playa). The playas themselves were generally located near an area suitable for grazing, and frequently there was a major drainage nearby. In support of this, it was learned that roughly the same pattern prevails in the Llano Estacado. Wendorf and Hester state that in that area, "campsites tend to occur on ridges, dunes, or hills which overlook either a stream channel or pond, at a distance of several hundred yards to a mile" (1962:166).

2. Interpretation of Aerial Photos and Maps:

Given the discovery of the playa-ridge-drainage pattern, the problem was one of locating these constellations of features in the research area and surveying them. In a region the size of the one under consideration here, this would be virtually impossible to accomplish without some sort of initial selection. It was therefore decided to utilize aerial photographs and topographic maps to locate the features initially. Thus the second step consisted of a systematic and thorough analysis of aerial photographs of the survey area in order to isolate those locations which satisfy the topographic requisites for site location.

There are at least two advantages to utilizing aerial photographs as a primary source of analysis, supplemented by topographic maps. First, the aerial photographs show more detail in terms of subtle differences in elevation. For instance, one of the most important sites encountered (13GX5) is near a large, shallow playa which is not indicated on the topographic map of the site area. The playa does show, however, on the aerial photo. Secondly, in some areas the 7.5 minute topographic maps have not yet been published, while photographs are available. It should be noted, though, that 7.5 minute topographic maps are extremely helpful as supplementary aids. In the central Rio Grande case, some of the aerial photographs were taken so long ago that the roads are no longer in the same location and in some instances it was impossible to locate photographic features on the ground without the aid of a topographic map. In addition, the topographic maps are

very useful for recording site locations.

3. Location of sites:

The next step is to list the potentially suitable site areas de-

rived through the analysis above, and then visit these areas and survey

them for actual sites. It should be mentioned here that it is important

to record all areas which exhibit potential even if they do not yield

sites when surveyed. I believe it is just as important and necessary

to explain the absence of sites as it is to interpret their presence.

This, then, is basically how the site pattern recognition tech-

nique works in an archeological survey and it was employed quite

successfully in the present study. It is readily apparent, however,

that from the standpoint of sampling the technique has a built-in bias.

That is, only those sites which satisfy the pattern requisites will be

located. For this reason, the following measures were taken to

counteract this bias.

In order to investigate the possibility of sites being located in

areas other than those indicated by the site pattern recognized, a sys-

tem of probability sampling was employed. This involved the imposi-

tion of a grid system over the survey region, the selection of a random

number of grids, and the intensive surveying of the selected grids for

sites which might exits in extra-pattern situations. This was carried

out as follows:

Utilizing a 1:250, 000 topographic map composite of the survey region, a grid system of 1-inch squares was imposed over the survey area. At this scale each grid unit equals 16 square miles. This size was selected for convenience both in setting up the grid and in surveying. In that the survey area is irregular in shape, many squares along the perimeter were not complete, and these were not counted in the grid since it would involve an arbitrary decision as to which to use and which not to use. The complete squares were numbered sequentially, yielding a total of 146 squares. Next, by consulting a table of random numbers, a sample of 20% (29 units) of the total grid count was selected randomly for intensive investigation. A map of the grid system and the squares selected is presented in Figure 2.[1]

As the survey progressed, each one of the selected grids was surveyed as intensively as possible to determine if any PaleoIndian sites were located in areas other than the regular site pattern areas. A total of 465 square miles was surveyed in this manner. All sites which could definitely be attributed to PaleoIndian that were found in the selected grids conformed generally to the site recognition pattern.[2]

---

[1]Grid units were numbered sequentially starting at the bottom and working from left to right, 1-146. The table of random numbers consulted was that presented in Edwards (1967:Table 1). A total of 29 numbers were obtained in two sets of replacement sampling through random selection of the following block-row-column sets: 1st. set (20 numbers): 01-17-03; 2nd. set (9 numbers): 03-01-30.

[2]It should be pointed out that the author did not, and could not, accomplish this by himself. Many of these areas were surveyed over a period of time by other fieldworkers; notably Ele Baker, Jerry Dawson,

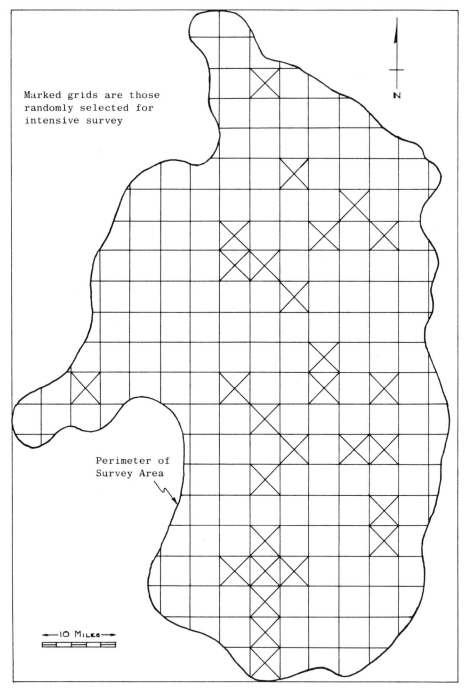

Figure 2. Grid System Ultilized for Objective Survey.

These two techniques were employed in conjunction with each other in order to attain objective sampling while at the same time acquiring as much data as possible. In the first technique--site pattern recognition--complete site discovery and collection was attempted by the most efficient means possible. The second technique--probability sampling--was designed to compensate for the bias inherent in site pattern recognition. I feel that the utilization of both these survey techniques has resulted in the recovery of an adequate, unbiased sample of the PaleoIndian sites in the survey region.

In retrospect, it is possible to check the effectiveness of the site pattern recognition technique based on the results of random sampling. In the 29 randomly selected grids, a total of 16 PaleoIndian occupational loci were recorded. Since the 29 grids represent 20% of the population universe, one would expect to find a total of 80 occupational loci in the survey area. Actually a total of 59 were found by the site pattern recognition method. This is 74% of the presumed total and represents, I feel, a sample sufficient to permit reliable generalization.

Survey Methodology

The present study was organized and initiated in the winter of 1967. At that time the survey technique was formalized and data on

Ted Reinhart, and Dennis Stanford; at times independently and at times with the author.

the existing site knowledge of the area assembled. The field survey was carried out intensively during the spring and summer of 1967, then intermittently until the following summer when it again became intensive. Meanwhile, the analytic portion was carried on throughout this period. An initial report on the analytic phase was presented at the 33rd. Annual Meeting of the Society for American Archeology (Judge 1968).

Approximately 930 hours were spent by the author in the field on site survey. I was rarely alone, and would like to acknowledge my debt of gratitude to Ele Baker, Terry Booth, Jerry Dawson, Bill Roosa, and Dennis Stanford for their volunteer assistance without which the study could not have been undertaken. My time in the field is in addition, of course, to the months spent in the area by Baker and Dawson prior to the formal initiation of the survey. If there is a message here for future researchers, it is simply that a survey of 3,000 square miles is an enormous undertaking.

Aerial photographs were purchased in the spring of 1967. It was found that the Soil Conservation Service Mosaic photographs (2" = 1 mile) were the most convenient to use. In addition, the available 7.5 minute U.S.G.S. topographic maps were purchased at this time.[3] This combination of sources provided excellent coverage of the survey area.

[3]The maps and aerial photos were purchased with the aid of a grant from the American Philosophical Society. Their support is genuinely appreciated.

Once these photographs had been interpreted in terms of the known site patterns, a list of potential areas was established and where applicable, permission to visit the locations was obtained from landowners.

It was decided that in order to make the survey as objective as possible, the selection of potential site locations would not be limited to the playa-ridge-drainage pattern alone. These areas would be visited first in order to gain an adequate sample of artifacts as rapidly as possible, but eventually an attempt would be made to survey all recognizable playas in the survey region. As it turned out, this was effective in the long run since some of the sites did not conform to the primary pattern.

Fortunately, innumerable small dirt roads interlace the survey region. Few potential site locations were more than a half hour walk from one of these roads, thus facilitating the initial and subsequent checking of the area. When a location was visited, it was surveyed intensively. All blowouts, ridge surfaces, and arroyo cuts were checked thoroughly for evidence of PaleoIndian occupation. If a site was found, cultural material was collected and environmental data recorded (see below). If no site was located, this fact was recorded and an intensive search of the adjacent areas was undertaken. In addition, all site areas (both with positive and negative yield) were revisited a number of times, during which the adjacent areas were surveyed for additional cultural evidence. I feel that this method added to the objectivity of

the survey, since a number of sites were located which did not conform
to the primary pattern, and a number of locations were encountered in
which the pattern requisites were satisfied more than adequately, yet
no evidence of PaleoIndian occupation was found.

PaleoIndian sites were recognized as such primarily through the
location of partial or complete projectile points. The PaleoIndian
cultural stage is defined in the literature on the basis of point typology
(Wormington 1957), and this definition is adhered to herein. With some
practice however, it became quite easy to recognize a PaleoIndian site
even though no points were found on it initially. This was possible due
to three distinctive attributes exhibited by PaleoIndian assemblages
in the survey area. First, transverse flake scrapers (endscrapers)
are in this region almost exclusively obtained from PaleoIndian sites.
This is a function not of the PaleoIndian assemblages themselves, but
of the fact that the later Archaic cultures in the central Rio Grande
valley used a different type of scraper; one which was frequently dis-
coidal or semi-discoidal and exhibited a very high profile. In this
respect the survey area differs considerably from the Plains, where
transverse scrapers were a part of the cultural assemblage until
modern times.

Second, the PaleoIndian sites yielded lithic debitage generally
distinct from that of the Archaic cultures. Specifically, flakes of bifacial retouch with heavily ground striking platforms are not commonly

encountered in Archaic assemblages in the survey area. This is perhaps an anomaly, since Jelinek (1966:403) has found them significant
in the Archaic both in the Pecos Valley and in the Llano Estacado.
Nevertheless they are rare here, and when encountered in a non-
PaleoIndian site situation, it is generally Basketmaker II. Obviously
a site would not be labeled as PaleoIndian on this basis alone, but it
was recorded as a distinct possibility, and was revisited until diagnostic
artifacts were encountered.

The third means involved the nature of the lithic raw material.
Archaic cultures in the area most frequently chose a low-grade, gray,
dendritic chalcedony--known locally as Rio Grande chalcedony--for the
manufacture of many of their tools, and almost exclusively used obsidian or basalt to produce their projectile points. Thus sites which
yielded these two materials to the exclusion of others generally proved
not to be PaleoIndian. Again, the Basketmaker II assemblages differed
in this respect, and in fact were frequently similar to PaleoIndian in
the nature of the raw materials utilized. PaleoIndian assemblages,
while at times employing the Rio Grande chalcedony, emphasized the
more exotic jaspers, cherts, and silicified woods, and in general
only occasionally made projectile points of obsidian.

Regarding the actual collection of cultural materials, all visible
artifacts and debitage were picked up from the PaleoIndian sites. This

satisfied the requisite of an adequate number of items for analysis while at the same time permitting us to assess the degree to which materials were being uncovered by on-going deflation. One of the assumptions of the survey especially relevant to the analytic phase was that the arti- facts recovered from each site represented a reliable sample of the total site assemblage. In the absence of actual excavation of the site, there is no way of assessing this reliability. It is simply an assump- tion which is inherent in a survey which derives data from surface collection. I do not pretend to have collected all the artifacts left by the various PaleoIndian hunting groups, nor can I maintain that the sample I have is mathematically random. I can only state that the sample recovered is a function of the specific location of deflated areas within the sites themselves. If this technique would in any way result in the recovery of a biased sample, the reasons are not immediately apparent.

I should add that no attempt was made to attain intra-site control over the location of artifacts. I feel this will be detrimental to future research in the area in the long run, but it was a necessary sacrifice in the interest of the time and financial resources available. Intra- site sampling techniques, such as those outlined by Binford (1964:435) and termed "controlled surface pickup" by Streuver (1968:143) should be utilized systematically wherever possible. They are, however, exceedingly time-consuming when a region of this extent is under analysis. Furthermore, there is the question of whether artifacts in this region, presently exposed by deflation and quite possibly deflated a number of times since their original deposition, are still in their original context. If not, intra-site control over artifact context would be of limited value to cultural interpretation.

Following the collection of artifacts from the site, the environmental data were recorded. The particular form utilized for this survey is presented in Figure 3. As indicated, attention was paid to those variables particularly relevant to locational analysis. Not all of these variables were found to be useful in later analysis, but they were nevertheless recorded during the survey. Completion of the form in the field involved obtaining these data, making a sketch map of the site on graph paper, and photographing the site and its surrounding topography.[4] Final completion of the form was done in the laboratory following the analytic phase of the research.

Finally, each site location was recorded on the appropriate 7.5 minute topographic map, and was assigned a site number. A system of site designation was adopted specifically for use in this survey. This system involves the employment of alphanumeric symbols in assigning

---

[4]Photographs were taken with a Yashica twin-lens reflex camera. They were found for the most part to be of little value. The topography of PaleoIndian sites in this area is of such low relief that it cannot be significantly defined photographically. The use of a 35-mm. camera equipped with a telephoto lens resulted in only slight improvement (Jerry Dawson, personal communication).

SITE SURVEY FORM

Date: Site No:
Other Name or No: Site Type:
Location: Elevation:

I. Check List (Data recorded elsewhere)   Location of
                                                materials:

    1. Inventory sheet no:
    2. Projectile point analysis form:
    3. Artifact analysis form:
    4. Scraper analysis form:
    5. Scraper data sheet:
    6. Sketch map:
    7. Photographed:

II. Location Analysis

From site to nearest:	Distance:	Direction:
1. Pond	___	___
2. Playa	___	___
3. Arroyo	___	___
4. Fresh water	___	___
5. High ridge	___	___
6. Lookout point	___	___
7. Grazing area	___	___
8. Trap area	___	___
9. Site of same type	___	___
10. Vertical distance to water	___	___
11. Other	___	___

III. Site Description

    1. Land form at site:
    2. Dimensions and shape:
    3. Exposure:
    4. Degree of deflation:
    5. Soil type:
    6. Sheltered or exposed?
       a. From prevailing wind:
       b. From grazing area:
    7. Drainage pattern:
    8. Surrounding topography:
       NE 1/4
       NW 1/4
       SW 1/4
       SE 1/4

Figure 3. The Site Survey Form

site numbers (e.g., 13DR4). To derive the number, each topographic map was divided into 25 grids, each grid into 25 units, and each of these units in turn into 9 units. The topographic maps were each assigned a number; for instance in 13DR4, the 13 refers to the map number. Each of the 25 grids were lettered A - Y, as were each of the 25 units within each grid. Thus, in the example, D refers to the grid letter, and R to the unit letter within the grid. The final symbol refers to the appropriate 9-unit number in which the site is located, in this case unit number 4.

Though seemingly complex this system is quite easy to use, and permits the accurate location (within 100 yards) of any site on a standard 7.5 minute topographic map simply by reference to the number. Artifacts collected were then numbered sequentially as they were derived, e.g., 13DR4.1, 13DR4.2 . . . 13DR4.n. The single disadvantage to the system is in a potential confusion of letters and numbers (for instance, I and 1), but with a minimum of caution in lettering, this can be avoided.

CHAPTER IV

The Empirical Material: Description and Summary

Introduction

At the time of the termination of survey activities, a total of 59 PaleoIndian occupational loci had been recorded (Figure 4). A number of other sites, primarily Archaic and Basketmaker, plus a number of isolated artifact finds, were also encountered during the course of the survey and were recorded. Descriptive information regarding all of these, 119 in total, is on file at the Maxwell Museum of Anthropology, University of New Mexico, Albuquerque.

The term "occupational loci" is used because of the apparent qualitative and quantitative variation in the nature of the PaleoIndian data recovered. For purposes of analysis only, these loci were arbitrarily divided into two analytic categories: PaleoIndian sites and PaleoIndian localities. Within each cultural assemblage, loci which each yielded more than 2% of the total number of artifacts recorded for that culture were considered sites. This resulted in a total of 30 sites which underwent intensive analysis for the interpretive portion of the present study.

The PaleoIndian localities were not analyzed intensively due to the low artifact yield. I would suggest that these localities represent

63

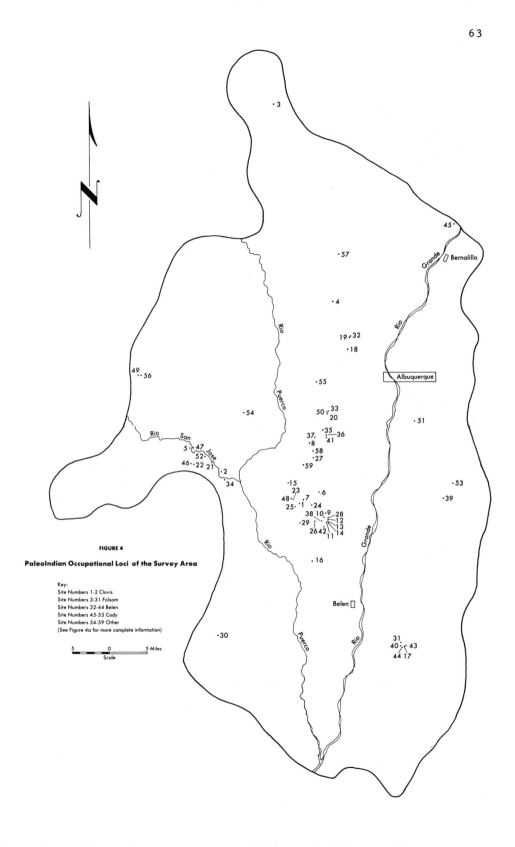

FIGURE 4

PaleoIndian Occupational Loci of the Survey Area

Key:
Site Numbers 1-2 Clovis
Site Numbers 3-31 Folsom
Site Numbers 32-44 Belen
Site Numbers 45-53 Cody
Site Numbers 54-59 Other
(See Figure 4a for more complete information)

5   0   5 Miles
Scale

1.	13JB5	Clovis site
2.	12QY3	Clovis locality
3.	2GD2	Folsom site
4.	9CM3	" "
5.	12OA3	" "
6.	13BA3	" "
7.	13ES8	" "
8.	13FR1	" "
9.	13GX5	" "
10.	13LC8	" "
11.	13LH9	" "
12.	13LI4	" "
13.	13LI7	" "
14.	13LN1	" "
15.	13XP3	" "
16.	18AG7	" "
17.	19JM9	" "
18.	9DQ2	Folsom locality
19.	9SI9	" "
20.	9VH6	" "
21.	12QA7	" "
22.	12TH7	" "
23.	13DS3	" "
24.	13FC9	" "
25.	13IJ5	" "
26.	13KI9	" "
27.	13KR6	" "
28.	13LI2	" "
29.	13OL4	" "
30.	17GA-E	" "
31.	19JC4	" "
32.	9SJ5	Belen site
33.	9VD9	" "
34.	12WG5	" "
35.	13BR3	" "
36.	13BX9	" "
37.	13FJ8	" "
38.	13LG9	" "
39.	14CS5	" "
40.	19JL5	" "
41.	13GD5	Belen locality
42.	13LM8	" "
43.	19JN5	" "
44.	19JR1	" "
45.	5DR1	Cody site
46.	12FT9	" "
47.	12JV5	" "
48.	13DR4	" "
49.	45JP9	" "
50.	9VD7	Cody locality
51.	10UY7	" "
52.	12KX2	" "
53.	14XN4	" "
54.	8XK8	Proto-Folsom site
55.	9GU3	Multi-component site
56.	45JR4	Unclassified Paleo site
57.	4MI8	Unclassified Paleo locality
58.	13KC5	Multi-component locality
59.	13TD7	" " "

Figure 4a. Key to Sites Numbered in Figure 4.

one of two things; either they are areas of extremely limited activity on the part of the PaleoIndians, or they may be indicative of larger artifact assemblages which are not yet uncovered by deflation. Although it is difficult to generalize about the localities, I feel that having examined the nature and extent of the deflation in these areas, many can be considered loci of very limited activity.

As categorized below, a total of 1,513 PaleoIndian artifacts were recorded in the survey, exclusive of debitage. Included in this are artifacts from those private collections analyzed by the author. Of this total, 1,269 artifacts are included in the 30 sites which underwent intensive analysis. The sites thus yielded an average of 42.5 artifacts apiece. I offer this information by way of comparison with the estimated artifact frequencies of selected PaleoIndian sites elsewhere in North America. Wilmsen (1967:28) presents the following data on assemblage sizes, based on his analysis of several sites: Lindenmeier, 7000; Vernon, 2334; Williamson, 1500; Shoop, 800. I feel that the rather large quantitative variation here merits explanation, and I will offer suggestions along this line in the concluding chapters of this study.

The commonly-accepted cultural divisions of the PaleoIndian stage in North America are discussed in detail elsewhere (cf. Wormington 1957, 1965, Mason 1962), and I will accept these divisions as a basis for analysis and chronological ordering. Employing this classification, the following PaleoIndian cultural manifestations were recorded by the survey (listed in order of relative abundance):

1. Folsom:

A total of 15 sites and 14 localities can be attributed to the Folsom

occupation of the survey region (Figure 5a, b). All of these can be

included under the category "classic Folsom" as derived from such

sites as Lindenmeier, Folsom, and Blackwater Draw. In fact, some

of the Folsom points which have been recovered here exhibit a quality

of workmanship which equals or surpasses that revealed elsewhere.

Chronologically, Folsom is considered to have occupied the western

North American plains between 9000 - 8000 B.C. based on the radio-

carbon dating from the Lindenmeier, Brewster, and Lubbock sites

(Haynes and Agogino 1960, Agogino and Rovner 1964, Sellards 1952).

For purposes of establishing relative chronology in the survey area,

it will be assumed that similar dates would be derived from the Folsom

occupation of the central Rio Grande valley, were datable organic

material available.

Perhaps the primary difference between the data derived from the

survey and that occuring elsewhere in the Plains and Southwest is the

increase in information about campsites. As mentioned previously,

most of the data on PaleoIndian culture has been derived from kill

sites, thus biasing considerably the sample of artifacts. Wendorf and

Hester (1962:162-63) noted only three published Folsom campsites in

1962, and their own survey of the Llano Estacado yielded limited topo-

graphic information on 13 more. Thus the present survey has in effect

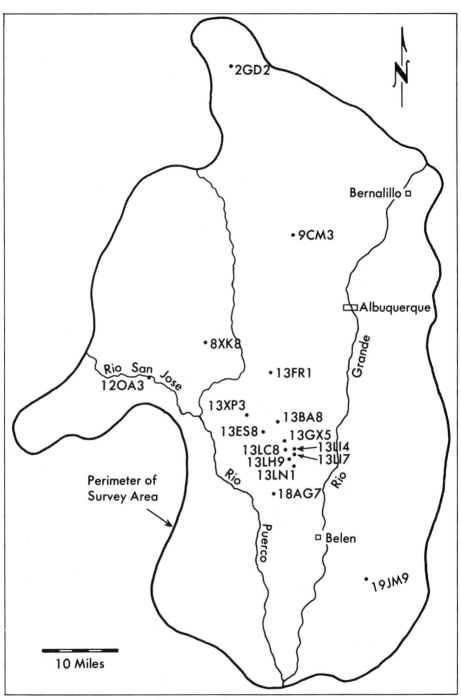

FIGURE 5a. Location of Folsom Sites.

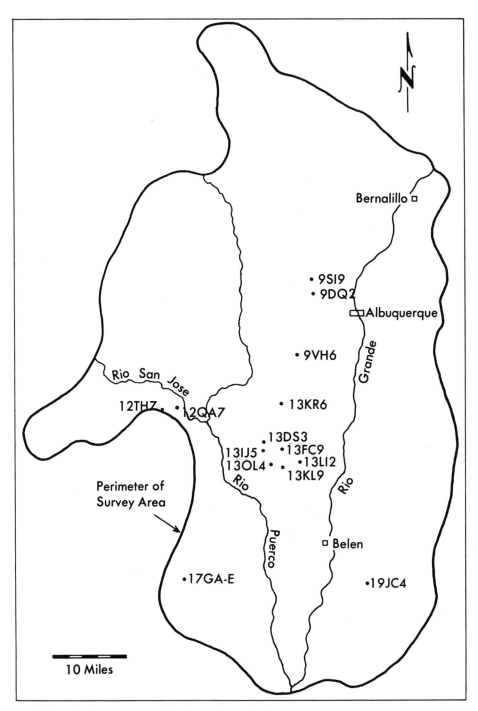

FIGURE 5b. Location of Folsom Localities.

almost doubled the total number of Folsom campsites for which cultural

and environmental data are now available.

One site (8XK8) has yielded fluted points which cannot be classi-

fied as "classic" Folsom and thus was not analyzed with the other sites.

The 8XK8 points exhibit some characteristics of Clovis manufacture,

and could possibly be transitional in the survey area between Clovis and

Folsom (Dawson and Judge 1969:153). There is also an equal possibility

that these points could be quite widespread in North America. On the

basis of published illustrations there are similar points found in Ohio

(Prufer 1962:numbers 494, 501; Prufer 1963:numbers 514, 523) and

in Michigan (Mason 1958:Plates II, III, and VII). No definite assump-

tions should be made on the basis of illustrations alone, yet I would

consider the evidence strong enough to warrant further investigation

of a possible widespread "proto-Folsom" complex from which a rela-

tively specialized Plains "classic" Folsom was derived.

2. Belen:

A total of 9 sites and 4 localities are attributed to a cultural

stage which will be referred to as "Belen" (Figure 6). When I first

began to analyze the Belen material, I felt it was most probably a

local Rio Grande variant of the Milnesand category found in eastern

New Mexico (Sellards 1955, Warnica and Williamson 1968). However

Ele Baker, who found the first Belen sites and named the type, has ex-

amined the original Milnesand collection in addition to the Plainview

70

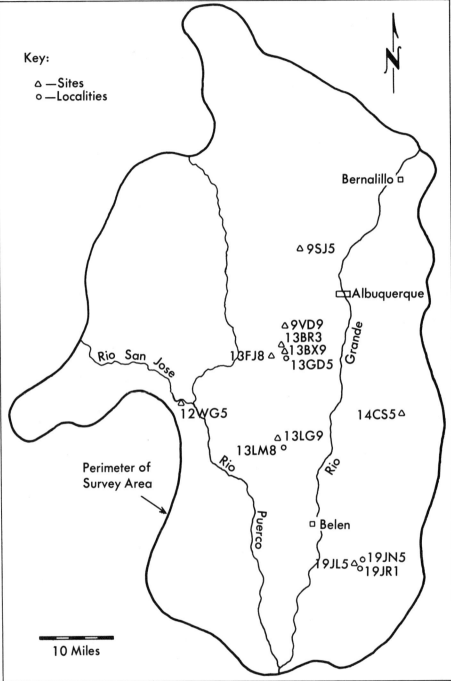

FIGURE 6. Location of Belen Sites and Localities.

and Midland collections, and has presented his interpretation that the
Belen points are indeed different (Baker 1968). I will, therefore, recognize the category Belen herein as an analytic type which differs sufficiently from other such types to warrant an explanation in either cultural or environmental terms. I should qualify this acceptance with
the statement that much further analysis will be necessary before any
final taxonomic categorization can be made.

Regardless of whether Belen will eventually be found to be more
closely associated with Plainview, Midland, or Milnesand, there is
little doubt that it forms part of a relatively generalized "tradition"
in the west, termed "Plano" by Mason (1962). Unfortunately, the Plano
tradition has become a catch-all category and exhibits at the moment
a pressing need for further research and clarification. Based on a
number of carbon dates, the Plano period is bracketed between 8000
and 5000 B.C. It is generally held that the Midland and Plainview types
occur near the beginning of this period, and that the Cody Complex
(Eden and Scottsbluff) types occur toward the end of it. Milnesand
points have not been dated, but the Portales Horizon at Blackwater
Draw has yielded a rather late date of 4500 to 4200 B.C. (Wormington
1957:112). The Portales Complex is felt to be similar to Milnesand.

Thus in attempting to orient the Belen assemblage chronologically,
one is faced with the enigmatic situation of typological similarities
which cover the whole range of the Plano cultural period. To

temporarily solve this problem, I will arbitrarily place the Belen type chronologically prior to the Cody Complex in the survey area. This assessment is based on the relatively early dates for the typologically similar Midland and Plainview, the lack of positive dating for Milnesand, and the generally late date acknowledged for the Cody Complex. Furthermore, I feel that evidence will result from analysis of the survey data which may tend to support this judgment. Positive chronological positioning of the Belen material will, of course, have to await the excavation and recovery of datable remains.

3. Cody Complex:

The survey revealed a total of 5 sites and 4 localities which could be assigned to the Cody Complex (Figure 7). Four of the sites yielded Eden point types, and the other site was assigned to the Cody Complex on the basis of the occurrence of Cody knives. It should be noted that no site manifestations of the Scottsbluff type were found in the survey area. This fact may eventually prove pertinent to the clarification of the distinction between Eden and Scottsbluff elsewhere in the Plains area.

The Eden points are generally similar to those found in well-known Cody Complex sites such as Claypool, Finley, Horner, and Olsen-Chubbock. If any distinction can be isolated, it would be in terms of the presence of lateral serration and basal concavities on the survey points, although it is somewhat difficult to generalize about the

73

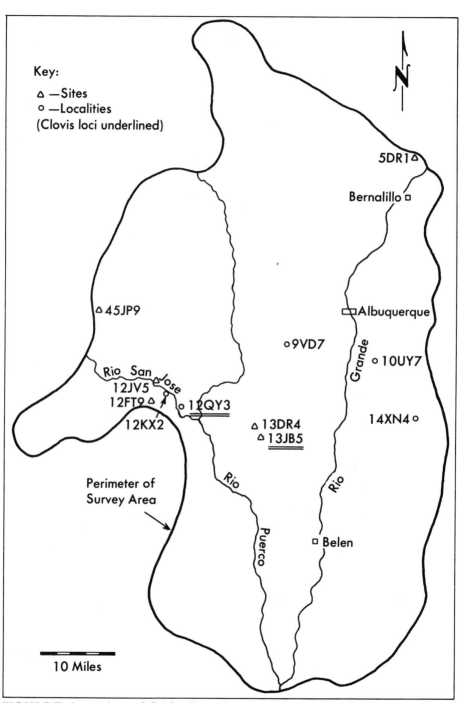

FIGURE 7. Location of Cody Complex and Clovis Sites and Localities.

survey sample. Lateral serration of Eden material may be more widespread than reported (Ruthann Knudson, personal communication), and
may even be functional with respect to the use of points as knives. The
basal concavities which occur frequently in the survey sample of Eden
points may prove to be a more significant difference, since this type
of basal modification may be a function of slight variation in hafting
methods. As far as I know, however, no extensive analysis has been
undertaken to determine the degree to which this trait occurs elsewhere
with respect to Eden material.

Radiocarbon dates from Cody Complex sites fall into the late
part of the Plano period. Perhaps the date of 6640 B.C. from Hell
Gap (Wormington 1965:23) can be considered broadly representative
of the Cody occupation of the Plains. For purposes of this survey,
the Cody Complex manifestations in the central Rio Grande will be considered definitely later than Folsom, and probably also post-dating the
Belen occupation.

4. Clovis:

Only one Clovis site and one Clovis locality were defined on the
basis of the survey data (Figure 7). A number of isolated finds of
Clovis points, both broken and complete, were recorded in the course
of the investigation. The Clovis material represented here is comparable morphologically and technologically to that from Clovis sites found
elsewhere in the west such as Dent, Blackwater Draw, and in southern

Arizona. The primary difference is that the Clovis site here is a campsite, possibly quite a large one.

Clovis campsites are very rare in the west, probably because many of the points have been located through discoveries of mammoth bones (i. e., kill situations). Wendorf and Hester (1962:162) listed no published Clovis campsites, and their own survey of the Llano Estacado revealed only three, two of which were mixed with later PaleoIndian material. Recent work at Murray Springs has revealed both camp and kill locations (C. Vance Haynes, personal communication). Aside from these locations, the only other Clovis site which is yielding information about activities other than kill situations is the Mockingbird site, some 60 miles south of the survey area. Under the direction of Robert Weber, this site is presently being excavated and the results are expected to provide a very important contribution to our knowledge of Clovis settlement activity.

Chronologically, the Clovis materials are probably the most well-defined of the PaleoIndian sequence. Radiocarbon dates have been derived from the Naco, Lehner, Dent, and Blackwater sites which indicate an accepted minimal antiquity of 9, 000 - 10, 000 B. C. for Clovis (cf. Haynes 1964). An age of this order will be assumed for the Clovis materials in the survey area.

5. Sandia:

An unexpected anomaly in the results of the survey was the total absence of Sandia sites. The type site, Sandia Cave, is situated on the northeastern periphery of the survey area and the single other

known Sandia location, the Lucy site, is only about 55 miles east.

These have been reported by Hibben (1941) and Roosa (1956a), the ori-

ginal investigators of the two sites. The position of the Sandia material

in the New World cultural sequence has been debated considerably

(cf. Mason 1962), an event which is not surprising due to the indications

of considerable antiquity which accompany the assemblage. Radio-

carbon dates from the cave and from the Lucy site suggest that Sandia

may predate Clovis in the PaleoIndian sequence (Hibben 1955, Roosa

1968).

Clarification of the Sandia situation depends upon the discovery

of new information, and it is for this reason that we were disappointed

in the lack of data revealed by the survey. One possible explanation

for this lacuna, as suggested by Dawson and Judge (1969:151), is that

the Rio Grande may have been a significant barrier at the time of

Sandia occupation. Since most of the survey area lies west of the

river, the absence of Sandia sites might possibly be explained on this

basis.

6. Other PaleoIndian Material:

No campsites of other cultures commonly accepted as PaleoIndian

were found in the survey area. The only possible exception to this is

site 14P05, which may be a Simonsen site similar to that reported by

Agogino and Frankforter (1960) in Iowa. The survey site has yielded

corner-notched points in association with the type of endscraper which
for the rest of the region is a horizon marker for PaleoIndian.

The original Simonsen site, and also the association of corner-
notched and lanceolate (Cody) points at the Renier site in Wisconsin
(Mason and Irwin 1960), raises the important question of the precise
definition of the PaleoIndian period; in particular its terminal boundary.
Should one define the limits of the PaleoIndian tradition on the basis
of lanceolate points, radiocarbon dates, faunal association, or on some
combination of the three? To my knowledge this question has not been
answered satisfactorily, and it has important implications for the
eventual explanation of the cultural transition from PaleoIndian to
Archaic in the Plains area. The Simonsen site falls within the Paleo-
Indian temproal sequence, having been dated at 6,471 B.C. (Agogino
and Frankforter 1960). Corner-notched points, however, are not
generally considered part of the PaleoIndian cultural inventory. The
faunal association at Simonsen (Bison occidentalis) has been questioned
because of the difficulty in distinguishing this species from B.
athabascae (Mason 1962:272). Until this question has been resolved
satisfactorily through further research in the Plains, I do not feel it
legitimate to consider 14P05 as a PaleoIndian site for the purposes of
this study.

There were a few isolated finds of projectile points other than
the types discussed above; specifically Agate Basin, Midland, and

Plainview, but no evidence of site association was encountered with these finds. The major point type missing from the survey assemblage is the Hell Gap type (Agogino 1961). There is, however, prolific evidence of a morphologically similar point type which proved to be post-PaleoIndian in age. This is a large stemmed point, variously referred to as Jay, Bajada, or Rio Grande. Regardless of the morphological similarity of this type to Hell Gap, examination of the associated utility implements indicated that it was not to be included in the Paleo-Indian sequence. Investigations by the Anasazi Origins Project verified that it overlies the Cody Complex stratigraphically at the Dunas Altas locality (Cynthia Irwin-Williams, personal communication). Eighteen of the Jay sites were recorded in the course of the survey, and there are doubtless many more since no attempt was made to concentrate on them. In the future, some effort should be made to examine this occupation more thoroughly in the survey area, since it is undoubtedly critical to an understanding of the PaleoIndian-Archaic transition in the region. [1]

7. Summary:

A summary of the PaleoIndian occupational loci of the central Rio Grande valley is presented in Table 1, arranged in the chronological order explained previously. Six sites and localities are listed

----

[1]For a discussion of the occurrence of this type of material elsewhere see Honea (1969).

Table 1: Summary of the PaleoIndian Occupational Loci of the Survey
Area

Cultural Type	Sites	Localities
A. Classified PaleoIndian		
Clovis	1	1
Folsom	15	14
Belen	9	4
Cody Complex	5	4
Subtotals	30	23
b. Other Data		
Proto- Folsom	1	0
Mixed Assemblages	1	2
Unclassified PaleoIndian	1	1
Totals	33	26

Total Occupational Loci: 59

80

separately because they either exhibit mixed data (more than one culture represented), do not fit into the accepted pattern (proto-Folsom),
or have not yet yielded sufficient diagnositc artifacts to permit classification.

It might be well to comment at this point on the differential quan-
tities of sites per culture, as revealed by the survey data (Table 1).
Folsom quite obviously predominates, followed by Belen, Cody, and
Clovis. There are two possible interpretations of this variation. One
is that the survey technique resulted primarily in the discovery of the
Folsom and Belen settlement strategies, thus biasing the sample toward these two cultures. Acceptance of this interpretation would include the assumption that additional Clovis and Cody sites will be found
when more is known regarding their settlement strategies.

In my opinion, a more plausible explanation is that these figures
represent in gross terms the intensity of occupation of the survey area
over a period of time by each of these cultures. This interpretation
is buttressed by the results of the probability sampling, but only time
and continued research will resolve the question.

Description of the Lithic Data

The following section will include a description of the various
functional categories of lithic implements found in the survey, with
the frequency of occurrence of each type. A summary of these data
will be provided at the end of the section. In general, I have tried to

follow the implement classifications which exist in the literature (cf.
Irwin and Wormington 1970); however, in a number of instances I felt
that these were inadequate and have supplied my own classifications
with descriptions.

1. Projectile Points:

PaleoIndian projectile points are generally larger and exhibit
superior craftsmanship to those of the Archaic cultures which followed.
They are characteristically lanceolate in outline, and one of the particularly distinguishing features is the presence of abrading or grinding
along the lower lateral edges, and frequently in the base of the point.
A commonly encountered explanation of this grinding is that it prevents
the lateral edges of the point from cutting the sinew used to secure it
in the haft (e.g., Mason 1958:10). I question this on a number of
counts. For instance, if this were true, why would the basal concavity
of certain points be consistently ground, or why would not other hafted
implements (scrapers, drills, etc.) also exhibit this type of abrasion?
In addition, later points (both dart points and arrowheads) were hafted
with sinew and do not exhibit the grinding.

I would suggest that we must look to a more intensive analysis
of the data in order to explain this phenomenon, and in the interpretative portion of this paper I will offer some hypotheses which will lead
to a more reasonable explanation. I should point out here, though,
that one frequently finds that the length of this lateral grinding is

considered a significant attribute of PaleoIndian point types. Except for the indented-base points, the utility of this measurement as an accurate indication of hafting length can be questioned. These points were ground by using a motion parallel to the long axis of the point, thus making it difficult for the producer of the point to limit the grinding length to any fixed degree. Thus for the purposes of this paper, the length of the lateral grinding will not be considered a significant variable, except for the indented-based points which were of necessity ground perpendicular to the long axis of the point.

One of the characteristics which defines two of the point types considered here (Folsom and Clovis) is that of fluting. In one context, fluting is simply another means of thinning the basal portion of the point, presumably to facilitate hafting. As such, it is difficult at times to distinguish poorly fluted, or multiple fluted points from basally thinned points. This distinction becomes important when attempting to determine whether a point found in the Arctic, for instance, is fluted or basally thinned (cf. Humphrey 1966). In reviewing the literature dealing with fluted points, I was unable to find an adequate definition of fluting, although Mason (1958) does discuss the proper method of measuring the length of the flutes. In the absence of any accepted standard for distinguishing these two factors, I will adhere to the following definition of fluting in the present study:

A projectile point will be considered fluted when there is evidence of consistent, careful preparation of both the preform (including the bifacial shaping of the surface from which the flutes will be removed) and the striking platform (including beveling or nippling by careful retouch), for the purpose of removing single thinning flakes with maximum efficiency.

Such a definition avoids basing the distinction on the length of the removed flake, since there is considerable variation of this attribute.

The bases of PaleoIndian lanceolate points are frequently straight or concave, and less frequently convex. In considering the significance of these attributes, it must be remembered that often the basal concavity is a dependent variable, that is, its presence is a function of the fluting or thinning process. This is especially true with Folsom and Clovis points.

Another attribute frequently encountered in data on projectile points is their length. It is true that PaleoIndian points are generally longer than later ones. Considerable caution must be exercised, however, in the correlation of the length variable among PaleoIndian points, since points were frequently resharpened, and this reduced the length of the point in many cases. Most of the projectile points analyzed in this study were not complete, but were broken bases left at the campsites during the process of rehafting. For this reason, and because of the resharpening factor, the length of points is not here considered a reliable attribute for analysis.

It is presumed that the primary function of the projectile point was the killing of animals, and in the case of the PaleoIndian, this probably included large game animals. Nevertheless, one should not neglect to consider possible secondary functions of the points in meeting hand-held piercing and cutting needs.

One of the most perplexing questions regarding PaleoIndian weaponry is whether or not the use of the spearthrower was known, and if so, what type of mechanism was involved in the attachment of the point to the main spear shaft? Regarding the spearthrower, it is presumed that this implement was used but there is no definite evidence for it prior to the time of the Cody Complex. An atlatl hook was found in situ at the Jergens site in Colorado, thus confirming the knowledge of the spearthrower during Cody times (Joe Ben Wheat, personal communication). At present we have no incontrovertible evidence of the spearthrower at any earlier time, although I feel that an intensive analysis of the points themselves may reveal characteristics attributable only to the use of such weaponry, and I will offer suggestions to this effect in the interpretive section that follows.

Another assumption is that some sort of foreshaft was used to attach the projectile point to the mainshaft. Such foreshafts could have been made of bone, wood, or antler. The advantage of this type of weapon configuration is that it permits the retrieval of one component of the system (the mainshaft) even if a kill is not made. In addition, the weight provided by a relatively heavy foreshaft (such as hard wood, bone, or antler) may be critical to the ballistic factor of the weapon assemblage, especially if a light point, such as Folsom, is being utilized.

A total of 179 projectile points were retrieved from the 30 sites analyzed in the survey. This total includes all broken points and point fragments, as well as complete specimens. The cultural distribution is shown in Table 2, at the end of this section. Representative points and point bases from each culture, and from the proto-Folsom site (not included in the totals) are illustrated in Figures 8 and 9.

2. Blanks and Preforms:

The term "blank" is used quite extensively in the literature to describe the flake or core lithic unit from which artifacts are made. As more data have been analyzed and more tool types encountered, it has become necessary to categorize an intermediate stage in the manufacture of lithic implements. The term "preform" will be used here to represent that stage, following the terminology adopted at the 1964 Les Eyzies conference on lithic technology (cf. Fitting, et. al. 1966:39). However, I shall modify these definitions somewhat in order to make explicit some of the results of the data obtained from this survey.

The term "blank", as used herein, will refer to the lithic unit from which the preform is made or from which the artifact is made, if there is no preform stage. A number of different types of implements can be made directly from unspecialized blanks. A "preform"

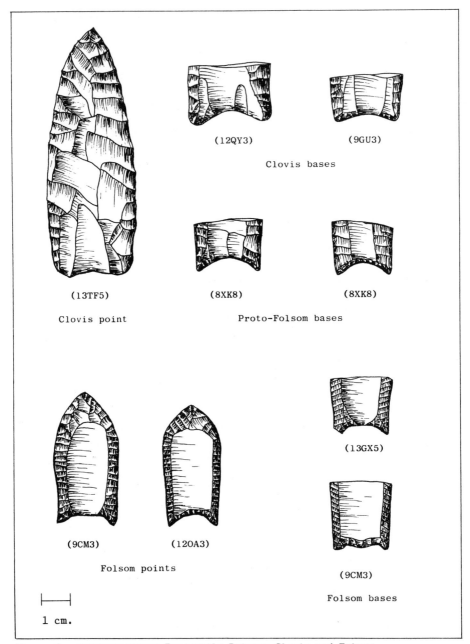

(12QY3)   (9GU3)

Clovis bases

(13TF5)   (8XK8)   (8XK8)

Clovis point   Proto-Folsom bases

(13GX5)

(9CM3)   (12OA3)

Folsom points

(9CM3)

Folsom bases

1 cm.

Figure 8.   Representative Projectile Points: Clovis and Folsom.

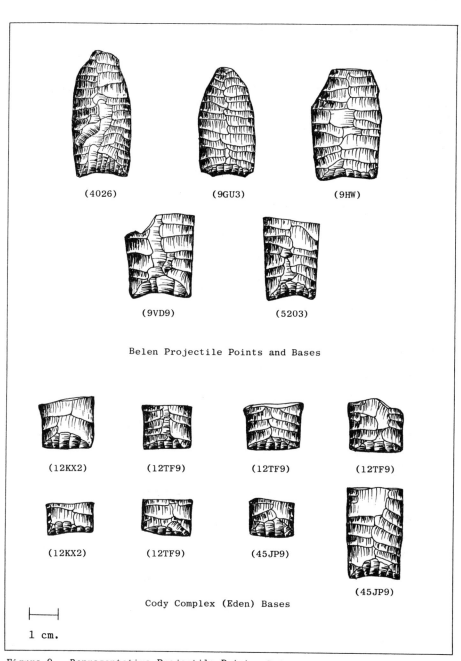

(4026)   (9GU3)   (9HW)

(9VD9)   (5203)

Belen Projectile Points and Bases

(12KX2)   (12TF9)   (12TF9)   (12TF9)

(12KX2)   (12TF9)   (45JP9)

(45JP9)

Cody Complex (Eden) Bases

1 cm.

Figure 9.   Representative Projectile Points: Belen and Cody Complex.

on the other hand, refers to a distinctive intermediate stage of manufacture in which the blank is modified in a specific manner necessary for the eventual production of a specific implement. Such implements can only be produced from specialized preforms. For example, Folsom point preforms, made from flake blanks, were designed specifically for the manufacture of fluted Folsom points.

Another reason for establishing an intermediate category is that in the case of the survey material, there is good evidence for the use of the preform itself for various functions prior to its modification into a given artifact. Fitting (Fitting, et. al. 1966:39) has noted that the Holcombe preforms were not generally used. In contrast, the central Rio Grande data indicates that for Folsom at least, the preform was itself a functionally important tool, and this may have held for other cultures as well. Elsewhere, I have indicated the importance of considering this function in the formulation of reliable taxonomic categories of projectile points (Judge 1970).

Flake blanks for the production of PaleoIndian points were generally struck as very large flakes or blades. Although we hear much about the use of blades and the blade technique by various PaleoIndian groups (especially Clovis), I feel this is somewhat of an over-reaction to the quest for specific Old World ties. I would suggest that most point blanks were originally flakes rather than blades, based on the existing evidence we now have from the Folsom data. Furthermore,

I think the evidence points strongly toward the use of a Levallois-like technique for the removal of these flakes, since this is one of the most efficient means of deriving a large, relatively thin flake, with minimal "trajectory" or curvature (see Chapter 6). Of the various PaleoIndian assemblages, I would suggest that only Eden points might have been derived from blade blanks.

Blanks were worked into bifacial preforms primarily through the use of soft hammer percussion. Of the techniques utilized in point production, most is known about the Folsom method, since 91% of the preforms recovered were from Folsom assemblages. The Folsom technique is a very highly specialized process which will be discussed in detail in Chapter 6.

In terms of primary function, the preform obviously served as a source for a projectile point. However, secondary or related functions should not be overlooked and there is a good deal of evidence, again based primarily on the Folson data, that the preforms were utilized as effective cutting implements prior to their transformation into points. A total of 141 preforms were recorded from the survey, and as shown in Table 2, 128 of these were from Folsom sites. Included here are broken as well as complete specimens, and in the case of Folsom I have included the descriptive categories of hinged preforms and snapped tips, which will be explained later. Illustrations of this material are presented in Figure 10.

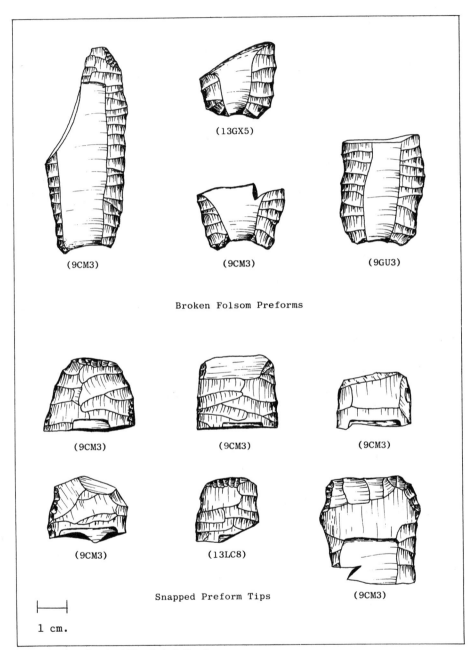

(13GX5)

(9CM3)   (9CM3)   (9GU3)

Broken Folsom Preforms

(9CM3)   (9CM3)   (9CM3)

(9CM3)   (13LC8)

Snapped Preform Tips   (9CM3)

1 cm.

Figure 10. Projectile Point Preforms.

3. Transverse Scrapers:

As mentioned previously, the transverse scraper or "endscraper" is a horizon marker for the PaleoIndian stage in the survey area, and it is by far the most abundant item in the lithic tool assemblage. For these two reasons, the transverse scrapers were analyzed intensively in this study in order to determine the more subtle changes in lithic technology occurring in the PaleoIndian sequence, which might not be overtly reflected in the projectile point typologies.

Prior to describing the generalized PaleoIndian transverse scraper I would like to present the basic flake terminology employed in this study to clarify the distinctions which will be made in this and ensuing descriptions. A flake is simply a piece of lithic material which is removed from a larger lithic unit, here termed a core. Methods of detachment commonly include direct percussion, indirect percussion, and pressure. Direct percussion includes the use of a hammerstone to remove the flake, or the use of a material (wood, bone, or antler) softer than the core. The latter technique will be termed "soft hammer" percussion. Indirect percussion utilizes an intermediary or "punch" to remove the flake, and the pressure technique involves pressing the flakes off rather than striking them. The point of detachment on the flake is termed the striking platform, and it is frequently prepared prior to flake removal by careful retouch, grinding, or both. The end of the flake exhibiting the striking platform (or if the latter is absent, the end from which the flake was removed) is termed the proximal end, and the opposite the distal end. The outer surface of the flake (i.e., the original core surface) is termed the dorsal surface, and the smooth inner surface of the flake is its ventral side. The two edges between the distal and proximal ends are called the lateral edges. The term blade is used here in the Old World sense; it is simply a specialized flake which is twice as long as it is wide. A prismatic blade is one with a single dorsal ridge, resulting in a triangular cross-section.

The basic transverse scraper morphology is that of a unifacial flake, roughly triangular in outline with the narrow apex at the proximal end. The distal end is modified by soft hammer retouch into an arc-shaped working edge, transverse to the main axis of the scraper. It is this modification which gives the implement its name. From this basic structure, transverse scrapers are modified in a number of different ways, presumably to satisfy different functional needs. For instance, they may be modified unilaterally or bilaterally with high or low angle retouch; one or both distal corners may be modified into a sharp point called a spur; and single or multiple notches may be chipped into either or both lateral edges. Some scrapers exhibit large, well-flaked notches which may have functioned as spokeshaves, and less frequently there are delicate gravers worked into one of the lateral edges.

These scrapers may have been used either as hand-held or hafted implements. Direct evidence for hafting is difficult to determine and is best inferred by analyzing a number of factors, such as the degree of divergence, proximal modification, type of notching, and lack of lateral wear. Almost certainly these items were important tools, serving a number of generalized functions such as scraping, cutting, slashing, gouging, and "burin" incising.

A total of 557 transverse scrapers were recorded by the survey from the 30 PaleoIndian sites, and the cultural distribution of these is shown in Table 2. For purposes of analysis, the scrapers were divided into three readily apparent categories based on lateral modification: unmodified (TU), unilaterally modified (TS), and bilaterally modified (TB). Illustrations of representative scrapers of these categories from each culture are presented in Figures 11 and 12.

4. Side Scrapers:

Side scrapers are defined as flakes which exhibit concentration on the modification of the lateral, as opposed to distal, edges. Generally the modification occurs on only one lateral edge of a relatively large flake, although at times both edges will be modified. The scraping edge is usually either straight or convex. In their review of Paleo-Indian tool types, Irwin and Wormington (1970) divided side scrapers into single and double-edged categories, and from these derived a

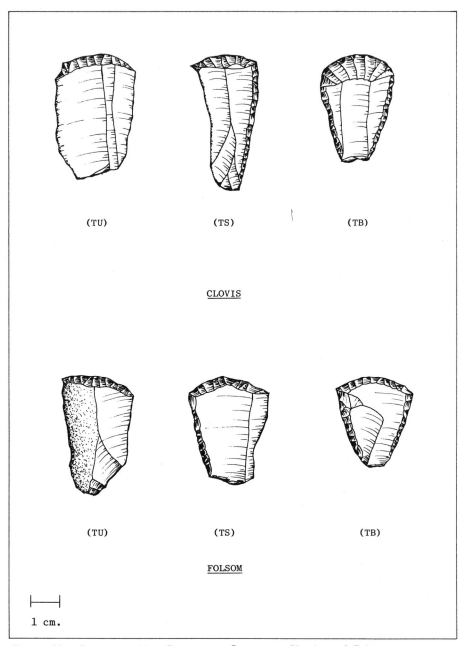

(TU)   (TS)   (TB)

CLOVIS

(TU)   (TS)   (TB)

FOLSOM

1 cm.

Figure 11.   Representative Transverse Scrapers: Clovis and Folsom.

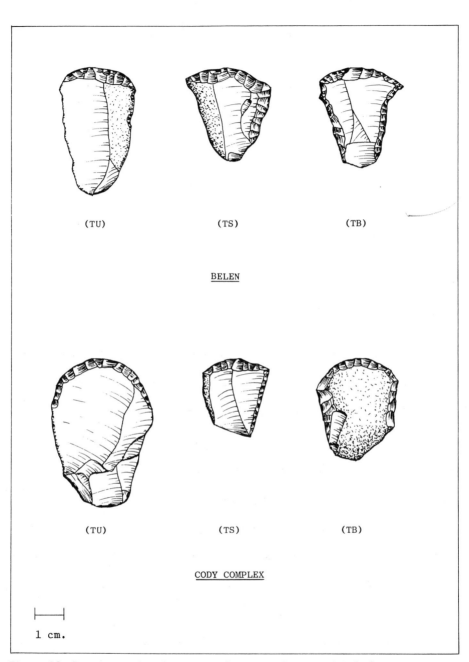

Figure 12. Representative Transverse Scrapers: Belen and Cody Complex.

total of 12 types of implements. I did not attempt any such extensive

classification with the rather limited sample I had from the survey.

It is interesting to point out that of the Clovis and Folsom samples

Irwin and Wormington (1970:30) investigated, the ratios of side scrapers

to end scrapers differ considerably from my data:

	Clovis	Folsom
Irwin & Wormington:		
Side scrapers	75%	40%
End scrapers	19%	40%
Survey Sample:		
Side scrapers	26%	09%
End scrapers	42%	32%

The large percentage of side scrapers found by Irwin and Wormington

in the Blackwater (Clovis) and Lindenmeier (Folsom) tool kits is simply

not manifest in the survey sample. I would suggest that this can even-

tually be explained in terms of different activity loci represented at

the different sites. Blackwater was a kill site, and Lindenmeier was

evidently a combination kill-camp site. The survey sample comprises

campsites only. This would be a starting point from which to explore

the true meaning of the various configurations of tool types represented

in the different assemblages.

One specialized type of side scraper was recognized in the survey

data, although it was limited to the Folsom and Belen assemblages only.

I could find no previously recorded occurrence of this implement, so I have arbitrarily termed it a "tabular" side scraper (Figure 13). These are generally made from wide, flat, thin flakes from which both the distal and proximal ends have been removed (snapped off) in a manner which forms a rough triangle. The wider of the two lateral edges is modified by steep retouch to produce a scraping edge. When first noticed it was felt that these specimens were simply side scrapers broken in usage, but more careful examination of wear patterns revealed the consistent usage of the "pointed" edge (i.e., the one opposite the retouch). It would seem, then, that these are somewhat specialized implements although at the moment their precise function remains undetermined. Tabular side scrapers comprise 27.5% of the total number of side scrapers in the Folsom and Belen assemblages.

Functionally, the category "side scraper" seems oriented more toward a single generalized purpose than the transverse scrapers, primarily because they lack the various modifications (spurs, spokeshave, etc.) which occur on the latter. Since they would be difficult to haft, I would consider their function primarily in terms of hand-held scraping uses. It should be remembered, though, that if only one lateral edge is retouched, that edge can be considered the functional equivalent of a "backed" surface to permit knife usage of the opposing lateral edge. Thus the possibility that they were used as backed knives must also be considered.

Including the tabular forms, a total of 142 side scrapers were derived from the survey, and the cultural distribution of these is shown in Table 2. Illustrations are provided in Figure 13.

5. Knives:

This is a rather amorphous category based primarily on the thinness of the use edge. Quite obviously, any relatively thin edge, either bifacial or unifacial, could have been used for cutting purposes (cf. Crabtree and Davis 1968). The determination of what edge angle distinguishes knives from scrapers becomes somewhat arbitrary since the higher angle (thicker) edges could have been used both for scraping and heavy cutting functions. Wilmsen (1967:139) found in his analysis of edge angle distribution that the values clustered trimodally at 26°-35°, 46°-55°, and 66°-75°. He suggests that the first range was associated with cutting functions, the second with scraping and heavy cutting (also edge blunting), and the third with wood and bone working, and heavy shredding (ibid:140). I did not take edge angle measurements on implements other than scrapers due to limited samples. Nevertheless, the specimens which I term knives herein are those which exhibit working edges of the order of Wilmsen's first category.

Acknowledging the fact that any thin unifacial edge on an implement would permit its use as a knife, I have nevertheless limited the category to those tools which are bifacially worked, since these seem to have been made specifically for knife use, as opposed to multiple

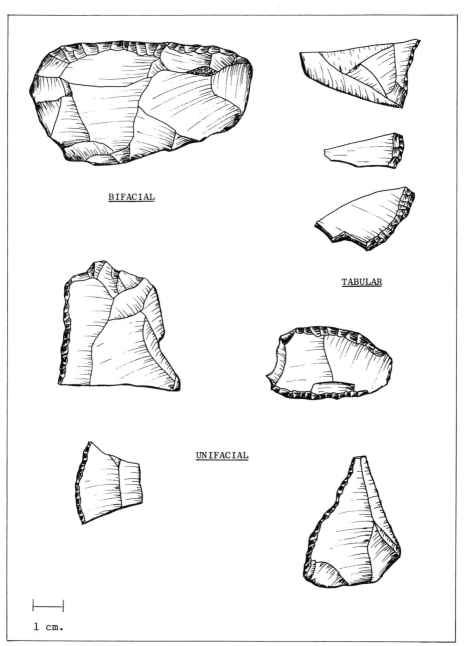

BIFACIAL

TABULAR

UNIFACIAL

1 cm.

Figure 13. Representative Side Scrapers.

function. Thus an implement with both a scraping edge and a thin un-worked edge is classified as a multipurpose scraper, while a tool bi-facially worked to a thin edge is called a knife. The one exception to this in my classification is the Folsom channel flake, which is a uni-facial blade. A very high percentage of these small blades exhibit microscopic knife wear, and some have macroscopic notching or irre-gular serration resulting from use. Thus I have included channel flakes as a specialized class of knives applicable to the Folsom assem-blages only (no Clovis channel flakes were found in the survey).

Of the bifacially worked knives, there seem to be two major categories. One is a large, heavy, bifacially-worked flake which fre-quently exhibits a projection on one side (Figure 14). This is termed a primary butchering tool, since wear pattern analysis shows it to have been used for very heavy cutting and chopping functions such as those associated with the initial butchering of large game. The other type is the thin bifacially-worked flake, termed simply a bifacial knife, which was used for lighter cutting functions, presumably those associa-ted with meat and hide severing. These are the only named categories of knives. It should also be recalled that both end and side scrapers, as well as preforms, points, and miscellaneous flakes, could effec-tively satisfy numerous cutting needs.

A total of 67 bifacially-worked knives (both categories included) were encountered in the survey data. In addition, 195 Folsom channel flakes were found. Of a sample of the latter, approximately 80% exhibited wear when examined microscopically. The cultural distribution of knives is presented in Table 2, and illustrations in Figure 14.

6. Gravers:

A graver is simply a flake, one end or side of which has been chipped into a very fine point. These are generally made from small, thin flake blanks, and the graving tip itself is produced either by careful pressure flaking or by the removal of two single spalls. The graver tips generally show wear microscopically in the form of a polish.

The pressure-worked graver is often found on larger flakes, and this type of graver tip is sometimes worked into other artifacts, such as scrapers, broken projectile points, and channel flakes. The single-spalled graver tips are found only on flakes thin enough to permit this type of modification.

One subcategory of gravers which may be distinguished is that of the double graver. This is simply a flake which has two graver tips instead of one. In the survey sample, double gravers were found in the Folsom assemblage only, of which they comprise about 10%. The cumulative graphs presented by Irwin and Wormington (1970), indicate that this type is not too frequently encountered in PaleoIndian assemblages.

The function of gravers has perplexed archeologists for some time, possibly because they are not commonly encountered in later cultural assemblages. Roberts (1935, 1936), in first noting the

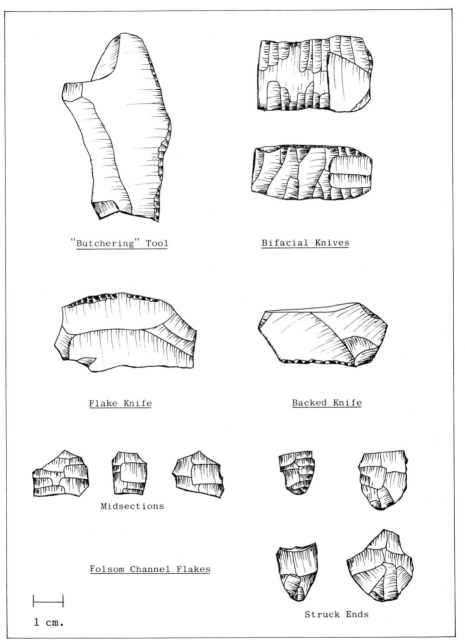

"Butchering" Tool

Bifacial Knives

Flake Knife

Backed Knife

Midsections

Folsom Channel Flakes

Struck Ends

1 cm.

Figure 14. Representative Knives and Channel Flakes.

presence of these items in the Lindenmeier assemblage, suggested both the incising of bone and tattooing as possible functions. Wendorf and Hester (1962) suggest possible uses in butchering and hide-dressing, although Hester found no apparent use for them in experiments in butchering deer. Irwin (Irwin and Wormington 1970:30) has experimented with them in the production of eyed needles and bone blanks. In my own experiments, I have found that the accuracy with which a bone rib can be cut, either longitudinally or crosswise, is in part a function of the accuracy with which the original line in incised. Once the original incision was made with a rather delicate, graver-like tip, the groove could be progressively deepened until it could be quickly cut with the use of a more durable implement such as a scraper spur. I also found that although easy to make, gravers are quite easy to break, and I feel that the sample we have from PaleoIndian sites probably represents only a small portion of those actually used.

I think the most likely use of the gravers was in the hand-held incising of bone for the initial production of bone implements. It is possible that they also served to perforate hides, but the latter is a function which could have been performed with greater efficiency by the use of a needle. It is doubtful that gravers were hafted. Double gravers were evidently limited to Folsom assemblages, at least in the central Rio Grande area.

We should not minimize the importance of gravers to the Paleo-Indian tool kits, since I feel an intensive analysis of this particular item may provide valuable clues to the relative importance of bone-working by PaleoIndian as opposed to later cultures. A total of 111 gravers were located by the survey, and their distribution is shown in Table 2. They are illustrated in Figure 15.

7. Chisel Gravers:

These implements are frequently included as a subcategory of gravers, but I have given them separate status here because I feel the term "graver" may misrepresent their actual function. Frequently, only the broken "chisel" tip is found, thus making it difficult to determine the techniques of production involved. Of the complete ones found, some were made on flakes, others on prismatic blades. In either case, the distal portion is unifacially worked into an elongated, narrow scraping tip by pressure modification. Of the complete specimens recovered, none yielded positive evidence of hafting, and it is presumed they were handheld.

These are not common items in the survey assemblages, and this fact plus their unique morphology would indicate a highly specialized function. I would suggest hand-held gouging of wood or bone in deep, narrow places such as that necessary to hollow out the distal end of a main shaft to receive the pointed foreshaft. In fact, one of the chisel gravers obtained from a Folsom assemblage exhibited wear identical to that found on drills and was reclassified as a drill. The gouging

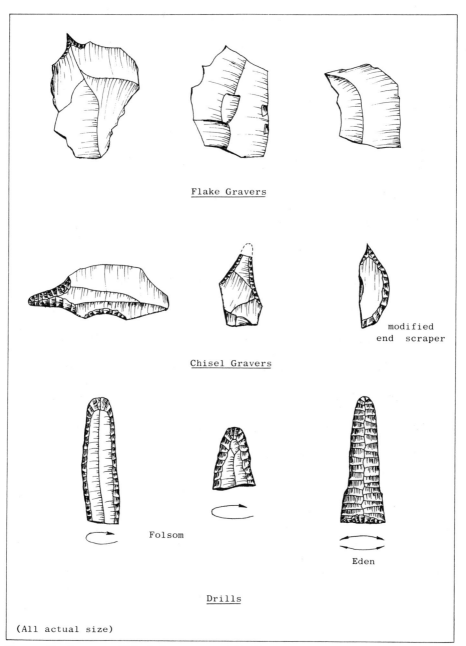

Figure 15. Gravers, Chisel Gravers, and Drills.

required to hollow out a shaft end would produce wear similar to that of a drill. Although this usage cannot be confirmed at this time, I feel that it was the lateral edges, rather than the tip, which were the important functional components of the tool. Thus the term "graver", which implies usage of the tip, may be a misnomer.

Thirteen chisel gravers were found in the survey data, distributed as indicated in Table 2. Examples are illustrated in Figure 15.

8. Drills:

Drills are not frequently encountered in PaleoIndian assemblages, at least those reported in the literature. I think this reflects less the actual usage of drills during this period than it does the results of not employing functional typologies. As mentioned above, one of the Folsom chisel gravers from the survey revealed usage similar to that found on drills, and was subsequently reclassified as a drill in functional terms. Morphologically, drills are generally thought to be bifacially worked to an elongated point, i.e., they approach the morphology of the ethnographical equivalent. This type of drill does occur in PaleoIndian assemblages, though it is generally related to the Plano horizon and the Cody Complex in particular. In the case of the latter, a number of drills have been found which are evidently projectile points reworked into the drill morphology. Such drills may have been hafted when used.

Wear patterns on those drills examined revealed use in both hard and soft materials. I would suggest primary use in wood or bone, again possibly to form the hole in the distal end of a mainshaft, or perhaps the distal end of the foreshaft where this type of hafting is used. I think that the two categories of drill and chisel graver should be re-examined in PaleoIndian assemblages, since the unifacial-bifacial distinction which separates them now may turn out to be largely irrelevant to the eventual formulation of a functional taxonomy.

As indicated in Table 2, only 6 drills were encountered in the survey sites, including the Folsom chisel graver. Examples are illustrated in Figure 15.

9. Spokeshaves:

A spokeshave is simply a concave scraping surface which has been carefully worked into the distal or lateral edge of a fairly thick flake. Irwin and Wormington (1970:29) found that the arc radius of these concavities clustered around 2.5 cm. I did not attempt to calculate the arc radius on the survey specimens, but did measure the distance between the two edge-points of the concavity. The mean of this distance was 15.05 mm., but there was a large amount of variation involved (s=5.79 mm.). It would be difficult, therefore, to attempt inferences as to the diameter of shafts which were being smoothed on the basis of the limited spokeshave data available. However, it should be remembered that a shaft can be worked with any type of scraper

(e. g., a side scraper, or the lateral edge of an endscraper) which exhibits a fairly marked curvature or trajectory. Thus in order to be used efficiently, spokeshaves must have been made for the final rounding process, and should be reliable indicators of shaft sizes if an adequate sample can be obtained.

As indicated, the function of these implements was probably oriented toward the final smoothing of weapon shafts or tool handles. Irwin and Wormington (1970:29) suggest also their use in the shredding of plant fibers. Twenty-one spokeshaves were found in the survey, and their cultural distribution is provided in Table 2. A typical spokeshave is illustrated in Figure 16.

10. Utility Flakes:

This category comprises a new tool type, which as far as I am aware has not yet been recognized in PaleoIndian assemblages. It is not my intention to contribute to the proliferation of invalid type categories. However, when a particular constellation of functional elements occurs with consistency, I feel it should be brought to the attention of investigators so that its validity can eventually be determined. Unfortunately, this tool type was not recognized early enough in the analysis to permit an accurate tabulation of its total occurrence in the survey sites. An adequate sample was obtained, however, and the following generalizations are based on the sample.

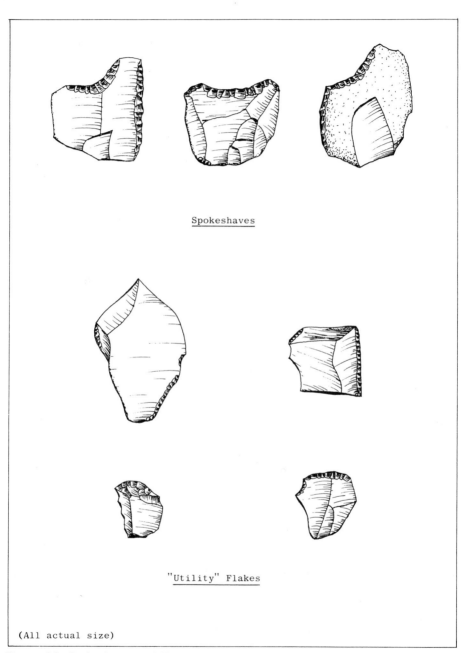

Spokeshaves

"Utility" Flakes

(All actual size)

Figure 16. Spokeshaves and Utility Flakes.

I have arbitrarly termed these implements "utility flakes" because they were apparently multipurpose tools. They are generally made on rather small, thin flakes, most of which still retain the striking platform. On either one lateral edge of the flake, or on its distal end, a scraping edge has been produced by steep retouch. A graver tip is generally worked into one side of the distal edge. The side opposite the scraping edge is generally unmodified, leaving a low-angle natural flake surface. This latter edge was used for cutting and exhibits knife wear when viewed microscopically. It is the combination of scraping, graving, and cutting functions which define the flake. At times, not all three elements are present, and combinations of any two have also been found.

The total occurrence of utility flakes in the sites surveyed is unknown, however a sample of 43 were distributed as indicated in Table 2. It is presumed they were used for light scraping, piercing, and cutting functions, and were hand-held. Typical examples are illustrated in Figure 16.

11. Debitage:

All flakes, chips, and lithic shatter were collected from the survey sites, but were not analyzed intensively. A meaningful analysis of lithic debitage would require either a complete assemblage, or a known sample thereof, in order to determine the variables relevant to the lithic technologies they represent. Furthermore, reliable data as to the contextual attributes of the debitage is virtually essential to the determination of activity loci at the intrasite level. Since individual specimens of debitage are generally quite small, they are susceptible to both alluvial and eolian movement, and thus the context is impossible to attain in the absence of controlled excavation of in situ material.

One possible analysis which could be undertaken on debitage exposed through deflation is that of material type. However, this was precluded in the present survey due to the wide variety of materials available, the difficulty in deriving an objective classification of material types, and the heterogeneity of the materials present in the debitage.

All the debitage collected was separated into four major classes which might be useful for future analysis should any of the sites be excavated, or should the survey material be re-examined:

1. Modified Flakes: These are flakes which exhibit purposeful retouch of one or more edges to provide a working surface, presumably to satisfy a specific functional need.

2. Utilized Flakes: These are flakes which were not purposefully modified, but which exhibit edge flaking as a result of use.

3. Non-utilized Flakes: Those which exhibit neither retouch nor use scars, and therefore were evidently not used.

4. Scraper-sharpening Flakes: These flakes are the very distinctive results of soft-hammer sharpening of a transverse or side scraper. Remnants of the old working surface remain on the dorsal portion of the proximal end.

With the possible exception of the fourth, each of these categories can in turn be subdivided into flakes which retain the striking platform, and those without the striking platforms.

Given these basic categories, meaningful analyses can be carried out on materials for which there is adequate contextual information (cf. Fitting, et. al. 1966; and White, Binford, and Papworth 1963). An identification and description of scraper-sharpening flakes is presented in Jelinek (1966), and an excellent analytic treatment of the same is found in Frison (1967).

12. "Burned" tool tips:

There is one final lithic category to which I would like to call attention, since it is previously unreported in the literature. In analyzing the Folsom survey assemblages, I noticed that a number of artifacts which had sharp protrusions exhibiting a reddened area on these sharp tips. Although this peculiar characteristic was noticed relatively late in the process of analysis, I reviewed that material available to me at the time and found that it occurred only on Folsom artifacts, and then primarily on the brown or tan denritic jaspers. A total of 21 artifacts had the reddened tip, distributed among the tool types as follows:

Knives	6
Gravers	5
Transverse scrapers	4
Point bases (ears)	2
Channel flake	1
Snapped preform tip	1
Side scraper	1
Utilized flake	1

Crabtree and Butler (1964) have experimented with the heat treatment of cryptocrystalline materials, and in disucssing this with Crabtree (personal communication), I suggested that the Folsom items might represent the purposeful heat treatment of the tips of these specimens in order to harden them for heavy incising. Crabtree confirmed my opinion that the reddened portions represented heat treatment (evidently oxidation of the ferric component of the raw material), but disagreed that this could indicate heating after the artifact had been manufactured. He suggested instead that the reddened tips represent those areas of the raw material which were near the surface of the heating pit, and were thus oxidized to yield the isolated red color.

I respect Crabtree's judgment of this phenomenon, however I also feel that the consistency of the occurrence of this coloration on the sharp tips of various types of tools warrants further explanation. This opinion is buttressed by more careful examination of two of the artifacts in question. One, a side scraper (Figure 17), has reddened tips on opposing edges. Another, a channel flake, was broken in half, and only one of the points at the break exhibits the characteristic red. It would seem, then, that this is sufficient evidence to require further analysis of this phenomenon in the future, with the hope of an eventual explanation.

Again, the distribution of this trait is limited to the Folsom assemblages in the survey sample. About 2% of the total number of

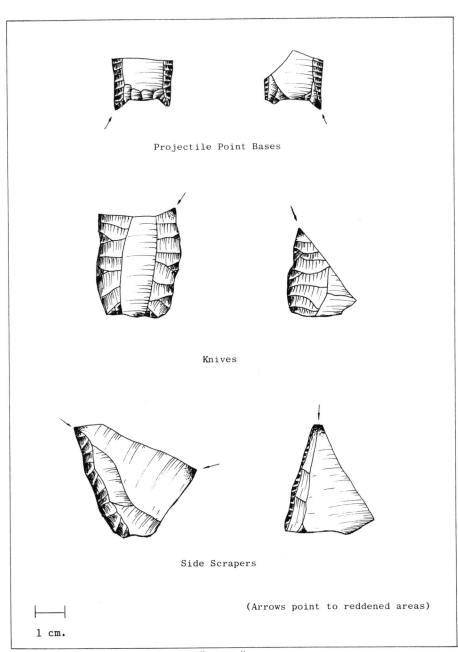

Projectile Point Bases

Knives

Side Scrapers

(Arrows point to reddened areas)

1 cm.

Figure 17. Implements Exhibiting "Burned" Tips.

Folsom artifacts have reddened tips. Some typical examples are illustrated in Figure 17.

13. Summary of Tool Types:

The distribution of the 10 primary categories of PaleoIndian tools described above is summarized in Table 2. Both total numbers and percentage frequencies are given. Channel flakes, a category limited to Folsom only, are listed but not included in calculating frequency distribution.

A cumulative graph of the percentage frequencies indicated in Table 2 is presented in Figure 18. The numbers of the tool types correspond to those described in the text above, and listed in Table 1. Of interest in the graph is the closeness of the curves of Belen and Cody, and the distinctiveness of Clovis and Folsom, both from each other and from the other two assemblages. Although the Folsom, Belen, and Cody samples are adequate for this type of graphic representation, it should be remembered that the Clovis plot is based on a sample of only 43 implements, and thus is not altogether reliable relative to the others.

In order to facilitate the analysis of the correlation of the lithic and environmental components, an index of the frequency of occurrence of each implement type on each of the 30 primary sites was calculated. These indices are presented in Table 3. Each index is computed by dividing the number of each tool type recovered from a site by the total number of artifacts at the site. The latter figure is also recorded in

Table 2: Cultural Distribution of Lithic Implements[a]

Tool Types	Clovis		Folsom		Belen		Cody		Total	
	N	%	N	%	N	%	N	%	N	%
1. Proj. Points	8	18.6	117	14.4	29	11.8	25	14.9	179	14.1
2. Preforms	3	07.0	128	15.8	9	03.5	5	02.9	145	11.2
3. Trans. Scrapers	18	41.9	308	38.0	139	56.4	92	54.9	557	43.9
4. Side Scrapers	11	25.6	80	09.8	31	12.6	15	08.9	137	10.8
5. Knives	0	00.0	45	05.5	8	03.2	11	06.5	64	05.1
6. Gravers	2	04.6	79	09.8	16	06.5	8	04.7	105	08.3
7. Chisel Gravers	0	00.0	8	01.0	3	01.2	1	00.6	12	01.0
8. Drills	1	02.3	2	00.3	0	00.0	3	01.8	6	00.5
9. Spokeshaves	0	00.0	10	01.2	7	02.8	4	02.4	21	01.7
10. Utility Flakes	0	00.0	34	04.2	5	02.0	4	02.4	43	03.4
Total	43	100.0	811	100.0	247	100.0	168	100.0	1269	100.0
Folsom Channel Flakes			217						217	
Total Artifacts (30 sites)									1486	

[a] This distribution is for the 30 primary sites only (see Table 1).

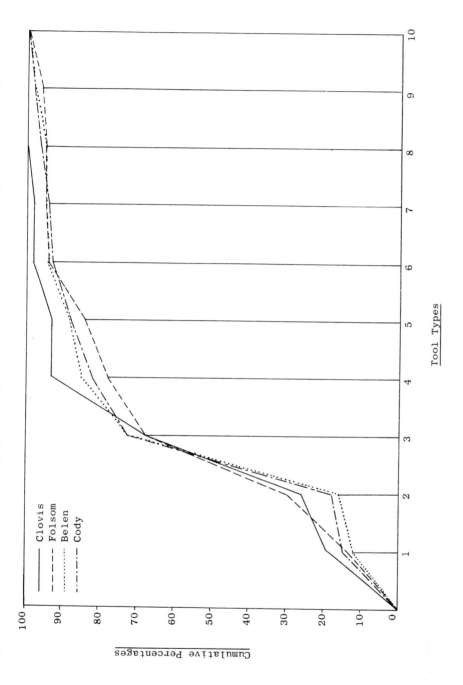

Figure 18. Cumulative Graph of Cultural Distribution of Lithic Implements.

Table 3: Implement Frequency Index for 30 Sites[a]

Site Number	Proj. Points	Preforms	Trans. Scrapers	Side Scrapers	Knives	Channel Flakes	Gravers	Chisel Gravers	Drills	Spokeshaves	Utility Flakes	Total Artifacts
A. Clovis:												
1. 13JB5	.19	.07	.42	.25	.00	.00	.05	.00	.02	.00	.00	43
B. Folsom:												
2. 2GD2	.03	.05	.58	.10	.08	.05	.08	.00	.00	.00	.03	38
3. 9CM3	.16	.09	.42	.04	.05	.16	.06	.01	.00	.01	.00	230
4. 12OA3	.15	.17	.35	.13	.02	.07	.09	.02	.00	.00	.00	103
5. 13BA8	.08	.17	.63	.12	.00	.00	.00	.00	.00	.00	.00	24
6. 13ES8	.12	.07	.17	.02	.00	.45	.12	.05	.00	.00	.00	42
7. 13FR1	.02	.05	.10	.05	.14	.51	.12	.00	.00	.00	.01	43
8. 13GX5	.08	.04	.27	.16	.08	.10	.14	.00	.00	.04	.09	220
9. 13LC8	.05	.36	.07	.12	.03	.28	.07	.00	.00	.00	.02	86
10. 13LH9	.08	.23	.53	.00	.00	.08	.08	.00	.00	.00	.00	26
11. 13LI4	.23	.03	.12	.03	.03	.56	.00	.00	.00	.00	.00	34
12. 13LI7	.15	.21	.21	.01	.00	.39	.03	.00	.00	.00	.00	75
13. 13LN1	.29	.19	.19	.00	.00	.33	.00	.00	.00	.00	.00	31
14. 13XP3	.05	.30	.35	.10	.05	.15	.00	.00	.00	.00	.00	20
15. 18AG7	.08	.15	.15	.00	.23	.23	.08	.00	.00	.00	.08	13
16. 19JM9	.03	.08	.35	.03	.00	.48	.03	.00	.00	.00	.00	37
C. Belen:												
17. 9SJ5	.04	.04	.39	.13	.04		.22	.00	.00	.04	.09	23
18. 9VD9	.06	.00	.29	.29	.18		.12	.00	.00	.00	.06	17
19. 12WG5	.05	.00	.65	.05	.15		.05	.00	.00	.00	.05	20
20. 13BR3	.09	.00	.65	.22	.00		.04	.00	.00	.00	.00	23
21. 13BX9	.04	.07	.57	.14	.00		.11	.00	.00	.07	.00	28
22. 13FJ8	.21	.10	.51	.18	.00		.00	.00	.00	.00	.00	51
23. 13LG9	.17	.00	.54	.08	.00		.13	.00	.00	.08	.00	24
24. 14CS5	.21	.00	.61	.00	.00		.00	.09	.00	.09	.00	23
25. 19JL5	.08	.03	.75	.05	.03		.03	.03	.00	.00	.00	37

(continued next page)

Table 3: (Continued)

Site Number	Proj. Points	Preforms	Trans. Scrapers	Side Scrapers	Knives	Gravers	Chisel Gravers	Drills	Spokeshaves	Utility Flakes	Total Artifacts
D. Cody Complex:											
26. 5DR1	.16	.10	.54	.12	.02	.02	.02	.02	.00	.00	50
27. 12JV5	.16	.00	.64	.08	.12	.00	.00	.00	.00	.00	25
28. 12TF9	.11	.00	.66	.11	.04	.04	.00	.00	.00	.04	46
29. 13DR4	.10	.00	.60	.03	.10	.03	.00	.00	.14	.00	29
30. 45JP9	.31	.00	.13	.06	.13	.25	.00	.13	.00	.00	16

[a]Index obtained by dividing the frequency an artifact occurs in a site by the total number of artifacts from the site.

Table 3. It should be noted that for the Folsom sites, channel flakes have been included in the total artifact count, and the indices for channel flakes are recorded.

Description of the Environmental Data

All the data related to the environmental components of the survey were recorded on the Site Survey Form (Figure 3). An initial analysis of the completed forms indicated that not all the variables would be significant, in that some exhibited little or no variation. Other information recorded was determined not to be relevant to the present study, but is being kept on file for future reference.

Those environmental variables relevant to the analytic portion of the present paper are presented in coded form in Table 4 for the 30 primary sites analyzed in the survey. An interpretative key to the symbols used is given at the end of the table. Five major categories of environmental components are included, comprising a total of 18 variables. These are described below:

1. Nearest Water:

At each site, an effort was made to determine the source of the nearest water at the time of PaleoIndian occupation. A variety of sources were found, including playas, arroyos, rivers, and springs. By definition, playas are basin-shaped depressions with interior drainage, and thus probably held stagnant water at the time of occupation. Since a number of sites were found in locations where a playa was not

Table 4: Environmental Variables of the 30 Primary Sites

Site Number	Nearest Water				Overview			Hunting Area			Potential Trap Area			Discrete Variables				
	1 Type	2 Horiz. Dist.	3 Direction	4 Vert. Dist.	5 At site?	6 Distance	7 Direction	8 Type	9 Distance	10 Direction	11 Type	12 Distance	13 Direction	14 Landform	15 Soil Type	16 Exposure	17 Visible?	18 Playa near?
Clovis																		
13JB5	A	15	W	5	N	100	NE	Mi	1320	SW	L	880	W	F	SL	D	N	N
Folsom																		
2GD2	A	150	E	50	N	200	NW	Mi	1760	W	A	1000	S	S	SG	E	N	N
9CM3	A	25	N	20	Y	-	-	Ma	3520	S	A	1760	S	S	S	S	Y	Y
12OA3	R	100	E	15	N	50	W	Ma	440	SW	A	-	-	S	S	E	N	Y
13BA8	P	00	-	00	N	170	NW	Mi	880	SW	A	300	SE	F	SL	D	N	Y
13ES8	P	00	-	00	N	100	E	Ma	1320	SE	L	440	S	S	SL	W	N	Y
13FR1	P	200	SW	20	Y	-	-	Mi	1320	SE	N	-	-	F	S	D	Y	Y
13GX5	A	60	NE	10	N	440	SE	Ma	1760	S	L	440	SW	S	SG	S	N	Y
13LC8	P	25	SE	15	N	200	SW	Ma	880	S	L	440	NW	F	S	D	N	Y
13LH9	P	00	-	00	N	100	NE	Ma	880	SW	L	1760	NW	S	SG	W	Y	Y
13LI4	P	150	N	20	Y	-	-	Ma	1320	SW	A	880	NE	S	S	W	Y	Y
13LI7	P	25	SW	15	N	75	N	Ma	440	SW	A	880	NE	S	S	S	Y	Y
13LN1	P	200	NW	15	Y	-	-	Ma	880	SW	A	1320	NE	F	S	D	Y	Y
13XP3	P	250	W	15	N	40	E	Mi	1760	S	N	-	-	S	S	S	Y	Y

(continued next page)

Table 4: (continued)

	1	2	3	4	5	6	7	8	9	10	11	12	13	14	15	16	17	18
18AG7	P	300	NW	15	Y	-	-	Mi	440	SW	N	-	-	F	S	D	Y	Y
19JM9	P	150	NW	15	Y	-	-	Ma	1760	SE	N	-	-	F	S	D	Y	Y
Belen:																		
9SJ5	P	300	SE	40	Y	-	-	Mi	1760	SW	N	-	-	F	SL	S	Y	Y
9VD9	P	125	SW	15	N	250	SW	Mi	1760	W	N	-	-	F	S	S	N	Y
12WG5	R	50	N	60	N	50	E	Mi	880	NE	N	-	-	F	SL	D	N	N
13BR3	P	50	N	10	N	150	SW	Mi	2460	SW	N	-	-	F	SG	D	N	Y
13BX9	A	100	E	40	Y	-	-	Mi	1320	W	N	-	-	F	SG	Y	Y	N
13FJ8	P	50	S	15	Y	-	-	Mi	880	S	N	-	-	F	SG	D	Y	Y
13LG9	P	25	N	30	N	25	S	Ma	880	SE	L	880	W	F	S	D	N	Y
14CS5	S	300	SW	40	Y	-	-	Ma	880	SW	N	-	-	F	S	D	Y	N
19JL5	P	440	E	20	Y	-	-	Ma	1760	E	N	-	-	F	S	D	Y	Y
Cody:																		
5DR1	R	880	E	150	Y	-	-	Mi	4400	SW	A	880	W	F	SL	D	Y	N
12JV5	R	100	W	40	N	100	SE	Ma	440	NW	A	440	W	F	SL	D	Y	Y
12TF9	S	440	NE	40	Y	-	-	Ma	2640	NW	A	-	-	F	S	D	Y	N
13DR4	P	440	S	10	N	200	SE	Mi	site	-	L	440	W	F	S	D	Y	N
45JP9	A	350	E	65	N	100	N	Ma	5280	S	A	880	SE	S	S	S	N	N

(continued next page)

Table 4: (continued)

Key to interpretation of Table 4:

Column 1: Type of nearest water. A = arroyo, P = playa, R = river, S = spring
" 2: Horizontal distance to nearest water measured in yards
" 3: Direction to nearest water (cardinal points & combinations thereof)
" 4: Vertical distance to water measured in feet
" 5: Is the site at an overview? N = no, Y = yes
" 6: Distance to overview measured in yards
" 7: Direction to overview
" 8: Type of hunting area. Ma = major, Mi = minor
" 9: Distance to hunting area measured in yards
" 10: Direction to hunting area
" 11: Type of trap area. A = arroyo, L = lava shelves, N = none present
" 12: Distance to trap area in yards
" 13: Direction to trap area
" 14: Landform at site. F = flat, S = sloping
" 15: Soil type at site. S = sand, SG = sand & gravel, SL = sand & lava
" 16: Exposure. D = direct, N, E, S, W = cardinal directions
" 17: Is site visible from hunting area: N = no, Y = yes
" 18: Is there a playa in the vicinity? N = no, Y = yes

only the nearest, but also the only source of water, it may be that the PaleoIndians did not consider fresh water essential to the selection of a campsite.

Present-day arroyos may well have been small streams at the time of occupation, but were recorded as arroyos in the survey. Some evidence was found of shallow arroyos which may have been blocked in the past, and these were recorded as ponded arroyos, rather than playas or ponds. Present rivers (i. e., those in which water runs throughout the year), and springs were recorded as such. In each case, the distance to the closest source of water was measured in yards, and recorded. The direction from the site to the water was also noted.

Although the elevation of each site was recorded from the information given on the topographic maps, this number in itself was insufficient to describe the vertical relationship of the site situation relative to the surrounding terrain. In order to adequately describe the site in three-dimensional space, an index of vertical distance was needed. To satisfy this requisite, the vertical distance (measured in feet) from the site to the nearest playa was recorded. It was found that the most convenient and accurate method of establishing this distance was to read it directly from the topographic map upon which the site had been accurately located. If there was no playa in the immediate vicinity, the distance was taken from the site to the other nearest source of water. However, playas were used wherever possible in order to standardize the measurement.

The data on the nearest source of water comprise the first four variables (columns) presented in Table 4, including the type of the source (column 1), the horizontal distance to the source in yards (column 2), the direction from the site to the source (column 3), and the vertical distance index of the site in feet (column 4).

2. Overview:

At each site, data were recorded on the view of the surrounding topography afforded by the site situation. Special attention was paid to the view of the nearest large hunting area (see below). This was done by recording the distance and direction to the nearest ridge and to the nearest lookout point, the latter being defined as a high point in the site vicinity which would afford a good view of all the surrounding terrain.

An initial analysis of the survey data revealed that sites were frequently located on ridges which afforded a suitable view, especially with reference to the hunting area, thus indicating that the site itself was at a lookout point. It was thus possible, for analytic purposes, to combine the two categories "nearest ridge" and "lookout point" from the survey form into one component, termed "overview".

As indicated in Table 4, the overview component comprises three columns. The first (column 5) refers to the location of the overview.

If the site itself is at a lookout point, the "Y" (yes) is recorded in column 5, and the next two columns are left blank. If the site is not at a suitable overview, the "N" (no) is recorded and the distance from the site to the overview in yards is presented (column 6), as well as the direction (column 7).

3. Hunting Area:

It was noted previously (Chapter 2, Figure 1) that there are four major plains-like areas in the survey region. It is with reference to these areas (termed "hunting areas") that the major site concentrations are located. This is not to imply that these areas were the only ones utilized by the occupants for hunting purposes. Certainly if the Pleistocene megafauna behaved in any way similar to modern herbivores, they would not have been limited to these areas. Instead, the term "hunting area" is employed descriptively to convey the idea of a large, relatively unbroken region which could accomodate large concentrations of gregarious animals. Grasses were probably abundant in these areas, as were sources of water in the form of the numerous playas. From the standpoint of hunting, perhaps the most accomodating aspect of these areas was that due to the low relief, game could be spotted readily at quite some distance.

For analytic purposes, the four main areas have been termed the "major" hunting areas. In addition to the clusters of sites found oriented toward the major areas, many sites were found to be near similar topographic areas of much smaller size. These have been termed "minor" hunting areas. Again, the predominant feature of low relief characterizes the minor hunting areas, as well as numerous playas. The distinction is thus quantitative, not qualitative, and it is presumed that ecologically the two types of hunting areas were virtually identical.

In Table 4, the type of hunting area near each site is listed, along with the direction and distance. The type (column 4) is given as either major or minor. The distance (column 9) is measured in yards. Wherever possible, this distance was determined by actual measurement, either with a vehicle or on foot, then confirmed with reference to the topographic map. If actual measurement was prohibited, the distance was derived from the topographic map alone. The distance indicated is that between the site and the edge of the hunting area, as determined by the beginning of the low topographical relief. The direction from the site to the hunting area is given in column 10.

With respect to hunting areas, the one exception situation occuring in the survey data is that of site number 13DR4, a Cody Complex site. This site was located in the middle of one of the minor hunting areas, and was not elevated in relation to the area. Thus under column 9, the term "site" has been recorded for 13DR4.

4. Potential Trap Area:

Large game animals can be killed by any number of means, but as evidenced by the numerous bison "drive" or "jump" sites in North

America (Anell 1969:Map 3), the most efficient means of killing them was frequently sought. There is at least one instance of a bison drive utilized in PaleoIndian times (Wheat 1967), and more will undoubtedly be found in the future. As the environmental data were recorded for each site, an attempt was made to locate possible areas in the vicinity which would facilitate the efficient killing of large game animals. In that not all were similar situations, they were recorded as "potential trap areas."

Many of the situations found suitable for game traps were a function of the volcanic activity so prominent in the central part of the survey region. As a result of this activity, there are numerous lava flows which terminate in "tongues", forming small, semi-circular enclosures. Although predating the PaleoIndian occupation, these lava flows are not old enough to have eroded significantly, and still exhibit relatively steep sides with prominent lava boulders. It would have been relatively easy to contain animals in any of these numerous enclosures, where they could have been killed from either above or below with minimal effort.

Other trap situations recorded were arroyos over which the animals could have been driven, or which might have provided enclosures similar to the lava tongues. Any situation which could involve the driving of game over a steep escarpment or bank was so noted on the survey forms, but for purposes of analysis was recorded as an arroyo in Table 4. In many instances, no possible trap situation could be seen in the vicinity of the site area, indicating that the trap feature was not necessarily essential to the selection of a camp site. This was especially true in the case of Belen.

Whenever possible, the potential trap areas were walked and checked for evidence of bone or other material indicating possible use as a kill. In only one instance was any bone found, and it occurred in unidentifiable fragments. No cultural material accompanied it. This lack of evidence may be attributed to a number of factors: 1) those areas which we have termed "trap areas" were simply not used by the PaleoIndians and have no relevance to the locations of sites; 2) too few of the areas were checked thoroughly enough to discover the evidence; 3) there has not been sufficient erosion in the trap areas to expose the material; or 4) decomposition took place at a more rapid rate than deposition, thus destroying the evidence.

In Table 4, the type of potential trap area is listed in column 11 as either an arroyo or a lava tongue. If no trap situation could be located, the site is listed as having none. Distance and direction from the site to the trap area are listed in columns 12 and 13 respectively.

5. Discrete Variables:

The last major category of environmental components presented in Table 4 comprises 5 variables which could not easily be quantified, and are thus termed discrete. The first of these (column 14) is the landform at the site. This term refers to the nature of the terrain within the immediate vicinity of the site itself; in other words, the microtopography of the site situation. Although a number of different types of terrain were recorded, it was found that they could all be subsumed under the general categories of either flat or sloping. Those sites which were situated on the tops of ridges, or on level shelves protruding from ridge slopes, were recorded as having a flat landform. Those sites which were on the ridge slopes, or on the sloping edges of playas were classified as having a sloping landform. In no instance were the sloping site locations on very steep slopes; all were fairly gentle in nature.

The type of soil presently existing at the site was also recorded (column 15). One particular type of soil is very common throughout the survey region. This is a reddish-brown sandy clay which forms a fairly compact surface when exposed and dried. A light brown, wind-deposited sand overlies the sandy clay in most of the survey area. Many of the areas of deflation which have exposed the PaleoIndian material are characterized by this reddish sandy clay, and this is listed simply as "sand" in Table 4. However, in a number of areas, especially in the central part of the survey region, this sand is thoroughly mixed with rather small lava rocks. The latter have not eroded sufficiently to remove the sharp edges, and without some sort of protective footwear they would cut the skin quite severely. This type of soil is listed in column 15 as "sand and lava". The third type of soil frequently encountered in the sites is that of sand mixed with small, rounded pebbles. This last soil type is listed as "sand and gravel" in Table 4.

It should be noted here that these three different soil types may represent three distinct types of genesis of the site landform from the geomorphological standpoint, and this may have significance with re- gard to the criteria used for site selection at the time of occupation. At present, however, no correlation between site type and soil type is apparent.

Column 16 of Table 4 records the "exposure" of the site. This refers to the position of the site relative to the ridge and ridge slope upon which it is located. If the site is on top of the ridge, it is termed a "direct" exposure. If it is on the east slope of a ridge, it is termed an "eastern" exposure, and so on. Direct and southern exposures would take advantage of the position of the sun, but would not provide shelter from the wind. Northeastern exposures would provide the latter.

In that there may have been an effort on the part of those selecting the site locations to choose a place which was concealed in some manner, this variable was also recorded as part of the survey. Column 17 lists, either in affirmative or negative terms, whether or not the site is visible from the hunting area, and vice versa.

The final variable (column 18) indicates the presence of a playa in the vicinity of the site. In a number of instances other types of water sources were closer than a playa, yet the playa may have had something to do with the site selection. In order to determine this, the occurrence of a playa in the vicinity of the site was noted whenever present. In this case, the "vicinity" of the site refers to an area of about 3/4 of a mile. A playa much more distant than this would probably not be a critical variable in the determination of site location.

The environmental data presented in Table 4 can be considered the "raw data" for the 30 sites analyzed in the survey. As such, the data are quite variable in nature, and are difficult to visualize and interpret. I have therefore attempted to summarize Table 4 as concisely as possible, and the results of this attempt are presented in Table 5.

Table 5 summarizes the environmental data with respect to each of the four PaleoIndian assemblages. It should be noted that the Clovis data is based on one site only, and thus should in no instance be used for the implicit or explicit formulation of generalizations. It is included in Table 5 for illustrative purposes only. A number of categories were combined to permit condensation for the summary, and frequency indices were computed to facilitate intercultural comparison. These procedures warrant a brief explanation:

Under the category of nearest water, both arroyos and rivers were subsumed under the heading of "stream". Frequency of occurrence indices for playas, streams, and springs were calculated by dividing

Table 5: Summary of the Environmental Data[a]

Environmental Component		Clovis	Folsom	Belen	Cody
1. Water					
A. Type:					
	Playa	(.00)	(.73)	(.67)	(.20)
	Stream	(1.00)	(.27)	(.22)	(.60)
	Spring	(.00)	(.00)	(.11)	(.20)
B. Average Distance:					
	Horizontal	15	109	160	444
	Vertical	5	15	30	61
C. Direction:					
	NE quad.	(.00)	(.47)	(.67)	(.60)
	SW quad.	(1.00)	(.53)	(.33)	(.40)
2. Overview					
A. Type:					
	Site	(.00)	(.40)	(.56)	(.40)
	Ridge	(1.00)	(.60)	(.44)	(.60)
B. Average Distance:		100	73	53	80
C. Direction:					
	NE quad.	(1.00)	(.33)	(.11)	(.60)
	SW quad.	(.00)	(.27)	(.33)	(.00)
3. Hunting Area					
A. Type:					
	Major	(.00)	(.66)	(.45)	(.60)
	Minor	(1.00)	(.34)	(.55)	(.40)
B. Average Distance:		1320	1290	1395	2550
C. Direction:					
	NE quad.	(.00)	(.20)	(.34)	(.00)
	SW quad.	(1.00)	(.80)	(.66)	(1.00)
4. Potential Trap Area:					
	Present	(1.00)	(.74)	(.11)	(1.00)
	Absent	(.00)	(.26)	(.89)	(.00)
5. Landform					
	Sloping	(.00)	(.60)	(.00)	(.80)
	Flat	(1.00)	(.40)	(1.00)	(.20)
6. Exposure					
	Direct	(1.00)	(.40)	(.78)	(.80)
	NE quad.	(.00)	(.13)	(.00)	(.00)
	SW quad.	(.00)	(.47)	(.22)	(.20)
7. Visible?					
	Yes	(.00)	(.60)	(.56)	(.80)
	No	(1.00)	(.40)	(.44)	(.20)

134

Table 5. Summary of the Environmental Data   (continued)[a]

Environmental Component	Clovis	Folsom	Belen	Cody
8. Soil Type				
Sand	(.00)	(.66)	(.45)	(.60)
Sand & Gravel	(.00)	(.20)	(.33)	(.00)
Sand & Lava	(1.00)	(.14)	(.22)	(.40)
9. Playa in vicinity?				
Yes	(.00)	(.94)	(.66)	(.20)
No	(1.00)	(.06)	(.34)	(.80)

[a] Frequency of occurrence index shown in parentheses.

the frequency each one occurred as the nearest source of water in each culture by the total number of sites in that culture. These indices are presented in parentheses in order to facilitate visually their distinction from the other data. The average distance to the nearest source of water was calculated for each culture, and is presented as shown. The horizontal distance is in yards, the vertical distance in feet.

In order to facilitate the description of the direction to the various components, it was decided to divide the compass points into two categories relative to the prevailing wind, which is in a southwest to northeast direction. These two categories are termed "NE quad." and "SW quad." in Table 5. The former refers to those directions listed as N, NE, E, and SE on the data sheets, while the latter (SW quad.) includes those listed as S, SW, W, and NW. This arbitrary division is for analytic purposes only. Frequency of occurrence indices are presented for the direction to nearest water in terms of these two categories.

Under the category of "overview", the type of overview is indicated as either "site" or "ridge". The former refers to those site locations which are situated on overviews, while the latter indicates the overview is located on a ridge apart from the site. The average distance and direction to the ridge are also presented. Note that the directional indices do not all add up to 1.00, because some sites were situated at the overview itself.

The remaining indices were calculated in the same fashion as those previously and are self-explanatory. Average distances are given in yards. The component of "potential trap area" was found to be highly variable in terms of distance, direction, and type, and is therefore presented only as "present" or "absent".

This concludes the presentation of the empirical material derived from the survey. Only the data relevant to further analysis have been listed; the remainder is on file at the Museum of Anthropology, University of New Mexico, Albuquerque.

CHAPTER V

Analytic Techniques

Introduction

The purpose of the following section is to explain the techniques
employed in the analytic phase of the survey model. As noted in the
first chapter, the goal of the analytic survey model is the achievement
of taxonomic structures of the systems components, oriented toward
specific functions. Such structures, when investigated from the standpoint of covariation with other taxonomic categories, will lead to an
understanding of PaleoIndian settlement technology, an element considered integral to the eventual elucidation of cultural process. Basic
to the accomplishment of this goal is the systematic definition of subsystem components, subsystems, and systems, and an analysis of the
manner in which these variables articulate with reference to a specific
function.

The analytic technique will therefore consist of the following
phases relating to both the lithic and environmental subsystems represented in the survey data: 1) the identification of the subsystem components, including the initial segregation of the inessential from the
essential variables; 2) the analysis of the articulation of these components (essential variables) in the operational subsystem; and 3) the

isolation of the critical variables (those exhibiting minimal vascilla-
tion in the range of co-variation) responsible for a particular articulation which demonstrates patterning. It is this last phase that results
in the formulation of a functional taxon.

In order to avoid possible misunderstanding, perhaps I should
clarify what is meant by the term functional type or taxon as used in
this study. The problem of classification is probably the single most
perplexing, yet vital, problem in archeology, and academic disputes
over "real" versus "arbitrary" types are well-known. The problem
is no less complex in the field of PaleoIndian studies. Wormington,
eight years after writing her definitive work on PaleoIndian artifacts,
was prompted to note a "growing conviction that the aborigines who
made these implements did not share her system of typology, and it
is apparent that the problem is vastly more complicated than it appeared
to be eight years ago" (1965:15).

I would suggest that the pursuit of the question of whether our
present taxonomic system was shared by those who created the artifacts is an absorbing, but quite futile approach. Rather than quibbling
over the supposed reality of a given typology, we should be more concerned with how it is maintained and how it behaves. What are the
critical variables which constitute the typology, and how are they inter-
related? Under what circumstances do these critical variables change,
and under what conditions are they maintained? We must not be

satisfied with a typology just because it works, we must explain how and
why it works. In short, I feel that typologies should be treated as
heuristic devices integral to the generation of hypotheses relevant to
cultural process.

Typologies should be established during the process of analyzing
an archeological assemblage through the isolation of the key variables
responsible for maintaining a particular constellation of interacting
components. In terms of systems analysis, this is referred to as
identifying the constraints which characterize the "trajectory" of the
cultural system, or its variations in attribute states through time.
Such typologies should, I believe, be considered provisional only, and
I would prefer to term them "analytic types". It is important that the
types so constructed be based on the key variables as identified through
analysis of the total range of components or essential variables, rather
than on any preconceived notion of what the types should represent.
As Binford has pointed out: "What new information could possibly be
gained about variations in the activity systems of the past by simply
fitting archeological remains into types which are ordered in terms
of our preconceptions of what those activities were? " (1967:235).

These analytic types should be constructed for all possible components of the subsystem under consideration. In some instances this
may not be possible due to lack of adequate sample size. For example,
in the following pages it will be seen that samples of implements other

than projectile points and transverse scrapers were inadequate for the rigorous analysis necessary to formulate analytic types. Yet this fact does not preclude the necessity to perform the analysis on those implements which do provide sufficient data. More can be learned about the subsystem of lithic technology of a given group by the intensive analysis of a few implements than by the superficial consideration of numerous categories.

Once the analytic types have been constructed for a particular subsystem (e. g., the subsystem of lithic technology), then the articulation of these components must be analyzed to determine the nature of the constraints in the trajectory of that subsystem. Here again, key components must be identified and isolated, for it is these critical variables which are the elements responsible for the patterning exhibited by the subsystems trajectories (Clarke 1968:71). To the extent that the constraints defining a subsystem trajectory are purposely imposed, that subsystem is goal-oriented toward a given cultural function. This is the primary basis for terming taxonomies identified in this manner "functional" taxonomies. Function is here taken in the broad sense implying goal-orientation of a subsystem toward reducing relevant stresses imposed upon the system of which it is a component.

Formulation of analytic taxonomies through the identification of key attributes will permit the generation of hypotheses relevant to the explanation of systems constraints in functional terms. When tested, we can explain why a particular type of artifact, type of lithic technoloby, or type of settlement technology is maintained through time. Once the maintenance of a type is understood, we can analyze the changes in typologies through time by explaining the variations in elements of primary technological focus in terms of known variables in articulating cultural or environmental systems. I believe we can, and should, do this without being overly concerned about whether the analytic types which we derive are in fact replicas of extinct folk taxonomies. These analytic techniques are not devised primarily to reconstruct past cultural systems, nor do they claim to approach past reality. Binford has stressed the position that valid results can be obtained

> irrespective of the degree of conformity between our criteria and the cognitive systems of the manufacturers of the artifacts we study. It is, in fact, quite unlikely that the cognitive systems of extinct peoples would be in any way adequate to, or relevant for, modern scientific investigation of the processes responsible for observed differences and similarities between cultural systems (1967:234).

Thus the concept of functional taxonomies, as used herein, refers to the functional orientation of the particular subsystem or component trajectory under consideration. These taxonomies may, or may not, coincide with existing typological categories which have served adequately in prior studies.

Lithic Sybsystem: Analytic Techniques

In analyzing the lithic technology of the various PaleoIndian groups represented in the survey material, the first step will be to

identify, describe, and analyze all the components of the lithic subsystem in order to separate the essential from the inessential variables.

One of the values of the systems approach is that it permits the
use of the same analytic techniques at various systemic levels. The
survey sample is composed of various implements from which we wish
to derive information regarding the lithic technology of the people who
produced them. This is most easily attained by treating each implement as the end-product of a distinct cultural system itself, with its
own attributes, constraints, and trajectory. Each implement was
manufactured from a specific lithic material, by certain specific techniques, which resulted in a given morphology destined to serve a
certain function. Thus we can define the components of the lithic subsystem as 1) a material component, 2) a production component, 3)
a morphology component, and 4) a functional component. An adequate
understanding of the variables involved in the articulation of these
four components for each major implement class will result in an
understanding of the lithic technological subsystem of a given culture.
Techniques for analyzing these components will now be discussed in
more detail.

1. Material Component:

All lithic source materials used by PaleoIndians in the survey
area were cryptocrystalline silicates. The problem of analyzing such
materials is primarily one of classification of the various silicates

themselves. Such classification is facilitated in those areas where there is either a limited variety of source material, or where one particular variety predominates the assemblage under study (cf. Fitting, et. al. 1966; MacDonald 1968). Unfortunately neither of these circumstances prevail in the central Rio Grande valley. Here there is such a wide variety of source material that if there was positive selection of certain materials by the PaleoIndian occupants of the area, it is both difficult to determine and substantiate. Types of silica minerals which elsewhere would be termed "exotic" are commonplace in these PaleoIndian assemblages where relative to later cultural manifestations, the entire collections can be termed exotic.

The system of mineral classification adopted here is based on the translucency (or opaqueness) of the material, plus the amount of impurities in it.[1] Of the numerous possible categories based on these two variables, a total of nine were found useful in describing the survey materials: 1) Chalcedony is the most translucent of the rocks of nonvolcanic origin, and as used herein, is free of impurities. 2) Agate is the term for a chalcedony which exhibits impurities, generally in the form of dendritic inclusions. Agates and chalcedonies are found in numerous colors in the survey area. One particular form of agate

[1]Lacking experience in the taxonomy of minerals, I solicited the the aid of Dr. Robert Weber at the New Mexico Institute of Mining and Technology, who kindly allowed me the use of his own system of classification as a guide. Since classification of minerals is ultimately subjective, any errors incurred in the adaptation of his system to the present study must rest with me alone.

which is very common in later cultures, but also occurs in PaleoIndian assemblages, is known locally as Rio Grande Chalcedony. This is a grey or blue-grey mineral which under the present system is termed an agate due to the inclusions it contains. 3) Flint is free of impurities, but is more opaque than chalcedony and is also more waxy in texture. Flints are rare in the survey area and when occurring, are generally blue-grey. 4) Cherts are relatively free of inclusions, but are very opaque and less waxy than flint. The acute edge of a chert flake will not be translucent when held to the light. 5) Jaspers exhibit the same degree of opaqueness as does the chert, but have varying degree of impurities. Two common forms of impurities in jaspers are dendritic and round inclusions. Both cherts and jaspers are found in a wide variety of colors in the survey area. One common form in PaleoIndian assemblages is known locally as Chinle Chert, in that it was thought to have come from the Chinle formation in western New Mexico (Reinhart 1968:16). Under the system employed here, Chinle Chert is termed a jasper since it most frequently exhibits dendritic inclusions. It is usually brown or tan in color. 6) Quartzite refers to an opaque material with a very coarse texture, unlike the extremely fine-grained types above. Quartzite also comes in numerous colors in the survey area. Various hues of reds predominate, but greys are common, and green is found in the eastern part of the region. 7) Basalt is a black, opaque, very coarse-grained material of volcanic origin. Most

commonly used by the early Archaic cultures (Jay, Bajada, etc.) in
the area, it does occur in some PaleoIndian assemblages. 8) <u>Obsidian</u>
is the translucent volcanic "glass" so commonly used by later cultures,
although at times selected by the PaleoIndians for the production of projectile points. 9) The final variety of material used is that of petrified
or <u>silicified</u> <u>wood,</u> including palmwood, which occurs quite frequently
in PaleoIndian sites in a variety of exotic colors.

All implements analyzed were classified as to one of the above
nine categories of mineral type. The exact sources of these raw
materials are not known (except in the case of obsidian from the Jemez
Mountains), but it is felt that they were derived from the numerous
outcrops of the Santa Fe formation in the central Rio Grande valley,
since they occur in these gravels today. The Santa Fe formation is re-
deposited, thus the raw material occurred in the form of cobbles rather
than tabular cores, as evidenced by the rolled cobble cortex occurring
on many of the implements. The analysis of the lithic technology of the
PaleoIndians here assumes this type of core as a constant. It should
be noted that a different form of raw material (tabular cores) might
alter considerably the lithic techniques utilized, and this should be
taken into consideration when investigating PaleoIndian assemblages
elsewhere in North America.

2. Artifact Production Component:

Wherever possible, implements were analyzed in terms of their
techniques of production. This can be done in either (or both) of two

manners; analyzing implements recovered in various stages of manufacture, or analyzing the finished product for evidence of production
techniques. The terminology utilized in describing these techniques
was derived from a number of sources dealing with analyses of lithic
assemblages. The final descriptive system used herein represents
my own version adapted and modified from White (1963) and Honea
(1965). Basically it involves primary, secondary, and tertiary technologies. The latter, which has to do with artifact function, will be
discussed later.

Primary technology refers to the nature of the core utilized, the
treatment of the core prior to removal of flakes, the method of removing the flakes, and the selection of certain flakes as blanks (potential implements). The latter are termed "flake blanks" in this
study. In the absence of the examination of the cores themselves, none
of which were found in the survey, information regarding primary
technology is derived through examination of the striking platform and
dorsal surfaces of the flake implements. An analysis form was devised
to record this and other information, and is illustrated in Figure 19.
In the section of the form dealing with primary technology, most of
the variables listed are self-explanatory. The exceptions, perhaps,
are orientation, trajectory, and core facet angle. Orientation here
refers to the angle of flake removal with reference to the main dorsal
ridge of the flake. Trajectory refers to the amount of longitudinal

Date: <u>ARTIFACT ANALYSIS FORM</u>   Code No:
                                                            Artifact No:

Type: Cultural Affinity:
Provenience: Material:

Sketch: Notes:

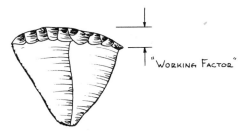

I. <u>Gross Morphology</u> II. <u>Continuous Variables</u> III. <u>Discrete Variables</u>

                                          A. Primary Technology:

1. Divergence Angle   1. Length   1. Punch or Baton Removal
2. Distal Configuration   2. Width   2. Platform Type
3. Corner Configuration   3. Thickness   3. Proximal Modification
4. Lateral Configuration   4. Working Factor   4. Dorsal Facets
5. Corner Sharpness   5. Distal Retouch Length   5. Cortex
                          6. Lateral Retouch Length   6. Orientation
                          7. Total Retouch Length   7. Core Facet Angle
                                             8. Trajectory
                                             9. Platform Width
                                         10. Platform-Facet Angle

B. Secondary Technology: C. Tertiary Technology:
   (Initial flaking)   (Secondary flaking)

                                          1. Distal
1. Modified from Wider Flake   1. Right Lateral   a. Polish or Grinding
2. Original Angle   2. Left Lateral   b. Gouging
3. Lateral Break   3. Notching   c. Step-Flaking
4. Lateral Shaping (Right)   4. Spurs   d. Undercut Edge
5. Lateral Shaping (Left)   5. Lateral Graver   e. Pressure Retouch
6. Ventral Shaping   6. Undercut Corner   2. Right Lateral
                          7. Ventral Treatment   a. Polish or Grinding
                                          b. Gouging
                                          c. Step-Flaking
                                          d. Undercut Edge
Other Notes: e. Pressure Retouch
                                          3. Left Lateral
                                          a. Polish or Grinding
                                          b. Gouging
                                          c. Step-Flaking
                                          d. Undercut Edge
                                          e. Pressure Retouch

Figure 19. Artifact Analysis Form.

curvature present in the flake, as evidenced by the ventral surface. The core facet angle is derived by measuring the angle at the covergence of the facets on the dorsal flake surface. This is termed "core" facet angle since it reflects the shape of the core prior to removal of the flake. In the case of a multifaceted dorsal surface, the angle cannot be taken.

The category of secondary technology refers to the techniques utilized in the modification of the flake blank into the particular morphology exhibited by the finished implement. Honea (1965) has distinguished between initial flaking and secondary flaking. This distinction was employed initially in the analysis, and later it was determined that for the purposes intended here the two types of secondary modification could be adequately subsumed under the heading of secondary technology. The relevant variables, shown in Figure 19, are generally concerned with modification of the lateral edges, notching, spurring, and retouch of the ventral surface of the flake. Included here are both modification for the general shaping of the artifact, and final modification of the shaped edges in preparation for use.

In that the secondary technology includes shaping the implement, another category of production technique should be noted here. This is the modification of finished artifacts following their use, which includes both the reworking of one type of implement into another (e.g., modifying a broken point into a drill), and resharpening the dulled edges of artifacts (scrapers, knives, etc.).

3. Artifact Morphology Component:

The morphological component of an implement, i.e., its shape in three-dimensional space, was analyzed from the standpoint of two major types of variables: continuous and discrete. An illustration of the recording of the variables is presented in Figure 20 for projectile points, and Figure 19 for other artifacts. In addition to the normally encountered continuous variables (length, width, thickness, etc.) a number of categories were developed to more completely describe certain types of artifacts, and these warrant further explanation.

In regard to projectile points (Figure 20), it was assumed that the fundamental characteristics of the basal morphology would be in part a function of the hafting methods. Since the latter is unknown, a number of measurements were devised with the specific intent of facilitating analysis toward the derivation of information on hafting techniques. One of the critical requisites was a standardized measurement which would represent attributes within the hafted portion of the base. To accomplish this, an arbitrary position (position "A") was established on each base at a distance along the lateral edge equal to one-half the basal width. Dimensions taken at this point were termed "hafting width", "hafting thickness", etc. In the case of those points which exhibit indented bases (e.g., Eden), the measurements were taken just below the point of indentation. All measurements of these and other variables were made with the use of a sliding caliper, and were recorded to the nearest 0.5 millimeters.

Date: PROJECTILE POINT ANALYSIS   Code No:

Type: Artifact No:

Provenience: Material:

Sketch: Notes:

Point "A" —

DISTANCE TO "A" EQUALS
1/2 BASAL WIDTH

EXAMPLE OF HAFTING WIDTH MEASUREMENT ON FOLSOM BASE.

Continuous Attributes: Discrete Attributes:

1. Maximum length: 1. Morphology:

2. Maximum width:
                                      2. Flaking:
3. Maximum thickness:

A. Hafting Data: 3. Degree of basal grinding:

   1. Basal width:
                                      4. Evidence of original facets:
   2. Length of "A":

   3. Width at "A":   5. No. of flutes:

   4. Max. thickness at "A":   Obverse: Reverse:

   5. Flute thickness as "A":
                                      6. Other:
   6. Flute width at "A":

   7. Concavity (convexity) length:

   8. Extent of basal grinding:

Figure 20. Projectile Point Analysis Form.

Regarding the analysis of other artifacts (Figure 19), a number of special categories of continuous variables were devised in order to insure an adequate description of the implements. Divergence angle refers to the angle described by the lateral edges of the flake implement, measured to the nearest 5°, with the proximal end of the flake toward the center of the protractor. Distal and lateral retouch refer to the length of the modified portions of the distal and lateral edges, respectively. The term working factor, adopted from White's (1963: 41) concept of "working length", refers to the length between the chord of the arc prescribed by the convex working edge of an implement and its distal edge (see Figure 19). This particular measurement was designed specifically as a standardized index of the working portion of transverse scrapers.

The other major category in the morphological component deals with discrete variables. As shown in Figure 20, this deals with such things as the presence or absence of basal and lateral grinding and the degree (heavy, light) of this grinding, for projectile points. For other artifacts, discrete variables include distal configuration (shape of the cross-section of the distal end of the implement), corner configuration (whether obtuse, right, or acute), and the shape of the lateral edges (cf. Figure 19:gross morphology).

4. Functional Component:

The final analytic component of the subsystem of lithic technology dealt with in this study is that of artifact function. Presumably, there

152

is an additional component not dealt with here; that of artifact style (S. R. Binford 1968, L. R. Binford 1962). However, stylistic attributes are those which are not explicable in functional or technological terms, and I do not believe that we have arrived at the point in the analysis of PaleoIndian materials which would permit us to deal effectively with the stylistic component. Analysis of the latter is predicated upon a thorough prior understanding of the functional and technological characteristics of PaleoIndian lithic subsystems, and to my knowledge such an understanding has not yet been achieved. Hoepfully, someday it will be, and we can then exploit the stylistic attribute analysis for more informative data at a higher socio-cultural level (Binford 1962:220).

Functional analyses carried out in the present study were of three basic types; primary, secondary, and related, functions. The primary function of a lithic implement refers to that function (or those functions) to which the subsystem trajectory of the artifact production was primarily oriented. Secondary function implies other uses for which a given implement may be employed. For instance, a projectile point is assumed to have a single primary function--that of the penetrating of an animal with the intent to kill it. However, it may also serve a number of secondary functions; e.g., use as a knife before the kill, or if retrieved, after the kill, and use as a piercing implement, etc. A transverse scraper may be intended primarily for utilization of the distally-modified end in hide-scraping functions, yet serve secondarily as a knife through utilization of the low-angled lateral edges. Other tools might well have numerous or multipurpose uses intended as the primary function.

Primary and secondary functions are analyzed through macroscopic and microscopic examination of the use surfaces. This is sometimes referred to as an analysis of "tertiary technology", that is, the flaking of an implement by utilization itself, as opposed to purposeful flaking in preparation for use. The microscopic examination of lithic material has become commonplace recently, primarily as a result of the initial work by Semenov (1964) in this field. The derivation of implement function through the microscopic analysis of the use surfaces requires experience which can be attained only by spending a considerable amount of time in actual practice. Also helpful is experimentation with artifact usage, and the examination of use surfaces of known function.[2]

In general, four types of wear can be distinguished through this type of analysis. The first is that of a high polish or sheen on the use surface which in its most distinctive state exhibits minute striae in the direction in which the artifact was used. In addition to Semenov (1964: 88), other investigators have noticed this characteristic (MacDonald

----

[2] When the intensive analysis of transverse scrapers for the present study was initiated, I spent an average of 45 minutes per artifact in attaining an adequate description of the wear patterns through microscopic analysis. After some 150 hours of practice, I was able to reduce the time spent to about 10 minutes per artifact.

1968:92, Wilmsen 1967:144). It is presumed that the luster or polish
on the working surface is a result of the scraping or softening of hides,
and that small silicate particles in the material being worked produce
the striations on the lithic implement. This type of wear is termed
"soft" wear herein, and it can also be ascertained on the edges of cutting implements which were used extensively on soft materials such as
hides or meat. A distinction was made in the analysis between "soft"
wear, in which the polish alone was present, and "heavy soft" wear
characterized by the additional presence of the striations.

A second type of wear observable under the microscope is that
which I have termed "grinding" wear. To my knowledge this is as yet
unreported in the literature. It is best described by noting its similarity to the grinding or abrading of the lateral edges of projectile
point bases. When viewed microscopically, the two types of wear are
virtually identical, thus the derivation of the term "grinding wear".
Endscrapers which exhibit grinding wear will also reveal this type of
abrasion in a flat plane when viewed laterally, thus defining the angle
at which the implement was used. Experiments have shown that grinding wear can be produced by the initial scraping of hard materials,
such as bone or antler, or by the extended scraping of some types of
wood. Presumably, grinding wear could not be produced by the scraping of hides, and by the same token, the extensive, heavy scraping of
very hard materials, though perhaps initially producing a grinding wear,
would eventually result in a different category of wear.

A third type of wear is that termed "step-flaking", and is the result of heavy scraping on a hard surface. Use flakes here terminate in a stepped or hinged fashion, making it difficult to distinguish these from resharpening flake scars on some artifacts (Crabtree and Davis 1968:428). On transverse scrapers, however, the process of resharpening involves the removal of a very distinctive flake (Jelinek 1966), much longer than those resulting from use. Step-flaking of the latter type is considered "hard wear" herein, and results from the heavy scraping of a hard material such as bone or antler, and possibly some of the harder woods. By heavy scraping, I am referring to the intended shaping of such materials, as opposed to merely smoothing them.

The final wear category distinguished here is that of "gouging". This refers to the irregular spalling of the working surface by use, which results in the formation of discontinuous gouges or serrations along its edge. Gouging can be of two types: unifacial and bifacial. Unifacial gouging may result from the scraping of a hard material with an edge which is too thin to withstand the stress, or, as Crabtree and Davis (1968:428) have pointed out, from mistakes made in the use of the implement when it is inadvertently allowed to strike another stone. Bifacial gouging results from the cutting of a hard material with a sawing action. For instance, bifacial gouging of the lateral edge of a flake can be produced by attempting to saw a piece of bone or antler in two. This, then, is another type of hard wear, but is generally confined to lateral edges of implements, e.g., those which are relatively straight and can be used for cutting, as opposed to the convex distal edge of a transverse scraper.

One final kind of variation should be mentioned in that it was recorded on the analysis forms. This is the variation of the degree to which a working edge may be undercut as a result of use. Both hard and soft wear can produce an undercut edge. In either case, if undercutting was pronounced (more than 90°), the adjective "heavy" was added to the type of wear present.

Although primary and secondary functions can be derived through microscopic examination, the determination of what is here considered "related" functions must rest on inferential evidence. By related functions, I am referring to such things as the hafting technology employed with projectile points and other hafted implements, and the ballistic factors which must be taken into consideration in the effective use of projected weaponry. Although such elements cannot be considered primary or secondary functional components themselves, they do condition the efficient utilization of implements, and are therefore included in this analysis as related functional components.

As mentioned previously, there has been no evidence recovered from PaleoIndian contexts in North America which would reveal indisputably the methods of hafting projectile points or other implements. A total of three cylindrical tapering bone artifacts have been found at

Blackwater Draw (Wormington 1957:48, Warnica 1966:351-2) and these were originally thought to have represented foreshafts. Later, the possibility was raised that they were bone points. Having personally examined the specimen described by Warnica, I would tend to favor the foreshaft interpretation. If PaleoIndian groups did utilize a bone foreshaft, this could condition very considerably the production of projectile points, since lithic material is less time-consuming to work than bone, and the points would probably be fitted to the foreshafts. As indicated, the analysis of projectile points in the present study was designed specifically to determine information of this nature.

Regarding ballistics, we do not know at present whether the spear-thrower was employed by all PaleoIndian groups, though as mentioned there is some evidence from the Cody Complex Jurgens site. If spearthrowers were used, it would condition numerous essential variables in the production of projectile points, since weight is a critical factor in the ballistics of a projected missile. Experiments by Jerry Dawson (personal communication) and the author have revealed that the weight must be concentrated at the distal end of the missile assemblage (dart/foreshaft/point). This would suggest, for instance, the need to use a heavy bone or antler foreshaft in combination with the relatively light Folsom point to provide adequate penetrating power. Again, such information can be derived through inference only at the

158

present stage of analysis, but the ballistics and hafting components must be considered in the final formulation of any functional taxon dealing with PaleoIndian projectile points.

Once the various lithic implements were analyzed in the manner indicated above, the articulation of the components comprising the lithic subsystem was considered (see Chapter VI). To illustrate this process, using Folsom as an example, the material, production, morphological, and functional components of Folsom projectile points were identified, separating the essential from the inessential variables. The articulation of the essential variables was then analyzed to determine those attributes critical to the definition of a Folsom point as a functional category.[3]

The same process was then carried out for Folsom transverse scrapers and wherever possible, other implements in the Folsom tool assemblage. Having identified the implements in terms of the four major components, the articulation of all the implements comprising the Folsom lithic technological subsystem was then considered in order to determine the key variables which characterize it, in other words, the elements of primary technological focus. The procedure was then repeated for the other cultures manifested in the survey

---

[3]The technique of component articulation involves the complete systems trajectories from the initial material selection to the finished artifact, and the taxonomy thereby derived is formed on much more than morphological attributes alone. It is, presumably, equally more reliable than the morphological taxon.

159

sample. Though time-consuming, this process results in a maximal understanding of the lithic technologies represented, at least within the limits of the potential afforded by the nature of the empirical material resulting from survey collection.

Wherever possible and practical, the articulation of the components was analyzed by quantitative methods. Such analyses were facilitated considerably by the use of computer facilities in the Department of Anthropology and the University Computing Center of the University of New Mexico. The quantification of data has become commonplace in archeological analysis, due in large part to the stimulus provided by Spaulding (1953, 1960). In regard to the selection of specific statistical methods, a number of authors have discussed the merits of the various alternatives available (cf. Johnson 1967:52-59, Tugby 1965, Cowgill 1968, and Clarke 1968:547-566). The techniques used in the present study were adopted after a careful review of the alternatives.

Unfortunately, an intensive component analysis could not be made of all the implement types recovered in the survey, due to inadequate sample size. Only transverse scrapers and projectile points provided sufficiently reliable data to permit quantification at the component

level. A total of 235 transverse scrapers and 115 projectile points
were submitted to intensive statistical analyses, including basic statistics, tabulation, correlation, and factor analyses. The results of
these analyses are presented in the following chapters. It should be
noted that it was necessary to augment the number of Clovis points
found in the survey by 13 specimens from outside the survey area, in
order to obtain a sample adequate for comparative purposes.[4] This
fact must be taken into account when the interpretation of the Clovis
component articulation is being considered.

The Environmental Components: Analytic Techniques

The continuous and discrete environmental components have been
adequately described in the preceeding chapter, and presented in visual
form in Table 4. Each of these components was analyzed separately
for each culture, in order to segregate the essential from the inessential attributes. The essential attributes were then analyzed from the
standpoint of component articulation to determine those key attributes
responsible for particular patterning. As indicated in Table 4, there
is insufficient data on the environmental components of each culture
to permit quantification of the variables. Analysis was performed
instead by visual inspection of the data, and analytic taxons were formulated on this basis. Once patterning of the environmental components

---

[4]I am deeply indebted to Dr. Robert Weber for permission to
examine and record metric data on some of the Mockingbird Clovis
material.

had been recognized, and the key variables isolated, the next step
was to consider the articulation of lithic and environmental components.
This was achieved by analyzing the combination of the data presented
in Tables 3 and 4. Again, the essential and inessential variables were
distinguished, and the key attributes responsible for discerned patterns
were isolated. The result of this procedure was the formulation of
functional taxons with respect to the settlement technology of each culture, which as stated previously, was one of the major aims of the
analytic survey model.

Following the identification of the elements of primary settlement
technological focus for each culture, the analytic sequence was carried
out at the next higher systemic level, that of cultural systems themselves. Analysis at this stage is at the intercultural level of comparison and the emphasis is on the identification of those key variables
responsible for changes in systems trajectories at the macrotemporal
scale, generally in terms of constraints imposed upon the systems by
known or inferred environmental variables. Generalizations formulated
at the intercultural level of analysis of survey data must necessarily
be made in the form of hypotheses suggested for empirical verification
by actual excavation at some future date.

This completes the discussion of the analytic techniques utilized
in the processing of the survey data. The next chapter will deal with
the actual analysis and interpretation of the data at the subsystemic

(intracultural) level, while Chapter 7 will involve the intercultural

analysis permitted by these interpretations and further quantitative

analyses.

CHAPTER VI

Intracultural Analyses and Interpretations

In order to facilitate the presentation of the interpretative material, the analysis of the four PaleoIndian cultural components will be
discussed in order of relative abundance of sites and cultural material
recovered in the survey, i. e., Folsom, Belen, Cody Complex, and
Clovis. An analysis and interpretation of the lithic and environmental
components of each culture will be presented, followed by an interpretation of the lithic and settlement technological subsystems.

The Folsom Occupation

A total of fifteen Folsom sites and fourteen Folsom localities were
recorded in the survey. Only the sites were submitted to intensive
analysis, which involved a total of 1,028 artifacts including channel
flakes. Tables 1-5 summarize this data, and more detailed information
will be presented in tabular form in this section.

A. Lithic Components:

1. Projectile Points and Preforms:

A total of 117 Folsom projectile points or fragments thereof, and
evidence of 128 preforms were located by the survey. These artifacts
comprised 14.4 and 15.9% of the total Folsom collection respectively.
Of the projectile points, most were broken and fragmented sections of

different specimens. A sample of 33 complete basal sections was selected for intensive analysis (Table 6) from which the following interpretations are in part derived.

As shown in Table 6, analysis of the material component indicates that 84% of the points in the sample were of chert, chalcedony, or jasper, with only a slight preference for chert. The rest of the points were of miscellaneous materials, including 2 of quartzite and one of obsidian. The production of a Folsom point from quartzite is no easy task, and may have been facilitated by the heat treatment of either the core or flake blank. There was no correlation evident between the type of material utilized and any of the other variables included in the projectile point analysis.

The production component is perhaps better-known for Folsom than for any other PaleoIndian projectile point. This is primarily due to the large number of preforms found, from which the techniques of manufacture have been reconstructed. Interpretations of this technique have been offered by Crabtree (1966) and Irwin (1968), but neither of these were based on the comprehensive preform data available as a result of the present survey, which has served to clarify considerably the actual method utilized. The following description is a result of the detailed examination of more than 450 Folsom artifacts representing almost all the stages of projectile point manufacture.

Table 6. Analysis of Folsom Projectile Points[a]

A. Continuous Variables: (measured in millimeters)

Attribute	Mean	Standard Deviation	Coefficient of Variation	Maximum	Minimum	Range
1. Basal Width	19.42	1.125	5.79	22.0	17.2	4.8
2. Hafting Width	20.58	1.329	6.45	23.6	18.1	5.5
3. Maximum Width	21.51	1.492	6.93	25.0	18.5	6.5
4. Hafting Flute Width	13.35	1.469	11.00	15.5	8.5	7.0
5. Thickness	3.83	.481	12.54	5.0	3.1	1.9
6. Hafting Thickness	3.49	.489	14.00	5.0	3.0	2.0
7. Hafting flute thickness	2.43	.442	18.15	3.5	2.0	1.5
8. Concavity depth	2.89	1.159	40.15	6.0	1.0	5.0

9. Hafting index = .169

B. Discrete Variables: (percentage occurrence)

	Chert	Chalcedony	Jasper	Miscellaneous
1. Material type	.39	.24	.21	.16

	Lateral	Concavity	Both	Absent
2. Basal Grinding	.67	.00	.30	.03

[a] N = 33

The first step in the production of a Folsom projectile point is the removal from the core of a large flake with a relatively flat trajectory. This flake is termed here the "flake blank." Presumably done at the quarry site, remnants of this process have either not yet been found, or not yet recognized in Folsom assemblages. However, remnant striking platform indications noticed on Folsom preforms suggest strongly that this was not a blade blank, but rather a flake blank due to the oblique location of the platform and bulb. I believe that in order to remove a flake of this size with minimal curvature, either a Levallois technique or a very close approximation thereof would have to be utilized. No historical connection between the New World and the Old World is implied by this statement. I would rather consider the Levallois technique simply another logical method of working stone, and the term is used here in the purely descriptive sense.

Once the flake blank has been derived, it is bifacially worked by soft hammer percussion into a rather rectanguloid preform, roughly twice as long as it is wide. A considerable amount of care is taken in the production of the preform to insure a symmetrical biconvex cross-section, since the success of the flute removal depends largely on the precision with which this flaking is done.

Once the desired shape has been obtained, the preform is prepared for fluting. This activity evidently took place at the site, rather than at the quarry, since large numbers of channel flakes were found in the site survey. The fluting process involves first the chipping of a "W"-shaped, nipple-like platform in one end of the preform. Observations indicate that generally the distal end of the original flake was used for this preparation, and that the flutes were removed toward the thicker portion (proximal end).[1] The distal end may have been selected in order to facilitate flute platform preparation, which was done by pressure flaking.

After careful preparation, the flute striking platform is heavily abraded, probably to prevent slippage of the point of the intermediary used to remove the flute. The actual technique used in the removal of the flute is not known, though presumably it is through the use of indirect percussion. Such a technique would permit greater control over the angle and direction of the removal blow. It should be noted that prior to flute removal, the distal end of the preform (proximal end of the original flake) was prepared by pressure-flaking a bevelled edge into the face from which the first flute was to be struck. Generally the dorsal facet of the original flake blank was selected for first flute removal. The angle of the bevel of the distal end of the preform was about 50°, and evidently this bevel served functionally in the support of the preform during the fluting process.

---

[1] This characteristic has been verified elsewhere, although not for Folsom. Mason (1958:14) mentions the fluting of Michigan points from the "tip" of the original blade, and MacDonald (1968:108) observed a similar orientation of the Debert material.

After the first flute was removed, the "W"-shaped platform was again chipped into the proximal end of the preform in preparation for removing the second flute. The preparation and removal of the first flute resulted in the formation of a concavity in the base of the preform, and the process of second flute removal served to enlarge this concavity. It can thus be seen that the characteristic "ears" and basal concavity of a Folsom point are in large part a function of flute removal. Once the platform had again been prepared and abraded, the second flute was removed, presumably by the same process as the first. In some cases the distal end of the preform was rebevelled on the opposite edge (e.g., the second flute surface) prior to removal of the second flute, and in other instances it was not. There is no conclusive evidence for consistency of this trait.

The end result of this procedure was a preform which was fluted on both faces for about 3/4 of its entire length. Both flutes generally terminated in hinge fractures, and the second flute was often slightly shorter than the first. I would assume that this was because more caution had to be taken in the removal of the second flute to prevent breakage of the preform. This point in the manufacturing process can be considered the final stage in the production of the preform, and it was this preform which was also utilized as an implement for cutting functions. In fact, many of the Folsom "knives" reported in the literature (cf. Roberts 1936:Plate 10h) are in reality Folsom preforms, either in the fluted or unfluted stage. One would assume that a number

of these implements would be carried with the hunter, each serving the

dual purpose of a knife and a potential projectile point.

At the time the projectile point was to be finished, the unfluted

tip portion of the preform was broken off at the location of the terminal

end of the shortest flute. The broken portion is referred to here as a

"snapped tip," and it is through the recovery of many of these

items that this unique manufacturing procedure was reconstructed.

The result of this operation is a preform which is fluted its entire

length on both faces, and it is this preform which is finally modified

into the shape characteristic of a Folsom point. This is accomplished

through fine pressure retouch along the lateral edges, and more exten-

sive flaking of the distal end into a point. Modification of the basal

concavity was limited to occasional removal of small flakes along the

edges of the flute scars, evidently to facilitate fitting into a haft (see

Chapter VII). The final stage of manufacture was the grinding of the

lateral edges of the basal portion of the point.

This, then, is the process involved in the production of a Folsom

point as reconstructed from the evidence revealed by the survey. The

ideal version has been described. Obviously there were a number of

variations on this procedure, and the ideal was not always attained.

Failures in flute removal were quite frequent, as indicated by the

relatively large number of broken preform bases recovered in the survey.

Broken specimens include those in which one of the flutes hinged through, thus splitting the preform, and others for which the reason of breakage could not be determined. Of the total of 245 projectile points and preforms found in the survey, 61 were broken basal potions. This would indicate roughly a 25% failure in attempts to finish the points from the unfluted preform stage of manufacture.

The procedure involved in the production of a Folsom point has been described here in some detail for two reasons. First, a description of this process involving the snapped tip of the preform is as yet unreported in the literature. Secondly, it is important to realize that a number of distinct functional stages are represented in the production of a Folsom point, rather than the simple modification of a flake blank into a point. This will be examined in more detail in the discussion of the functional components below.

Regarding the morphological component, the characteristics commonly employed to identify a Folsom point are well-known. The presence of fluting (generally a single flute on each face), the basal concavity and basal ears, and the very fine pressure retouch along the lateral edges are generally considered the key variables of a Folsom point.

As mentioned in Chapter V, when I undertook the analysis of these and other points in the survey, I attempted to obtain variables which I felt would be crucial in the hafting of the point, since variations

in basal morphology almost certainly reflect variations in hafting techniques (or vice versa). The results of a statistical analysis of the data
taken on the Folsom point sample are presented in Table 6. Two of the
statistics presented merit further explanation. The coefficient of
variation is calculated by dividing the standard deviation by the mean
and multiplying by 100. Its purpose is to facilitate the comparison of
the standard deviations of the attributes analyzed, by taking into consideration the wide range of variation of the means involved. For
instance, as shown by the table, maximum thickness (variable 5) has a
lower standard deviation than does basal width (variable 1), yet when
the disparity in means is compensated for by computing the coefficient
of variation, it can be seen that there is relatively less deviation in the
case of basal width.

The other element requiring explanation is the "hafting index."
This is computed by dividing the hafting thickness (variable 6) by the
hafting width (variable 2). This is presented primarily to permit
comparison of hafting data at the intercultural level. The hafting index
increases in degree as the hafted portion of the point becomes thicker
relative to width.

The continuous variables in Table 6 have been arranged in order
of increasing values of coefficients of variation. This order itself indicates the critical variables in the production of a Folsom point. Here,
basal width is the most critical variable in that it exhibits the minimal

range of variation of those attributes analyzed. It is interesting to observe that point thickness is less critical than point width, since one of the assumptions frequently made about Folsom points in order to explain the fluting process is that thickness (thinness) is of maximal importance (cf. Rovner and Agogino 1967).

In opposition to the very close tolerances required by the Folsom point manufactures regarding basal width, the depth of the basal concavity is the least critical of the continuous variables. This confirms the suggestion made earlier that this attribute is largely a function of the fluting process and would be expected to vary considerably.

Regarding the attribute of basal grinding, 97% of the points were ground laterally, and 30% exhibited basal concavity grinding. None were ground only in the base. Some of the concavity grinding is probably remnant of the abrading process in striking platform preparation, and thus is not a reliable attribute. The important factor is the high incidence of lateral grinding. Of those ground, 53% exhibited heavy grinding, as determined through microscopic examination, while 47% were ground only lightly. No correlation appeared between the intensity of the grinding and the basal width.

Not shown in the table, and difficult to describe adequately, is the exceptional technological ability demonstrated by retouch on many of the Folsom points. Fifty percent of the points had very fine and even pressure retouch along the lateral edges. Many of the retouch scars were as narrow as 1.0-1.5 millimeters, indicative of the superior form of craftsmanship.

In regard to the functional components of the Folsom preforms and points, the latter are by definition projectile points, and presumably functioned as such. There was no evidence of secondary function on the points themselves either in terms of secondary retouch or soft knife wear on the point edges. However it should be pointed out that secondary function would be apparent primarily on complete points, and that the latter comprise only 3% of the total number of Folsom "points" recovered in the survey. The majority of the points were broken bases, which would not yield evidence of secondary function such as knife wear. There is a possibility that the "ears" of broken Folsom bases were utilized for piercing or engraving functions, as evidenced by the "burned tips" mentioned previously. Verification of this will have to await clarification of the heat treatment factor.

In the case of the preforms, however, there was ample evidence of multiple usage. The preform edges exhibit soft knife wear, and some were retouched bifacially to facilitate cutting functions. The majority of the channel flakes also show use, again generally in the form of soft knife wear. Thus the preform served both gross and fine cutting functions. The snapped tips reveal multiple usage, both in terms of retouch and actual wear. Many exhibit unilateral retouch of one face, suggesting function as a side scraper. Others had soft and hard knife wear. One had a "burned tip" on one of the sharp snapped edge points, and this plus further microscopic examination of the wear patterns indicated possible use as a hand-held burin for the working of bone.

Regarding related functions, no direct evidence of either hafting techniques, or information on ballistics was derived from the survey. Interpretations of such functions will be offered as the morphological and production components are analyzed.

The articulation of the four major components (material, production, morphology, function) can now be examined. This is best done by viewing the finished Folsom point as the end-product of a specific cultural subsystem trajectory in which certain key variables are responsible for constraints which define or "chart" the particular path of the trajectory.

By definition, Folsom points are fluted. They are also defined as lanceolate, thin, as having a pronounced basal concavity, and generally fine marginal retouch (Wormington 1957:263). My analysis has revealed that not all of these factors should be considered critical to the definition of a Folsom point as a functional type. First of all, it was demonstrated that basal width reveals relatively less variation than does the thickness of the point at the haft. Secondly, the basal concavity was shown to be a function of the fluting process and is therefore not a key variable in the subsystem trajectory. It could be considered an essential attribute, but not a key attribute. The key variables in the Folsom trajectory are as follows: a functional preform; a minimal degree of tolerance in the basal width of the point; the presence of flutes; the presence of lateral grinding; and the absence of post-flute grinding in the basal concavity.

It is true that Folsom points are uniformly thin, and the hafting index is very low. This thinness is a result of fluting, but perhaps too much emphasis has been placed on this in the past. Fluting is only one of many ways to thin a point base. Laterally or vertically-directed soft-hammer percussion is a very effective method which would not involve the complex preparation and potential high rate of failure that is part of the Folsom fluting process. However, lateral thinning also involves the reduction of the width of the base, and basal width is a key variable in the trajectory. It is thus more probable that fluting was undertaken because it offered a concentrated, efficient method of thinning the base, while at the same time maintaining a desired basal width.

The presence of fine lateral retouch, fluting, and the limitations in basal width indicate that Folsom points were being produced to meet very specific hafting needs. I would suggest that the basal width factor indicates the points were being fitted to a previously made foreshaft, rather than vice versa. A bone foreshaft, or even one of relatively hard wood, requires much more work to produce than does a projectile point. It is logical, therefore, that once a foreshaft was manufactured, numerous points would be made to fit it. It may well be that the fore-shaft was of the socket type, and that the fine retouch and grinding of the Folsom lateral edges was to permit the relatively easy insertion and extraction of the point base into the socket haft. Ele Baker (personal communication) has suggested, and I agree, that a rib section of a large herbivore such as a bison would provide excellent source material for such a foreshaft, in that it would require only minimal work to produce a socket capable of receiving a point base with a relatively low hafting index.

The use of a bone foreshaft would in turn permit the maintenance of the proper balance of a dart projected by a spearthrower. Since Folsom points are small relative to many other PaleoIndian points, a heavy foreshaft made of bone, antler, or very hard wood would be a virtual necessity from the standpoint of concentrating the weight at the distal end of the missile. Unfortunately we have no definite evidence that the spearthrower was known to the Folsom people, but I feel it probable that future statistical analyses, based on a more thorough understanding of hafting techniques, will confirm this implement as part of the Folsom tool assemblage.

The systems trajectory represented by what we now term a Folsom point involved a series of highly complex technological stages, many of which required adherence to close tolerances on the part of the flintknappers. The possibility of failure was quite high. One can assume, therefore, that the systems trajectory itself must have been quite highly adaptive in order to have been maintained for almost two millenia. A review of some of the possible adaptations may prove instructive at this point:

For one thing, fluting permitted the use of a relatively thick flake blank to start with, and the latter may have been a technological requisite necessary to achieve a blank with low curvature. I feel the evidence indicates that this wide, thick flake blank was purposely selected by Folsom flintknappers for the production of preforms and finally points. After all, they could have selected thinner, more narrow flakes as blanks, and modified these directly into the Folsom morphology without fluting. In effect this is what a Midland point is, indicating that this more simplified means of production was selected at times either by Folsom people, or by cultures very closely related. Nevertheless, the Folsom trajectory was selected in the majority of cases, and once the thick flake blank was obtained, the most efficient manner of thinning it, while maintaining adequate width, was to flute it. Fluting required the production of a carefully-made preform, and this preform was utilized as an implement, as were the channel flakes derived from it. At the time of final point production, the snapped tip of the preform provided another usable implement. In short, the entire system trajectory comprised a number of distinct stages which were functionally adaptive, indicating that this was an extremely efficient means of utilizing a given amount of lithic material. The Folsom point as a functional taxon, then, becomes much more than a simple projectile point. Instead it can be considered part of a complex implement system in which efficiency in material utilization was maximized.

In fact it may well be that the key element in the Folsom trajectory was the preform rather than the point. Once the preform had been fluted, it could be made into a point quite easily. It was in the manufacture of the fluted preform that most risk of failure was encountered, and yet the potential adaptiveness of the preform, both as an implement and a potential point, insured its retention in the Folsom tool assemblage. I suggest that the fluted preform be considered the focal point in the Folsom trajectory, since from this particular constellation of attributes all other key variables were derived.

2. Transverse Scrapers:

As stated in Chapter 4, the transverse scrapers derived from the survey were arbitrarily divided into four types, based on the presence or absence of lateral modification. Table 7 presents a breakdown of the frequency of occurrence of each of the four types for each of the PaleoIndian cultures represented in the survey.[2] These types will be referred to here as "TU" (transverse unmodified), "TR" (transverse

---

[2]As indicated by the tabular information, only 235 scrapers (of 557 found on the 30 sites) were submitted to intensive analysis. In that the specimens were selected randomly, the analyzed scrapers constitute a reliable sample.

Table 7: Frequency of Transverse Scraper Types per Culture[a]

Analytic Type	Folsom	Belen	Cody	Clovis	Total
1. Unmodified (TU)	40 (.48)	25 (.48)	16 (.32)	16 (.32)	97 (.41)
2. Left lateral (TL)	9 (.11)	4 (.08)	5 (.10)	8 (.16)	26 (.11)
3. Right lateral (TR)	12 (.14)	13 (.25)	9 (.18)	6 (.12)	40 (.17)
4. Bilateral (TB)	22 (.27)	10 (.19)	20 (.40)	20 (.40)	72 (.31)
Total	83(1.00)	52(1.00)	50(1.00)	50(1.00)	235(1.00)

[a] Frequency of occurrence index in parentheses. Artifact count precedes this figure.

right laterally modified), "TL" (transverse left laterally modified),
and "TB" (transverse bilaterally modified).

As shown in the table, 75% of all Folsom scrapers are of the TU
and TB types. For this reason, only these two types will be discussed
in further detail from the standpoint of component analysis. Discussion
of the TL and TR types will be limited to interpretation of specific
function.

Table 8 lists the means and frequency of occurrence indices of
the continuous and discrete variables respectively of the two predominant
analytic types for each culture. It should be noted that Table 8 is
primarily a summary in that data had to be condensed somewhat to
permit tabular portrayal. The condensation for Table 8 took two
forms. First, only the two predominant scraper types of the four
possible are presented for each culture, even though all types were
analyzed and the "total" columns reflect totals of all the scraper
types. The particular types selected were derived from the data in
Table 7. Secondly, not all of the 35 variables utilized in the analysis
are presented. The method employed for selecting those variables
considered most important is a by-product of the statistical analyses
carried out at the intercultural level (Chapter 7). A factor analysis of
an initial sample of some 250 transverse scrapers was undertaken,
and from the resulting factors variables were selected which are taken
to best represent the total variation per factor. The variables selected

Table 8. Analytical Summary of Transverse Scrapers[a]

Attribute	Folsom (N = 83)			Belen (N = 52)		
	TU	TB	Total	TU	TR	Total
1. Length	32.83	33.51	32.44	32.62	28.08	31.23
2. Width	28.73	29.72	29.61	25.88	26.77	26.66
3. Thickness	6.56	7.40	6.87	7.28	5.54	6.70
4. Distal retouch	30.50	31.36	31.16	29.32	29.69	30.08
5. Divergence angle	30.50	33.31	32.30	24.80	39.61	30.67
6. Core facet angle	132	141	136	116	138	125
7. Striking platform	.75	.64	.70	.44	.31	.44
8. Cortex	.23	.18	.22	.52	.38	.44
9. Dorsal facets						
single	.03	.09	.04	.00	.20	.04
double	.50	.32	.47	.56	.69	.58
triple	.12	.18	.11	.24	.08	.13
multiple	.35	.41	.31	.20	.23	.25
10. Orientation						
across	.15	.09	.13	.12	.15	.10
parallel	.63	.58	.64	.72	.31	.60
away	.20	.23	.25	.16	.46	.25
11. Notching						
single	.55	.41	.42	.36	.15	.27
double	.25	.18	.20	.28	.46	.42

[a] Attributes 1-4: means given in millimeters
    "   5-6: means given in degrees
    "   7-17: frequency of occurrence indices

(continued)

Table 8. Analytical Summary of Transverse Scrapers (continued)[a]

Attribute	Folsom (N = 83)			Belen (N = 52)		
	TU	TB	Total	TU	TR	Total
12. Spur						
single	.57	.45	.51	.68	.85	.71
double	.08	.05	.07	.08	.00	.10
13. Undercut corner	.48	.26	.42	.64	.23	.43
14. Distal wear						
heavy soft	.10	.18	.16	.24	.15	.21
soft	.30	.18	.25	.16	.08	.13
grinding	.40	.36	.39	.56	.69	.60
hard	.17	.27	.19	.04	.08	.06
15. Right lateral wear						
grinding	.20	.18	.20	.24	.38	.35
gouging	.45	.55	.49	.52	.61	.54
bifacial gouging	.27	.05	.17	.24	.00	.11
16. Left lateral wear						
grinding	.10	.18	.16	.24	.38	.33
gouging	.52	.36	.43	.32	.31	.35
bifacial gouging	.30	.00	.18	.32	.15	.19
17. Material type						
chalcedony	.32	.36	.33	.16	.08	.11
flint	.03	.09	.06	.28	.46	.29
chert	.45	.45	.47	.48	.31	.48
jasper	.17	.09	.13	.08	.15	.11
quartzite	.00	.00	.00	.00	.00	.00

(continued)

[a]Attributes 7-17: frequency of occurrence indices

Table 8: Analytical Summary of Transverse Scrapers (continued)[a]

Attribute	Cody (N = 50)			Clovis (N = 50)		
	TU	TB	Total	TU	TB	Total
1. Length	31.22	34.68	31.74	34.16	32.83	33.29
2. Width	24.91	27.30	26.05	27.69	26.30	26.51
3. Thickness	7.46	7.30	7.04	7.78	7.25	7.41
4. Distal retouch	27.44	30.35	29.00	30.31	29.70	29.20
5. Divergence angle	21.25	34.50	30.60	28.75	31.00	29.64
6. Core facet angle	121	143	118	122	139	129
7. Striking platform	.38	.35	.40	.56	.55	.56
8. Cortex	.56	.20	.38	.25	.15	.26
9. Dorsal facets						
single	.00	.10	.06	.06	.10	.08
double	.44	.30	.38	.63	.40	.56
triple	.19	.05	.08	.12	.00	.06
multiple	.38	.50	.46	.19	.45	.28
10. Orientation						
across	.06	.00	.02	.12	.00	.04
parallel	.56	.50	.48	.69	.75	.70
away	.12	.20	.20	.19	.10	.18
11. Notching						
single	.19	.40	.38	.25	.30	.34
double	.12	.30	.16	.44	.30	.30

[a] Attributes 1-4: means given in millimeters
" 5-6: means given in degrees
" 7-17: frequency of occurrence indices

(continued)

Table 8. Analytical Summary of Transverse Scrapers (continued)[a]

Attribute		Cody (N = 50)			Clovis (N = 50)		
		TU	TB	Total	TU	TB	Total
12. Spur	single	.19	.60	.50	.69	.60	.58
	double	.06	.00	.02	.12	.10	.08
13. Undercut corner		.31	.45	.40	.50	.25	.40
14. Distal wear	heavy soft	.44	.25	.27	.12	.40	.30
	soft	.25	.35	.37	.19	.15	.16
	grinding	.30	.25	.30	.38	.10	.24
	hard	.00	.15	.10	.31	.25	.26
15. Right lateral wear	grinding	.00	.15	.12	.19	.05	.12
	gouging	.44	.85	.54	.44	.55	.46
	bifacial gouging	.25	.00	.12	.31	.00	.12
16. Left lateral wear	grinding	.00	.20	.08	.12	.15	.20
	gouging	.38	.50	.46	.37	.35	.36
	bifacial gouging	.19	.00	.10	.37	.00	.20
17. Material type	chalcedony	.44	.20	.22	.25	.20	.18
	flint	.00	.20	.14	.25	.05	.14
	chert	.31	.35	.42	.31	.20	.32
	jasper	.19	.15	.14	.12	.45	.28
	quartzite	.06	.10	.08	.06	.05	.04

[a]Attributes 7-17: frequency of occurrence indices

were those which exhibited the highest loadings in each factor. It is
these which are presented in Table 8. In addition, several more variables have been added to the "pure" measures in order to more
completely account for the variation in the functional components.
The following analysis is based on the tabular data.

Regarding the material component of the TU and TB Folsom
scrapers, except for the somewhat more extensive use of jasper for
TU scrapers, there is little difference between the two types, and
little to suggest that material was a key variable in the production of
transverse scrapers.

In terms of the production and morphological components, it can
be seen that the TU scrapers are generally smaller than the TB types
in all continuous attributes except length. The most significant distinction here is in the core facet angles. There is a difference of 12°
between the two types, with the TU scrapers exhibiting a much more
acute angle. This indicates that the more acute flakes were being
selected for scraper blanks in which the distal end only would be
retouched, leaving the lateral edges unmodified. The "flatter" flakes
would have been considerably wider and thus were modified bilaterally
to attain a given shape. A lower standard deviation exhibited by the
mean divergence angle of the Folsom TB scrapers tends to confirm
this.

The question can now be raised as to whether the scraper blanks were struck purposely to produce the variation in facet angle or whether they were simply selected from random flakes resulting from a standard-ized method of working a core? The similarity in orientation between the two types, as well as the general lack of cortex on both would suggest similarity in core treatment for the production of both. This is strongly reinforced by observing the thickness variable (attribute 3). Given a standardized core treatment, narrow flakes are necessarily thinner than wide flakes, and this is evident in the narrower TU and wider TB types. In order to alter this characteristic covariation, the core treatment must vary also. Thus the evidence in this case indi-cates that Folsom scraper blanks were generally selected following removal from the core, and there was no determined effort to dress the core in a manner which would provide a specific type of scraper blank.

Elements of secondary modification which distinguish the two types are rather slight variations in notching and the presence of the spur. The TU scraper is more consistently notched and spurred than is the TB type.

Regarding the functional component, there is no definite associa-tion between either of the two types and any specific type of distal wear. The ratio of hard to soft distal wear is about 3:2 for all Folsom trans-verse scrapers, and the TU and TB types follow this ratio in general.

In terms of lateral wear, the unmodified TU scraper revealed bifacial gouging of the edges, especially the left lateral. The TB scrapers exhibited heavy unifacial gouging of the right lateral edge, and relatively little wear of the left lateral edge.

The articulation of these components reveals no specific association of distal wear with either of the two types. The key variables seem to be the elements of divergence and facet angle, which would suggest differences in hafting potential. A scraper of relatively low divergence (e. g., tending toward parallel sides) would be easier to haft than one which is widely divergent. Thus here it would seem that a functional taxonomy of Folsom scrapers would almost certainly have to involve the related functional component of "haftability."

The two remaining scraper types, transverse left and transverse right, are not shown in Table 7 but an analysis of the same variables revealed considerable specialization in function. The TL scrapers (11% of the total Folsom sample) were quite large, thick, and parallel-sided scrapers which exhibited a high percentage of grinding wear. Presumably, they were hafted and used for heavy wood-working. The TR scrapers, on the other hand, were short, flat, and highly divergent, and had a high percentage of soft wear. These were evidently hand-held hide working scrapers in which the maximum advantage of the distal retouch length was utilized. It should be noted here that either of the singly modified scrapers (TL or TR) could have been, and probably were, used as backed knives, with the lateral edge opposite the modified edge serving for cutting functions.

In summary, an analysis of the transverse scrapers in the Folsom assemblage indicates the selection of scraper blanks from a random assortment of flakes, which were then modified according to need. The general lack of association between the dominant scraper types and specific wear patterns indicates an orientation toward the multipurpose use of these implements. In all probability, when hafting was necessary the TU type was chosen, yet such selection did not result in a significant variation in wear between types. If any pattern can be derived from the analysis of the Folsom transverse scrapers, it is the emergence of this implement as a generalized, multipurpose tool.

3. Other Artifacts:

The formulation of typologies within other implement classes was not attempted due to the small sample sizes involved, although a preliminary division was made of the side scrapers. In none of the other implement classes, however, was the sample size large enough to permit an intensive analysis of the material, production, and morphological components as in the case of the points and transverse scrapers. The percentage distribution per culture of these implements has already been presented (Table 2), and they will be discussed briefly.

It can be seen from Table 2 that Folsom has a slightly lower than average number of side scrapers. These were classified as unifacial, bifacial, and tabular (see Chapter 4) and the percentage occurrences of these subtypes were 61%, 13%, and 26% respectively of the total number of side scrapers. It is rather difficult to generalize about the wear patterns on these scrapers, but Folsom people seemed to use them primarily for working hard surfaces. Based on an examined sample of 46 (58% of the total) it was found that 59% revealed hard wear, 35% soft, and 6% had indications of both hard and soft usage. The tabular and bifacial side scrapers were used for both hard and soft functions about equally, but the unifacial types were used almost exclusively on hard surfaces. Presumably hand-held, side scrapers were evidently used less for the working of hide than for the shaping of wooden or bone implements.

Regarding the remaining tool types (knives, gravers, chisel gravers, drills, spokeshaves, and utility flakes), it can be seen from Table 2 that the Folsom assemblage contains roughly average numbers of these items, with the exception of gravers and utility flakes which run higher than average. Of the gravers, about 10% were double gravers of unknown function. Even if these were removed from the sample, the remaining gravers would comprise a higher percentage than normal for the PaleoIndian assemblages as a whole. Although the exact function of gravers remains an enigma, it was suggested that they may have been used in the working of bone. If so, we can assume that Folsom either worked bone more frequently than the other Paleo-Indian groups in the survey, or that the high frequency of gravers compensates for the lack of graving tips in the total tool assemblage. The latter hypothesis is partially supported by examining the frequency of spurs on Folsom transverse scrapers. As indicated by Table 7, Folsom has the second lowest incidence of spurred scraper corners. Only Cody Complex has fewer. Thus it may be that the increase in frequency of gravers as separate implements compensates for the low frequency of spurs associated with transverse scrapers.

Regarding the relatively high number of utility flakes in the Folsom assemblage, we can again postulate that functionally these tools may compensate for a deficiency elsewhere. Referring once more to Table 2, it can be seen that Folsom has the lowest incidence of transverse scrapers of the four cultures, and presumably this deficiency was buttressed somewhat by the higher number of utility flakes which provided hand-held scraping functions.

4. Component Articulation:

The examination of the articulation of the components described and analyzed above suggests certain generalizations regarding Folsom lithic technology as a whole.

A review of the material and production components indicates no particular preference in the selection of lithic material types, but instead a very definite orientation toward the efficient utilization of lithic material in general. An analysis of the morphological and functional components indicates that regardless of the more obvious morphological categories, most tools served multipurpose functions, again demonstrating the maximization of efficiency in utilization of raw material. There are relatively few highly specialized implements in the Folsom tool kit (such as chisel gravers, drills, and spokeshaves), and there are numerous tools such as the preform, transverse scraper, and utility flake, which serve multipurpose needs. Certainly the Folsom preform, itself a knife, with the potential of deriving channel flakes, a snapped tip, and a projectile point from it, was a highly efficient treatment of lithic material for a maximum of possible functions. Furthermore, an analysis of transverse scraper production techniques revealed that scraper blanks were not purposefully struck as such, but were instead selected from a variety of flakes and modified according to need. I would suggest that these flakes were by-products of the initial treatment of a core for the eventual removal of a preform flake blank. In other words the primary focus of core "dressing" was the removal of a large, flat, and relatively thick flake which could be modified into a preform, and the flakes which resulted from this specific type of core preparation were those utilized as blanks for other implements. This suggests that the derivation of the preform could be considered the element of primary technological focus in the Folsom subsystem of lithic technology.

The concept of the preform as a highly adaptive tool also explains its retention in the Folsom tool kit. As I have pointed out elsewhere

(Judge 1970) it is difficult to explain why Folsom people went to the trouble of preparing a preform carefully in order to flute it (and thus risk possible loss of the preform), when they could have quite easily selected thinner flake blanks to start with and modified them into the Folsom morphology (i. e., a Midland point). In the absence of noting the functional adaptiveness of the Folsom preform, one is hard put to explain its existence.

We can conclude, then, that Folsom people were quite conservative in their use of lithic material, and that this is manifest in the production of a preform as a primary focal unit. By-products of this process served as blanks for other tools, which then served multipurpose rather than specialized needs. It is tempting to suggest that this efficiency in utilization of raw material and the multipurpose usage of a minimum number of tool types represents an adaptation to a highly mobile way of life. This is certainly a possible explanation for this phenomenon in the central Rio Grande valley, but one should not generalize beyond the survey region. In fact, I would consider this one of the more important problems raised by this survey to be investigated through further research outside the survey area. Is this same efficiency manifest in Folsom assemblages elsewhere, or is it simply a function of the nature and sources of raw material in the Rio Grande area? If further research indicates that Folsom data exhibit the same degree of efficiency in lithic technology elsewhere as in the survey region, then it may eventually be shown that Folsom was in fact more mobile than other PaleoIndian groups, perhaps because of a food-procurement system which involved maximum exploitation of specific big-game such as bison, rather than the total spectrum of megafaunal species.

In any event, I feel that the intensive analysis of Folsom implements derived from this survey indicates maximum efficiency in lithic treatment here, and I would hope that investigations elsewhere would treat this factor with equal importance.

B.   Environmental Components:

The data on the environmental components for the fifteen Folsom sites are presented in Table 4, and summarized analytically in Table 5.   A more detailed examination follows which will serve to outline the very general components which the Folsom data reveal as critical to the establishment of an occupational location.   Following this discussion, the environmental and lithic component articulation will be considered, and several functional settlement taxons will be formulated.

1.   Continuous Variables:

Subsumed under this category are the type, direction, and distance to the nearest source of water, the nearest overview, and the grazing and potential trap areas.   Regarding the first variable (nearest source of water), the Folsom people chose playas 73% of the time, and streams for the remainder.   No Folsom sites were located near existing springs.

194

The average horizontal distance to water was 109 yards, the lowest average of the four PaleoIndian cultures with the exception of Clovis.[3] The range of variation was from zero to 300 yards.

For Folsom, the direction to the nearest water seems immaterial, the sites being split roughly evenly between the northeast and southeast analytical quadrants. Regarding vertical distance to water, Folsom exhibited the lowest mean (15 feet), again with the exception of Clovis. The range in this variable was from zero to 50 feet.

With reference to the overview component, 40% of the Folsom sites were located on an overview ridge themselves, while the remaining sites were an average of 73 yards away from the overview. There was little consistency to the direction of the ridge in the case of the latter.

Regarding the hunting area component, all but one of the Folsom sites were so situated that the hunting area was to the south, and in 80% of the sites, the hunting area was in the southwest analytical quadrant. The mean distance to the hunting areas was 1290 yards, ranging from a maximum of 3520 to a minimum of 440 yards. The majority of the sites were located near one of the four major areas of hunting.

---

[3]It should be recalled that the Clovis environmental data is based on information from one site only and is therefore not considered reliable.

Potential trap areas were found to be present in the vicinity of 74% of the Folsom sites, and were of either the arroyo or lava tongue type. Distance to these varied from 300 to 1760 yards, and there was no discernible consistancy in the direction involved.

2. Discrete Variables:

Sixty percent of the Folsom sites were found to rest on gentle slopes, generally on the side of a ridge sloping toward a playa edge. The remainder of the sites exhibited a flat landform, usually the flat top of a relatively broad ridge. Because of the predominance of the ridge slop location, the exposure of the sites varied somewhat, 40% being direct and 47% tending toward a southern exposure. Only 13% sought the northeast slope of the ridge which may have offered protection from the prevailing wind. Most (60%) of the sites were visible from the hunting area; they did not seek concealment in any discernible fashion. With reference to soil type, most of the sites were found in the red sandy clay typical of the later Pleistocene horizons in the area, although 20% were in a sand-gravel mix, and 14% were on fairly recent lava flows. Perhaps most significant in regard to the discrete variables, 94% of the Folsom sites were located in the vicinity of a playa, even though that playa might not have been the nearest source of water.

3. Component Articulation:

Viewing all the variables in terms of functional articulation, it seems evident that the single most critical variable was the necessity of having a playa in the vicinity of the site. Next to this in importance was the direction to the hunting area, which was generally to the southwest. Noting the frequency with which a location to the northeast of a hunting area was chosen, it can be suggested that there was a definite effort on the part of Folsom to remain downwind of the hunting area. Thus they apparently searched the general downwind locale of a major hunting area for a suitable site situation, which would have a playa nearby. In this general area, either the playa itself or a stream served as the nearest source of water.

A closer examination of the Folsom playa data revealed that 80% of the sites were located to the east or northeast of the playas, regardless of whether the latter served as the nearest source of water. This directional preference suggests strongly that the Folsom people were using the playas themselves as trap areas. In other words, camped downwind from the hunting area, they would either wait for the animals to come to water, or possibly drive them toward the playa area where they could be surrounded and killed. The proximity of other trap areas in the vicinity of many sites suggests these were alternatives held in reserve if the playa trap failed.

Finally, it should be noted that all the Folsom sites were either at, or within an average of 100 yards of, a topographical overview from which a good view of the hunting area was possible. Since relative to the rest of the PaleoIndian sites in the region this is not a minimum distance, it can be considered an essential, though not a key, variable for the selection of Folsom sites. Where ridges were selected for sites they were relatively low, as indicated by the mean vertical distance to water of 15 feet.

C. Folsom Settlement Technology:

In that there were more Folsom sites located by the survey than any of the other cultures represented, it was felt that the Folsom occupation offered the best potential for the initial understanding of Paleo-Indian settlement technology. Although the general Folsom pattern had been ascertained by analysis of the environmental components, it was felt that these generalizations may have masked more subtle variations in environmental utilization which might be associated with differences in cultural activity.

In order to verify this, it was assumed that the analysis of the articulation of the environmental and lithic components might reveal the selection of certain variables from each as critical for the performance of specific activities, resulting in particular constellations of variables exhibiting regularity. Analysis was started by comparing the implement frequencies among the Folsom sites, derived from Table 3. These data were modified by separating the category "projectile points" into two sub-classes; broken bases, and broken points (termed "point fragments"), and separating those transverse scrapers exhibiting hard distal wear from those with soft distal wear. This

resulted in a total of 13 categories of implement types, and the frequency of occurrence indices were then computed for these categories
for each of the 15 Folsom sites. Since each of the sites represented
a particular constellation of environmental variables, it was felt the
comparison of implement frequencies which were adjusted to maximize
the functional interpretation would be the best approach to the initial
analysis of the articulation of the environmental and lithic components.

Initial comparison revealed that three sites (9CM3, 120A3,
13GX5) comprised almost half of the total numbers of Folsom artifacts,
thus dominating the Folsom sample. These were set aside for further
analysis at a later time, and attention was directed to the remaining
12 sites. In order to facilitate comparison of the implement frequencies of the latter, a graph was plotted of the cumulative percentages
of the 13 categories of artifacts for the 12 sites. The original graph
cannot be presented here since numerous colors were used to separate
the sites, but it did afford a relatively fast method of initially analyzing
the variations in tool assemblages. [4]

Interpretation of the original graph suggested that the 12 sites
were grouped roughly into two major categories based primarily on
differences in the number of preforms, scraper wear patterns, and

---

[4]The use of the cumulative graph in archeological analysis was
initiated by Bordes (1952), and is discussed in Jelinek (1962) and
Irwin (1968).

other implement frequencies, particularly scrapers and channel flakes. The first category, based on a large number of preforms, a relative lack of soft scraper wear, and a large number of channel flakes, included seven Folsom sites. These were site numbers 13FRl, 13LC8, 13LH9, 13LI4, 13LNl, 13XP3, and 18AG7. Five sites made up the other category which included among other differences, fewer preforms, higher percentages of soft wear, and fewer channel flakes. These included site numbers 2GD2, 13BA8, 13ES8, 13LI7, and 19JM9.

The seven sites comprising the first category were combined, their total implement frequencies computed, and these were then plotted on a cumulative graph. The same was done for the 5 sites in the second category, and the graph is shown in Figure 21. The graph of the three most productive sites is included for comparative purposes. The distinctions between these categories of sites are readily apparent.

Given the variations resulting from the initial analysis, the articulation of environmental and lithic components was investigated more closely for each category in order to determine possible taxonomic structures. The three most productive sites, due to the large numbers of artifacts present and the variety of implements included, suggested a more intensive occupation relative to the other sites and were therefore labeled "base camps." All three of these are situated near and to the northeast of playas, although all utilized streams as the nearest source of water. All were located in relation to major hunting areas, rather than minor ones.

200

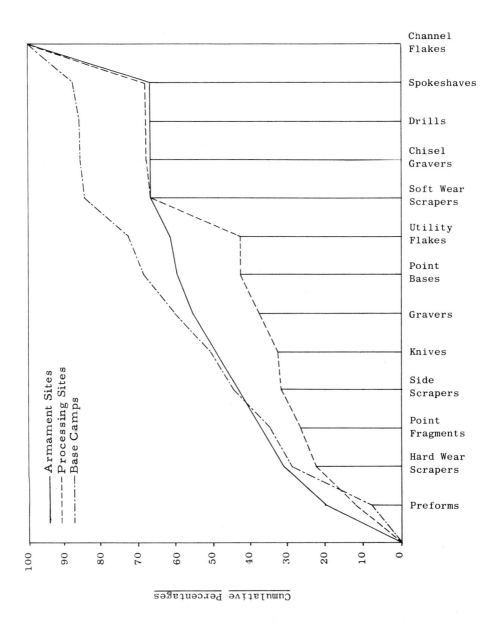

Figure 21. Cumulative Graph of Folsom Settlement Types.

The term base camp is employed cautiously here, and no direct association between the base camps and the other sites should be implied by the term itself. This particular point will be investigated later on. Evidently, the key variables in the selection of such camps by the Folsom people were 1) location relative to a major hunting area, 2) the presence of running water (for drinking?), and 3) the presence of a playa in the vicinity of the site. As shown in Figure 5a, these three base camps control the northern ends of the three main hunting areas west of the Rio Grande. No Folsom base camp has been found in relation to the major hunting area east of the river.

Regarding the other two categories of sites, it was noticed that the seven grouped in the first category were generally located near an overview. All but two of these sites were closer than average to an overview, and four were situated on the overview itself. One can assume, therefore, that the proximity of an overview was a key varia-ble in the selection of the location of these sites. The tool assemblages accompanying these sites, as indicated by Table 9, can be interpreted as revealing a primary concern with the preparation of weapons, particularly the final production of projectile points. In terms of Folsom lithic technology, this process involves the fluting and snapping of the preform, and the final shaping of the point. Thus one would expect channel flakes and snapped tips as debitage here, and this is indicated by the site totals. Also notable in these sites is the lack of

Table 9: Implement Frequencies of Folsom Settlement Types

Implement type	Armament sites[a]		Processing sites[b]		Base camps[c]	
	N	%	N	%	N	%
1. Preforms	54	(.21)	28	(.13)	46	(.08)
2. Point fragments	15	(.06)	9	(.04)	27	(.05)
3. Point bases	11	(.04)	11	(.05)	44	(.08)
4. Hard wear scrapers	27	(.11)	22	(.10)	125	(.22)
5. Soft wear scrapers	16	(.05)	51	(.24)	67	(.12)
6. Side scrapers	15	(.06)	10	(.05)	55	(.10)
7. Knives	14	(.06)	3	(.01)	31	(.06)
8. Channel flakes	83	(.33)	68	(.32)	66	(.12)
9. Gravers	14	(.06)	11	(.05	54	(.10)
10. Chisel gravers	0	(.00)	2	(.01)	6	(.01)
11. Drills	0	(.00)	0	(.00)	2	(.00)
12. Spokeshaves	0	(.00)	0	(.00)	10	(.02)
13. Utility flakes	4	(.02)	1	(.00)	20	(.04)
Totals	253	(1.00)	216	(1.00)	553	(1.00)

[a]Includes sites 13FR1, 13LC8, 13LH9, 13LI4, 13LN1, 13XP3, 18AG7.

[b]Includes sites 2GD2, 13BA8, 13ES8, 13LI7, 19JM9.

[c]Includes sites 9CM3, 12OA3, 13GX5.

soft wear on the transverse scrapers, and the lack of point bases. The former indicates primary scraper function in working hard materials, and the latter suggests that points were not generally being rehafted at these sites. Viewing the articulation of the environmental and lithic components for these sites, and taking into consideration the key variables of overview and point preparation, I have termed them "armament" or staging sites, with the implication that here activities centered around equipping implements in anticipation of a hunt. The overview itself would have served as a vantage point for the observation of game movements.

Regarding the five sites comprising the second category, it is somewhat more difficult to generalize about the environmental components although it appears that proximity to water is a key variable. The mean horizontal distance to water for these sites is 65 yards, and two of the sites are situated at the edge of playas. The mean horizontal distance to water for the preparatory sites is 161 yards. Furthermore, the overview situation is not critical here. All but one of the sites is further than the average distance away from the nearest overview, and three are out of view completely from the hunting area. Perhaps the single most critical variable for this category with reference to the lithic implements is the high percentage of soft wear on the transverse scrapers (Table 9), as well as the high frequency of these scrapers themselves. Thirty-four percent of the total tool assemblage consists of scrapers and of these roughly 75% exhibit soft wear. This factor becomes even more relevant when viewed in relation to the position of the transverse scraper in the Folsom assemblage as a whole. The Folsom complex exhibits the lowest frequency of these implements of all the PaleoIndian cultures in the survey, and a total of 58% of the Folsom scrapers indicated hard wear. The rather low incidence of preforms and the relatively high percentage of bases would indicate weapon renewal rather than prehunt preparation. The presence of fewer channel flakes substantiates the de-emphasis of preform production.

Based on this evidence, the sites grouped in the second category have been termed "processing" sites, in which activities centered around weapon renewal and hide-working, presumably in the aftermath of a successful hunt. Here the key environmental variables were proximity to water, probably for hide-soaking, and a general lack of concern with an overview. As was suggested earlier, there is a possibility that the Folsom hunters were using the playas themselves as game traps. If so, some of these sites could be post-kill secondary butchering stations, though there is no direct evidence of butchering activities.

In order to verify further these two functional categories of Folsom settlement types, the chi-square test of association was applied to the variables of hard and soft scraper wear, and the mean distances

to the overview and to the nearest source of water. The results of
these tests, both of which are significant at less than the .01 level,
are presented in Table 10. This indicates a definite association
armament and processing sites would be related to activities of a
more limited nature.

The formulation of these functional taxonomic categories comprising Folsom settlement technology is offered here only as an initial step
toward eventual understanding of Folsom and other PaleoIndian settlement patterns. It is, however, based on an analysis of the lithic
technology and environmental components which comprise the structure of this cultural subsystem. I feel that the taxons suggested here
are valid, although they may be mislabeled. Wilmsen (1967:151) has
suggested the use of "multiple activity locations" and "limited activity
locations" to characterize PaleoIndian sites. On this basis, my category "base camp" would be a multiple activity location, while the
preparatory and maintenance sites would be related to activities of a
more limited nature.

Though it may be somewhat far-fetched to suggest at this time,
I would think that there may possibly be certain socio-cultural implications in the functional taxons formulated by the foregoing study.
There is some evidence to indicate, for instance, that the selection of
the environmental components for the armament sites centered
around male-associated activities (weapon production), while in the

Table 10: Test of Association between Folsom Scraper Wear and Selected Environmental Components.[a]

A. Scraper Wear vs. Distance to Overview:

	More than average to overview		Less than average to overview		
	O	(E)	O	(E)	Totals
Hard wear scrapers	25	(33.8)	25	(16.1)	50
Soft wear scrapers	55	(46.1)	13	(21.8)	68
Totals	80		38		118

$\chi^2 = 12.476$ d.f. = 1   p. < .01

B. Scraper Wear vs. Distance to Nearest Water

	More than average to water		Less than average to water		
	O	(E)	O	(E)	Totals
Hard wear scrapers	33	(25.9)	18	(25.1)	51
Soft wear scrapers	27	(34.1)	40	(32.9)	67
Totals	60		58		118

$\chi^2 = 6.964$ d.f. = 1   p. < .01

[a]O = observed value.   (E) = expected value (in parentheses).

case of the processing sites, selection reveals a focus on female-associated activities (hide and food processing). This is not to imply that male-female associated activities were mutually exclusive in terms of site location. Rather, the primary foci of Folsom settlement technology may include emphases along these lines. To verify this suggestion, one would have to assume first that the armament and processing (limited activity) sites were associated with the base camps. In other words, groups of males and groups of females from the same base camp would be working in different environmental situations. As noted earlier, this is an assumption which cannot be made on the basis of the data available from the survey, but I would advance this as an essential hypothesis to test through actual excavation of sites in this region in the future.

One experiment was undertaken to initially test this hypothesis, but unfortunately the nature of the survey data precluded a completely thorough test. The experiment involved an attempt to match channel flakes and projectile points from different sites. To carry out this task completely would require that all the survey data be available in a given place at a given time, and such circumstances could not be attained in the present study. However, I was able to compare a sample of 41 Folsom points and 119 channel flakes from a total of 18 Folsom sites and localities. Preliminary analysis revealed the probable matching of five point-channel flake sets. Two of these indicated the possible association of base camp 13GX5 with armament site 13LI4, and processing site 13LI7. It should be noted that neither of these can be considered definite associations, since comparison was made on the basis of material type, rather than actual replacement of the channel flake on the point. The latter method, which would be the ideal manner in which to test the hypothesis, was precluded in this case due to the lack of the proper point and flake fragments. I would suggest strongly that future research in the area include tests of this sort, however, since it offers a good deal of potential in the interpretation of band structure, site utilization, and activity loci.

To summarize briefly, Folsom settlement technology is seen as a cultural subsystem comprising a number of essential environmental and cultural variables in which patterning is manifest in different arrays of environmental and lithic implement components. To comprehend the particular constellations of components, one must understand the lithic technology involved in the artifacts represented. Folsom lithic technology is seen to involve the very efficient utilization of raw material, focusing around the production of the bifacial Folsom preform. With few exceptions, most Folsom utility tools were multipurpose, and flakes at hand were modified to serve a variety of needs. Folsom people were more particular about the selection of environmental variables, however, and playa localities downwind (northeast) of major hunting areas were actively sought for campsite locations. Generally, playa areas surrounded by low ridges were preferred.

Within these general requisites, particular constellations of features were chosen for more specific activities. The processing of the preform, which is considered the element of primary technological focus, took place most frequently in those locations offering a good view of the surrounding terrain, particularly the hunting area. Proximity to water was not a key variable for these sites, which have been termed "armament" or "staging" areas. It was suggested that these sites focused around male-associated activities, perhaps in advance of a hunt.

Proximity to water was a key attribute of another group of sites, termed "processing" sites. Here multipurpose tools were employed in more specific functions such as hide-working, and there is evidence of limited weapon renewal in the form of point bases. However, the lower number of preforms, and higher incidence of transverse scrapers indicates that implement production was focused on non-weaponry artifacts. It was suggested that these processing sites were possibly post-hunt in nature, and that the selection of key environmental variables focused on female-associated activities.

Finally, the base camps were evidently multiple-activity locations of more intensive occupation. As noted, the three Folsom base camps are very strategically located with reference to major hunting areas, potential trap situations, and overviews. However the key variable common to all three seems to be the proximity of a source of fresh water in the form of a stream. This strongly suggests selection of a location with relatively more permanency in mind. Whether this means extended occupation by a single group, or multiple occupations by a number of groups remains one of the problems to be solved through continued research. Initial interpretation of the excavations at the Rio Rancho site, one of the base camps, suggested occupation by three distinct bands (Dawson and Judge 1969:159). In terms of total artifact composition, site 12OA3 more closely approximates Rio Rancho (9CM3) than does the other base camp, 13GX5. A cumulative graph (Figure 22) confirms the distinction of 13GX5. Its location is perhaps the most ideal in the total survey region from the standpoint of those variables essential to Folsom site selection, and I would suggest that the distinctiveness of this site is a function of extended temporal occupation by a number of Folsom bands. Unfortunately, this probably cannot be verified through excavation, since the site is almost completely deflated at the present time.

The Belen Occupation

A total of 9 sites and 4 localities attributed to the Belen complex were recorded in the survey. Of these, only the sites offered sufficient data for more intensive analysis. In all, 247 Belen artifacts were analyzed, and the interpretation of this analysis follows.

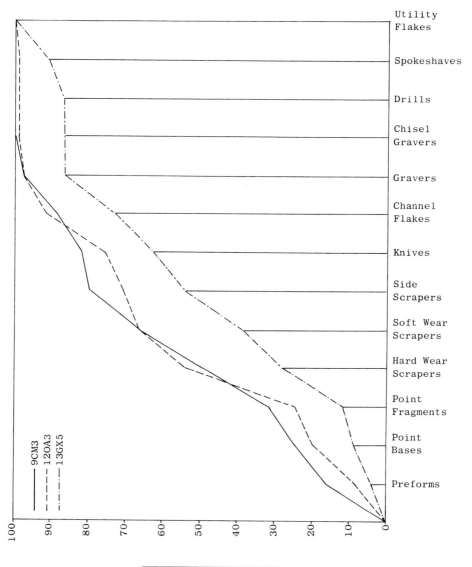

Figure 22. Cumulative Artifact Frequencies for Folsom Base Camps.

A.   Lithic Components:

   1.   Projectile Points and Preforms:

A total of 29 broken or complete Belen projectile points and nine preforms were found in the Belen sites under study.   These implements comprise 11.8% and 3.5% of the total number of artifacts in the nine site assemblages.   The 29 points, plus two more derived from the Belen localities, were submitted to the basic statistical analyses, the results of which are shown in Table 11.   The continuous attributes in the table are arranged in order of increasing values of the coefficient of variation.

In terms of the material component, chert dominates the Belen selection for projectile points, comprising almost half of the total number.   Chalcedony and quartzite follow, with jasper and flint included in the miscellaneous category.   The Belen preference for chert points may be an important consideration in the later analysis of transverse scrapers.

Regarding the production component, we unfortunately do not have the same amount of evidence for the production of Belen points that we have for Folsom, and therefore the techniques of manufacture are not as well understood.   Offsetting this somewhat is the assumption that production techniques were much less complex for other Paleo-Indian cultures than they were for Folsom.   Not much can be learned from an examination of the few Belen preforms available.   In fact, it

Table 11: Analysis of Belen Projectile Points[a]

A. Continuous Variables (measured in millimeters):

Attribute	Mean	Standard Deviation	Coefficient of Variation	Maximum	Minimum	Range
1. Maximum Width	22.75	2.198	9.66	27.1	19.5	7.6
2. Hafting Width	21.59	2.357	10.91	26.9	18.1	8.8
3. Basal Width	20.41	2.388	11.70	25.0	17.0	8.0
4. Hafting Thickness	4.45	.669	15.02	6.7	3.3	3.4
5. Maximum Thickness	5.19	.835	16.07	7.0	3.4	3.6
6. Concavity Depth	1.60	1.071	66.93	4.0	0.0	4.0

7. Hafting index = .206

B. Discrete Variables (percentage occurrence):

	Chert	Chalcedony	Quartzite	Miscellaneous
1. Material type	.48	.24	.16	.12

	Lateral	Concavity	Both	Absent
2. Basal grinding	.40	.00	.57	.03

	Present	Absent
3. Evidence of original facets	.16	.84

	Plano-convex	Bi-convex
4. Cross section	.55	.45

[a]N = 31

was even difficult to determine whether all the Belen preforms came from original flake blanks, or from core blanks. Sixteen percent of the finished points exhibited evidence of the original flake facet, so it can be assumed that at least that many were derived from flake blanks. In addition, 55% of the finished points exhibit a plano-convex cross-section, indicating a high probability of a flake blank as a source for at least half of the Belen preforms. However Ele Baker, who has studied the points thoroughly and has defined the type, has suggested that the original blanks may have been cores, and that they were purposely modified into a plano-convex cross-section through the use of strong laterally-directed soft-hammer percussion (Baker 1968). Perhaps ultimately, both flake and core blanks will be revealed in the Belen collections as further research in the form of excavation augments the existing data. Regardless of how derived, there is good evidence of a conscious attempt at achieving a plano-convex cross-section, if not at the middle of the point, at least at the base. Many of the bases reveal this cross-section as the result of purposeful thinning which was frequently directed vertically on one side and laterally on the other.

After achieving the final shaping of the point in the process of manufacture, the last step was basal grinding. A total of 97% of the points were basally ground, and 57% of them revealed grinding on both the lateral edges and in the basal concavity.

Morphologically, the Belen points resemble the Milnesand variety (Warnica and Williamson 1968), as noted previously. Most of the bases are concave, some as deep as 4 millimeters, although there is considerable variation in this feature and some of the Belen points are straight-based. Of the concave-based points, the point of maximum depth is frequently off-center, resulting in a barb-like appearance to the point base. These basal concavities are in fact a function of thinning the base by vertically-directed flakes, but the off-center concavity defies functional explanation at present, and may eventually prove to be stylistic.

As shown in Table 11, the coefficient of variation indicates the maximum width of the point to be the most critical variable, with hafting width and basal width following closely. Actually the attribute of maximum width may in this case be erroneous, in that 26 of the sample specimens were broken bases and only 5 were complete points. Thus the measurement of the "maximum" width was actually the width at the break in most cases, and it is felt that the hafting width is a much more reliable guide to the tolerances required in the manufacture of the points. As in the case of the Folsom points, here the width factors are more critical than those of thickness, and both are more important than the depth of the basal concavity. The hafting index is .206, quite similar to that of the Clovis points. In fact, the arrangement of the key continuous attributes here closely parallels that of Clovis.

Functionally the Belen points are projectile points by definition, but presumably could have served as knives in terms of secondary function. There was little evidence of knife wear on the points, but then the full complement could not be examined since mostly bases were present. Minute flaking along the lower lateral edges has been interpreted by Baker (1968) not as pressure retouch, but as spalling due to the lateral grinding. Grinding continued quite far up the lateral edges, but this length is a result of the use of the abrading implement in a longitudinal direction. These longitudinal abrasions can be seen microscopically on some specimens.

There is no direct evidence for hafting, but the use of a socket type haft may be tentatively inferred. Ele Baker (personal communication) has noted that the marrow cavity of the rib of a large animal exhibits a plano-convex cross-section and has suggested the use of such an item as a foreshaft. This would explain the conscious attempt at achieving this cross-section on the point bases.

Reviewing the articulation of the components discussed, it can be seen that the key variables involved in the subsystem trajectory of a Belen point were the attainment of a desired width, the grinding of the basal portion, and the achievement of a plano-convex cross-section at the base. This almost certainly indicates a concern with the necessity to shape the point base to a predetermined size, and it is suggested that this requisite is a function of the utilization of a bone foreshaft.

I would suggest that given the importance of the foreshaft, as inferred from this analysis and strongly supported by the statistical derivation of the key attribute of width, we should not consider the Belen point itself as a single functional type, but rather as part of a point-foreshaft combination of which the foreshaft was the primary component which regulated the final morphology of the projectile point.

2. Transverse Scrapers:

A total of 139 transverse scrapers were associated with the nine Belen sites, comprising 56.4% of the total tool assemblage. This was the highest scraper percentage of all four groups. A sample of 52 of these scrapers was selected for a more intensive analysis of the type performed on the Folsom scrapers. A summary of the initial statistical tests is presented in Table 8 for 17 selected variables. As in the case of Folsom, these variables were selected through the interpretation of a factor analysis which will be discussed in the next chapter. The same initial categories were used as before, that is, separation on the basis of the presence or absence of lateral modification. As shown in Table 7, the two highest frequency types in the case of Belen were the transverse unmodified (TU), and the transverse right laterally modified (TR). This was the only instance in the survey in which a single-edge modified scraper occurred more frequently than the double modified (TB) types.

In terms of the material component, chert, flint, chalcedony,
and jasper were popular materials for Belen scraper production, with
almost half (48%) of the specimens made of chert. It should be recalled
that the projectile point analysis revealed this same frequency of chert
as the preferred material. The TU scrapers follow this preference
closely, but it will be noted that the TR scrapers differ in that flint
was preferred over the chert. This suggests that in terms of the
material component, projectile points and TU scrapers may have been
made from the same cores, while the TR scrapers were produced
from different cores.

In terms of the production and morphological components, the
significant variables of the two types can be summarized from Table 8
as follows. The TU scraper is longer, thicker, and slightly more
narrow than the TR type. The latter is generally smaller and exhibits
most distinctiveness in being highly divergent (39.61°). The difference
in thickness between the two types is significant because one would
expect the thicker TU type to be the wider implement, given the same
core treatment for both types of scrapers. Here, however, the
thicker TU type is more narrow, thus we can look for evidence of
variation in core treatment between the types. There is no evidence
of variation in the number of dorsal facets (variable 9), and the high
incidence of double facets would initially point to similar core treatment. However, variables 6 and 10 do yield evidence of different core

treatment. The facet angles (variable 6) are extremely different between the two types. TU scrapers average 116° and TR scrapers average 138°. In addition, variable 10 (orientation) shows that the TR scrapers tended to be struck away from the line of the dorsal ridge, while the TU scrapers were struck parallel to it. This indicates a very distinct core treatment for the removal of TR scraper blanks, in which a shallow-angled core was prepared and the flake blanks struck in a manner which would yield a highly divergent, relatively thin flake, quite distinct from the TU type. In regard to the latter, it should be noted that 52% of the TU scrapers exhibited cortex on the dorsal surface, a very high incidence of this feature on PaleoIndian scrapers.

Also significant between the two types is the fact that while the TR types have the highest percentage (85%) of spurred specimens, the TU scrapers have a high frequency of corner undercut. This means that in the case of the TU scrapers, a shallow notch was chipped into the ventral side of the scraper just behind one of the corners along the lateral edge. This provides a very effective slashing tip or hook when the scraper is held ventral side up.

In regard to scraper function, there seems to be a distinction in use between the two types. The TR type was almost certainly intended to be a hard-wear scraper, since 77% of the distal edges revealed this type of wear. Further investigation showed a high percentage of both distal gouging and heavy undercut of the distal edge. The TU type, on the other hand, revealed 60% hard wear and 40% soft, a slightly higher than average amount of soft wear for the Belen scrapers. Thus it can be concluded that the TU type was a multipurpose scraper selected for use on soft materials when the occasion demanded. Lateral wear on both types is about normal, the unmodified TU type revealing the highest incidences of bifacial gouging as a result of knife usage of the lateral edges. The TR scraper does exhibit a high degree of gouging along the modified right lateral edge, which was evidently used for hard wear also.

In reviewing the articulation of the material, production, morphological, and functional components, there is evidence of functional separation of the two types, and in the case of the TR type there is evidence of specific production techniques leading to specialized usage. I would suggest that the TU types, which exhibit a high incidence of cortex, were modified from flake blanks derived from the initial processing of a cobble core. The similarity in material selection for points and the TU scrapers suggests that the scraper blanks and the point blanks were struck from the same cores, with a high percentage of decortication flakes being employed for TU scraper production. TU scrapers were retouched distally and used for scraping various surfaces, but were generally selected for soft wear when the occasion demanded. Corners were frequently undercut, permitting the very effective use of this laterally unmodified scraper as a slashing knife. Its low divergence angle permitted hafting when necessary for use in hide-softening.

The TR scraper, on the other hand, indicates selection toward specialized usage from the initial stages of production. The material sought was generally flint, and the production techniques indicate core treatment specifically for the removal of a thin, but highly divergent flake which was then modified along the right lateral edge and distal edge. The TR scraper was frequently spurred but not undercut, and was definitely a hard-wear scraper. I would suggest its use in hand-held wood and bone shaping, with the spur serving burin (engraving) functions. [5]

Finally, mention should be made of the other two scraper types in the Belen assemblage. The TL type comprised 8% of the Belen scrapers, and no specialized functions could be ascertained. The bilaterally modified (TB) scrapers made up 19% of the assemblage, and thus were important to it. These were quite similar to the TU types in production techniques, with the exception that flakes with a multi-faceted dorsal surface were chosen as scraper blanks. Evidence indicated that these were also by-products of core preparation for preform manufacture, and functionally were quite similar to the TU types. Seventy percent of the TB scrapers were made of chert.

---

[5]It is tempting at this point to speculate that the TR and TU scrapers are male and female associated implements respectively. This will have to remain speculation since I know of no way to verify it in the absence of more evidence of intrasite contextual variation between the two types.

3. Other Artifacts:

As in the case of Folsom, the incidence of other implements in the Belen assemblage was not high enough to permit an intensive analysis of the subsystem components. The frequency of occurrence indices presented in Table 2 will be reviewed briefly for comparative purposes. Significant is the high incidence (12.6%) of side scrapers in the Belen assemblage, second only to Clovis in this respect. Of the Belen side scrapers, 30% were tabular by my classification, and most were used on hard surfaces as indicated by the 75% frequency of hard wear. This high frequency of side scrapers is opposed in the Belen assemblage by a presently inexplicable low frequency of knives (3.2%).

With the exception of spokeshaves and drills, the remainder of the Belen implements do not exhibit significant variation from the numbers expected in the survey assemblages. There is a slightly higher incidence of spokeshaves (2.8%) for Belen, and drills are notable by their absence. In that no Belen drills were found in the survey sites, it is possible that chisel gravers served drill functions.

4. Component Articulation:

The lithic technology of the Belen culture emerges as quite distinct from that of Folsom, though the two are certainly similar within the generalized range of variation of all PaleoIndian assemblages. In fact, the differences between Belen and Folsom may be more a function of the distinctiveness of the Folsom complex itself. Clarification of this point will have to await further analysis of the remaining cultural assemblages.

In the case of Belen, the evidence does not point to the preform as an element of primary technological focus. As noted, the preforms may well have been produced from core blanks some of the time. There was a conscious attempt to derive TU scrapers blanks from the initial treatment of cobble cores, and probably TB scraper blanks from further treatment of these cores. In addition, there was specialized selection of both material and production techniques for the derivation of TR scraper blanks, which were then modified into specific-function scrapers. Thus the production of scrapers would seem to have been as important to the Belen people as the production of point preform blanks, suggesting that both points and scrapers were focal elements of technological emphasis.

It was stated that the Folsom complex stressed the highly efficient utilization of raw materials. It cannot be said that Belen technicians were any more wasteful, but I think the evidence strongly supports different methods of achieving maximum efficiency. For Folsom, the maximum utilization was attained through the production of multipurpose tools, especially the preform. The Belen people achieved efficient material utilization through the effective treatment of the cobble cores. I would suggest that this indicates a different type of core material for the two cultures, perhaps even different sources. This cannot be verified on the basis of the survey data, but I feel it should be considered an important problem requiring solution by actual excavation in the future. A detailed study of the debitage, emphasizing flake removal techniques and frequency of occurrence of cortex on flake surfaces, could prove highly instructive in ascertaining the nature of the core material utilized by the Belen culture. We may speculate that the cobbles utilized were considerably smaller than those used for Folsom preform derivation, perhaps not by choice but of necessity.

B. Environmental Components:

The data on the environmental components of the nine Belen sites are presented in Table 4, with an analytical summary in Table 5. These components will be examined in more detail in the following section.

1. Continuous Variables:

Though frequently found near playas, the Belen site locations do not reveal the same concern with the playa factor in the location of sites as did Folsom. Some 67% of the Belen sites utilized playa water as the closest source, while 22% were near streams and one site was situated on a ridge near a spring. The mean horizontal distance to the nearest water was 160 yards, while the average vertical distance was 30 feet. Direction to water was highly variable.

On the other hand, Belen sites reveal much more concern with the overview factor than did Folsom. Of the Belen sites, 56% were located at the overview itself, the highest percentage in the survey sample. Furthermore, the mean distance to the overview was the lowest in the survey sample (53 yards). Direction to the overview was in general southerly.

The data on the hunting area component reflect less concern with orientation toward the major hunting areas, and an increased utilization of the minor ones. Some 55% of the sites were located with reference to the latter. The average distance (1395 yards) to hunting areas was somewhat further than that for Folsom, yet the directions indicate a preference for a more lateral orientation with respect to these areas. The Folsom sites, it will be recalled, were generally located at the northern ends.

Regarding the potential trap situations, these are generally absent from Belen site locations, unless the playas themselves can be considered trap areas. Only one Belen site was located in the vicinity of a trap area, which in that case was a lava outcrop.

2. Discrete Variables:

There was no variation regarding landform among the Belen sites. All were situated on flat ridge tops or lower ridge shelves. None were found on playa or ridge slopes, as in the case of Folsom. Exposure was either direct, or in the case of shelf sites, southerly. All three soil types were represented in the sample, though the most predominant (45%) was the red sandy clay common to the late Pleistocene horizon. Six of the nine sites were situated in the vicinity of a playa, and in each of these instances the playa was the nearest source of water.

3. Component Articulation:

The key variables in the selection of Belen sites, as reflected by the survey data, were those associated with the presence of an over-view in the site vicinity. Of the nine Belen sites, five are located on the topographical overview, while two more are within fifty yards of the overview. The maximum distance to an overview is 250 yards, and as noted, the mean distance (53 yards) is the lowest in the survey sample.

The second most critical variable would seem to be orientation with respect to a hunting area, either major or minor. Here locations oriented more laterally than distally were sought by the Belen people. It should be noted that increased utilization of the minor hunting areas also provided increased topographic relief, in that the minor areas are located in situations of relatively high relief. Thus the factor of overview preference could be more easily satisfied by increased utili-zation of the minor areas.

Water availability was, of course, an essential variable, but the distance and nature of the source were not as critical as in the case of Folsom. Thus it is apparent that in selecting areas for campsites, the Belen people sought first a level ridge top or shelf commanding a view of a hunting area, frequently along its lateral edge. Though generally downwind of the hunting area, this direction was not a key factor in site selection. Water was evidently a secondary consideration. In other words, if the primary requisites could be satisfied, the nature of the nearest source of water made little difference. The availability of a potential trap area in the site vicinity was evidently an inessential variable in Belen settlement patterns.

C. Belen Settlement Technology:

In order to analyze the articulation of the Belen lithic and environmental components, the implement frequencies of each site were compared by the cumulative graph technique, as was done in the case of the Folsom assemblages. In this case, however, there were only ten implement categories, as opposed to 13 for Folsom. Due to the vary low frequency of point fragments found in the Belen sites, this and the category of point bases were combined into a single element "projectile points." Since no drills were found in the Belen assemblages, both this category and that of channel flakes (peculiar to Folsom) were omitted.

Preliminary examination of the cumulative graph revealed that patterning of the implement frequencies was not as readily apparent as in the case of Folsom. Nevertheless, two basic patterns were initially suggested, based primarily on the variation in transverse

scraper wear. An examination of the environmental components associated with these patterns indicated a possible correlation between sites
yielding soft scraper wear and location near to water, as was the case
with Folsom. To verify this, the association of scraper wear with
vertical distance to water was tested by the chi-square method, and
the results were found to be significant, as shown in Table 12. The
test was also carried out with respect to the distance to the overview
and the results were again significant (Table 12). Thus the data indicated a dual division; sites exhibiting predominant hard wear and
situated near or at overviews, and sites with predominant soft wear
located relatively closer to sources of water.

Two sites fit this dichotomy less well than the others, due primarily to less variation in the scraper wear patterns, a higher incidence of points and preforms, and higher total numbers of artifacts.
These two sites (13FJ8 and 19JL5) were singled out as probable base
camps. Together, they yielded 35.7% of the total number of implements
in the Belen site assemblages.

Of the remaining seven Belen sites, four clustered well in one
category, and three in the other. The first category comprised sites
9SJ5, 12WG5, 13BX9, and 14CS5. Three of these were located at
overviews themselves, and the fourth (12WG5) was within 50 yards of
an overview. Using the vertical distance to water as an index, all are

Table 12: Test of Association between Belen Scraper Wear and
Selected Environmental Components[a]

A. Scraper Wear vs. Distance to Overview:

| | More than average to overview | | Less than average to overview | | |
	O	(E)	O	(E)	Totals
Hard wear scrapers	7	(13.8)	52	(45.1)	59
Soft wear scrapers	13	(6.1)	13	(19.8)	26
Totals	20		65		85

$\chi^2 = 14.538$ d.f. = 1   p. < .01

B. Scraper Wear vs. Distance to Nearest Water:

| | More than average to water | | Less than average to water | | |
	O	(E)	O	(E)	Totals
Hard wear scrapers	46	(36.0)	13	(22.9)	59
Soft wear scrapers	6	(15.9)	20	(10.0)	26
Totals	52		33		85

$\chi^2 = 23.219$ d.f. = 1   p. < .01

[a] O = observed value   (E) = expected value (in parentheses)

further than average away from the nearest source of water.[6] At only

one of the four sites was there a playa in the vicinity, and this was

300 yards away (9SJ5).

The second category comprised three sites (9VD9, 13BR3, and

13LG9) which were all located in the vicinity of playas serving as the

nearest source of water. None were located at an overview, and only

one was closer than average to an overview.

A cumulative graph representing the artifact frequencies at these

three categories of Belen sites is presented in Figure 23, and the

implement frequencies are given in Table 13. As noted, the three

categories have been given the same labels as those in the Folsom

settlement types. The Belen armament sites are very distinctive in

the high frequency of hard wear scrapers and the association with over-

views. The processing sites, though somewhat less distinctive,

nevertheless exhibit a higher ratio of soft wear scrapers, and a high

incidence of side scrapers. Preforms are totally absent and all of

these sites are near water. For these reasons, I feel that the tenta-

tive labeling of these sites as "armament" and "processing" (as

described in the discussion of Folsom sites) is justified until further

research either verifies or invalidates these taxons.

---

[6]The vertical scale is used here in that it is a more reliable index of the accessibility to water. For instance site 12WG5 is only 50
yards from water horizontally, but access to the source required
descending a very steep 60-foot escarpment to the San Jose river.

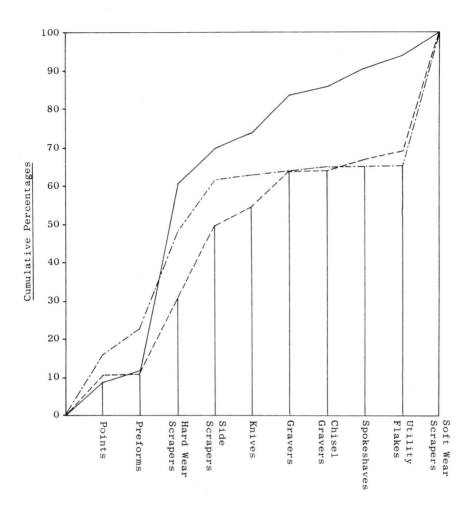

Key:

——————— Armament Sites
-------- Processing Sites
—·—·—·— Base Camps

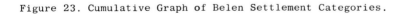

Figure 23. Cumulative Graph of Belen Settlement Categories.

Table 13: Implement Frequencies of Belen Settlement Types

Implement type	Armament sites[a]		Processing sites[b]		Base camps[c]	
	N	%	N	%	N	%
1. Projectile points	8	(.09)	7	(.11)	14	(.16)
2. Point preforms	3	(.03)	0	(.00)	6	(.07)
3. Hard wear scrapers	46	(.49)	13	(.20)	23	(.26)
4. Soft wear scrapers	6	(.06)	20	(.31)	31	(.35)
5. Side scrapers	8	(.09)	12	(.19)	11	(.13)
6. Knives	4	(.04)	3	(.05)	1	(.01)
7. Gravers	9	(.10)	6	(.09)	1	(.01)
8. Chisel gravers	2	(.02)	0	(.00)	1	(.01)
9. Spokeshaves	5	(.05)	2	(.03)	0	(.00)
10. Utility flakes	3	(.03)	1	(.02)	0	(.00)
Totals	94	(1.00)	64	(1.00)	88	(1.00)

[a] Includes sites 9SJ5, 12WG5, 13BX9, 14CS5.

[b] Includes sites 9VD9, 13BR3, 13LG9.

[c] Includes sites 13FJ8, 19JL5.

In the Belen armament sites, the overview was the critical environmental variable, and evidently operations associated with the preparation of weapons took place at these sites. The evidence of some preforms in association with point fragments indicates limited point production. However the high incidence of hard wear scrapers and relatively high number of spokeshaves also suggests the working of non-lithic implements at these sites, presumably those parts of the weaponry complex not produced from lithic material. It will be recalled that the Belen hard wear scrapers involved an emphasis on grinding wear (Table 8), such as results from the working of wood. I would suggest that the spokeshave-hard wear scraper combination at these sites indicates a primary focus on the working of wooden elements of weaponry, and that future excavation of this type of Belen site should attempt to verify this hypothesis. It should also be recalled that in addition to the production of points, scraper manufacture was an element of technological focus in the Belen case. If scraper discard is any indication of scraper renewal, one may assume that production of these implements was also one of the key activities at these sites.

In the processing sites, the soft wear scrapers predominate as well as a high percentage of side scrapers, which as noted previously were primarily hard wear implements. The critical environmental variable was the proximity to water. If we can assume the working of hides from soft scraper wear and the presence of water, then it would seem likely that these were post-kill sites utilized for hide processing and weapon renewal. The presence of bases indicates rehafting of points. I would suggest that these factors indicate not only the maintenance activities described, but also the specific working of bone into implements, as evidenced by the high incidence of side scrapers and the availability of bone in a post-kill situation. Again, verification of this will have to await excavation of this type of site.

Base camp functions were of the multiple activity type, as opposed to the relatively limited activities of the other settlement types. It should be pointed out, though, that there is not the wide variety of implements present here that there was in the Folsom base camps. This can be explained on the basis of either a limited sample, or that specialized tools such as gravers, chisel gravers, spokeshaves, etc., were utilized primarily in the limited activity sites rather than the base camps. Again, this is a problem which must await the acquisition of more data for ultimate solution. I feel the high incidence of bases and preforms at the base camps does indicate that the manufacture of both preforms and points took place more frequently at these sites than at the other two types. Finally, it should be noted that one of the base camps (19JL5) is located near the major hunting area east of the Rio Grande, indicating that the river was not a barrier to the Belen people.

The <u>Cody</u> <u>Occupation</u>

A total of five sites and four localities which could be attributed
to the Cody Complex were recorded by the survey. Only the sites
offered sufficient numbers of implements to permit further analysis
of the lithic material. Even here the sample is small, comprising
only 168 artifacts in all. These will be discussed in the following
section, followed by a general interpretation of the environmental variables associated with the Cody sites. There were not enough sites
represented to permit the derivation of meaningful statements on intracultural variations in site function.

A. Lithic Components:

1. Projectile Points:

Twenty-five projectile points were found by the survey. Of these,
23 were broken bases complete enough to permit further analysis. All
of these were of the "Eden" variety, one of the two primary types of
the Cody Complex. Data on the analysis of these points are presented
in Table 14.

Analysis of the material component reveals a wide variety of
material types selected for the production of Eden points. Chert,
obsidian, and chalcedony make up 78% of the total, while basalt,
pitchstone, and jasper comprise the remainder. Although 30% of the
points were made of chert, in general the Cody Complex lacks the
single material dominance evident in the other PaleoIndian types
surveyed.

Table 14. Analysis of Cody Complex Projectile Points[a]

A. Continuous Variables (measured in millimeters):

Attribute	Mean	Standard Deviation	Coefficient of Variation	Maximum	Minimum	Range
1. Basal Width	17.31	1.185	6.84	19.0	15.0	4.6
2. Hafting Width	17.73	1.302	7.34	19.7	15.1	4.6
3. Maximum Width	18.24	1.494	8.19	20.5	15.6	4.9
4. Maximum Thickness	5.72	.802	14.01	7.0	4.1	2.9
5. Hafting Thickness	5.48	.773	14.09	7.0	4.0	3.0
6. Hafting Length	12.34	2.027	16.42	15.5	7.6	7.9

7. Hafting index = .309

B. Discrete Variables (percentage of occurrence):

	Chert	Obsidian	Chalcedony	Miscellaneous
1. Material type	.30	.26	.22	.22

	Lateral	Concavity	Both	Absent
2. Basal grinding	.17	.00	.83	.00

	Concave	Straight	Convex	Unrecorded
3. Basal morphology	.48	.35	.09	.08

	Plano-convex	Bi-convex	Offset bi-convex
4. Cross section	.41	.45	.14

[a]N = 23

Regarding the production component, the question of the nature of the original blank used in producing Eden points remains an enigma. Of the points, 41% were plano-convex in cross-section, indicating that these at least, were probably produced from a flake blank, rather than a core blank. The points are thick (only Clovis points are thicker, and then by only a mean of .12 millimeters) and in relation to the reduced width this characteristic is even more pronounced. This is well demonstrated by the hafting index (.309), the largest in the survey sample.

In order to achieve the characteristic diamond-shaped cross-section, the Eden flintknappers must have started with a relatively large flake and worked it down bifacially to the finished product. Such a flake would have had to exhibit little or no curvature (trajectory). An alternative method would have been the use of a smaller but thicker prismatic blade as an initial blank. This could have been chipped ventrally until the bi-convex cross-section was obtained, then worked dorsally into the final form. However, there is nothing in the rest of the Cody assemblage which to my knowledge would indicate the extensive use of prismatic blades that one might expect from a well-developed blade technology. Thus I would suggest the use of a large flake blank as opposed to a prismatic blade in the production of Eden points. Core blanks could theoretically have been used, but it might have been difficult to control these to the extent that the generally fine Cody (specifically Eden) craftsmanship reveals.

Most of the bases were indented by means of pressure retouch, but in at least two of the sample points this indentation was a result of heavy lateral grinding alone. Wormington (1957:267) has reported some evidence of this also. Not all the points were straight-based, in fact 48% of the sample showed varying degrees of a basal concavity which on closer examination was found to result from vertical thinning of the base.

Morphologically, the continuous variables in Table 14 indicate that here also basal width required more critical tolerance on the part of the point manufacturers than did the categories of thickness. Furthermore, the coefficient of variation is quite low (6.84) and approaches that revealed by the Folsom data. Hafting length is the most variable of the continuous attributes, but here the coefficient of variation does not fall within the range of variation exhibited by the least critical attributes of the other PaleoIndian points studied.

Functionally, the Eden specimens are by definition projectile points, although it is only with some reluctance that one can attribute these exquisitely made implements a purely utilitarian function. Since only bases were recovered in the sample, it was not possible to determine if the points might also have served as knives. However, data from the Jurgens site in Colorado, a Cody Complex butchering site, does indicate the use of these points as knives, even to the extent of lateral modification through pressure retouch which at times altered the shape of the point (Ruthann Knudson, personal communication).

Regarding the related function of hafting, I would suggest again the use of a socketed haft, as evidenced by the close lateral tolerances required and the high (83%) incidence of lateral and basal grinding. Hafting evidently continued the length of the basal indentation since 68% of the bases were snapped at, or slightly below, the point of basal indentation, while the remainder were snapped slightly above this point. It should be noted also that on some of the obsidian specimens examined, vertical striations were evident on the dorsal and ventral basal surfaces, suggesting the close tolerances of this dimension when forcing the point into the haft.

Reviewing the articulation of these components, the Eden point emerges as the result of a fairly specialized system trajectory. Though no complete points were found in the survey, Eden points from elsewhere indicate that most are quite long, relative to width. This would explain the necessity for retaining point thickness, a factor required for strength. Assuming the validity of a socket-type haft of bone, the high hafting index (i.e., a thick, narrow base) required would have necessitated the use of a bone with a relatively large marrow cavity, quite different from those needed to haft Folsom and/or Belen points. I would suggest that this is the single most critical factor of point technology demanding explanation by further research through excavation of Cody Complex sites. An insight into this could be obtained by a careful analysis of those particular bones missing from kill sites, followed by an analysis of the potential hafting characteristics of these bones. For instance, Wendorf and Hester (1962:167) report that at the Olsen-Chubbock site, ribs and vertebrae (transverse processes?) were sometimes cut into segments and frequently ulnas were missing. I should think that a further examination of such data could yield valuable hypotheses regarding the derivation of potential foreshaft material from such parts of the animals killed.

2. Transverse Scrapers:

A total of 92 transverse scrapers were found on the Cody sites located in the survey, comprising 54.9% of the total Cody tool assemblage. Fifty of these scrapers were randomly selected for more intensive analysis, and the data on these is presented in Tables 7 and 8. As noted in Table 7, the unmodified (TU) types and the bilaterally modified (TB) types together comprise 72% of the total sample of Cody scrapers, thus these two types will be discussed in detail.

Regarding the materials selected for the production of scrapers, the TU types show a dominance of chalcedony (44%), while cherts were frequently used for the production of TB types (35%).

In terms of the production and morphological components, the TB scraper is generally the larger of the two types, and also the more highly divergent. Under these circumstances, one would expect a much higher core facet angle for the latter, which the data indicate to be the case. A difference in core treatment between the two types is indicated by the variation in dorsal facets, which indicates that the TU types are primarily double-faceted while the TB types are primarily multi-faceted. A difference is also reflected in the attribute of orientation, and most markedly in the high incidence of cortex found on the TU types. TU scrapers are rarely notched while TB types frequently are, and the same ratio applies to the presence of a single spur, and undercut corners.

Functionally, a separation between the two types is suggested. The TU scrapers exhibit predominant (69%) soft wear, with the emphasis on the heavy soft polish with striations, while the TB scraper reveals multi-purpose use of the distal end. It should be noted that soft wear predominates over hard for all Cody transverse scrapers, the only incidence of this ratio in the whole survey sample. Laterally, the expected knife usage of the unmodified TU scraper is confirmed by the data, and an unexplicably high incidence of right lateral gouging is evident on the TB types.

Reviewing the data in terms of component articulation, I think it can be determined that an analysis of material type, cortex, and dorsal facets indicates that the TU scrapers were not produced from the same cores as those being prepared for the derivation of projectile points. It is possible that the scrapers of the TB type were, though this cannot be determined at the moment. In general, the TU types were produced from primary decortication flakes. Their morphology would have permitted hafting without the need to notch the lateral edges, and they were selected when the need for working hides arose. The TB scraper was more a utility scraper, used for both hard and soft work, but was preferred when heavy hard work was necessary. The high incidence of notching of this type may indicate it was hafted when used for heavy hard scraping.

Of the other scraper types, the TL was relatively infrequent and demonstrates no special usage. The TR type comprised 18% of the Cody scrapers, and was primarily a hand-held hard wear scraper, with some evidence of left lateral bifacial gouging, indicating use as a backed knife.

3. Other Artifacts:

As in the case of the other PaleoIndian cultures studied, the sample of other Cody artifacts was too small to permit intensive analysis of subsystem components. However the total range of other implements is present, and with the exception of preforms and chisel gravers, they exhibit relatively high frequencies. Typologically there does not seem to be much difference between the Cody utility implements and those of other PaleoIndian assemblages, with the exception noted previously that the tabular side scraper occurs only in the Folsom and Belen assemblages and is absent in Cody and Clovis.

Two variations in the Cody material are worthy of note. First, there is a noticeably higher number of drills in the Cody assemblage than in other PaleoIndian. As indicated by Wendorf and Hester (1962: Table 2) in their review of PaleoIndian tool assemblages, this phenomenon is not limited to the central Rio Grande area. I have suggested previously that Folsom and Belen drills were unifacial and possibly mislabeled as chisel gravers, but this still does not explain the relatively high incidence of bifacial drills in the Cody assemblage. The other anomaly in the Cody material is the relatively high percentage of knives (6.5%) which is the highest of all the survey sample. I would suggest that this could possibly be explained by reference to the relatively low incidence of laterally unmodified transverse scrapers (which can double as knives) in the Cody assemblages. A further discussion of these phenomena will be offered in the following chapter.

4. Component Articulation:

It is difficult to generalize about the lithic technology of the Cody complex, partially because of the relatively low yield of this material in the survey area, and partially because of the nature of the components themselves. It should be recalled that no implements of the Scottsbluff variety were encountered in the survey, and only one site yielded Cody Knives. Thus, whatever conclusions are drawn would apply primarily to the Eden variety of the Cody Complex.

It is not possible at this time to derive from the data any particular process or implement type which could be labeled the element of primary technological focus in the Cody assemblage. If anything, it may be that here we begin to see an increase in the specialization of tools, that is, an increasing utilization of specially designed implements for single-purpose functions. The lack of multipurpose function is seen in the scraper wear patterns, and in the rather high percentages of other types of implements and the occurrence of the bifacial drill. Also it should be recalled that the Cody Complex is the origin of the evidently highly specialized Cody Knife. Thus if there can be any conclusions drawn about the focal point of Cody lithic technology, I would suggest that it was in the production of a variety of tools to meet a variety of different needs. The low incidence of preforms may actually substantiate this, in that if they were not used for purposes other than the derivation of points, there would be less chance of breakage, and thus a lower number discarded.

Though the specialization of tools is only hinted at here, I would consider this a fruitful avenue of investigation for further research into the Cody Complex, either through actual excavation in the survey area, or independent testing of the survey data. The latter approach is undertaken in Chapter 7.

B. Environmental Component:

There are not enough Cody sites to permit the formulation of functional settlement taxons within the Cody Complex as manifested in the survey area. I will, however, attempt to summarize the data available (Table 8), and point out two variations which do appear.

With regard to the component of nearest water, the playa was not as important in Cody times as it was earlier. Most of the sites were located near streams. The horizontal distance to water averaged 444 yards, the furthest of the survey sample, and the vertical distance was 61 feet, again the largest in the survey sample.

The overview was physically separated from three of the Cody sites, and at the site location itself for the other two. The average distance was 80 yards, and the direction generally in the northeast quadrants. The average distance to the hunting area, 2550 yards, was another factor which distinguished Cody sites from the other Paleo-Indian sites surveyed. This average distance was the largest of the survey sample, even considering the fact that one of the sites (13DR4) was situated in the middle of a hunting area itself and the distance there was counted as zero. Directions to this component were all in the southwest quadrants. Trap areas were also present in all of the site situations, and most were of the arroyo type.

Regarding discrete variables, the landform was generally flat, and exposure generally direct. Most sites were visible from the hunting area, and soil type varied between sand and lava, and sandy clay. Only one of the sites was situated in the vicinity of a playa.

In general, then, the factors distinguishing Cody sites from the other PaleoIndian sites surveyed are 1) vertical height and horizontal distance to the nearest source of water, and the nature of this source itself; and 2) the horizontal distance to the hunting area.

C. Cody Settlement Technology:

In reviewing the articulation of the lithic and environmental components, only limited generalizations can be made. Of the five Cody sites, two stand out as distinct within the Cody "pattern." As shown in Table 3, site 45JP9 exhibits quite distinct frequencies of artifact types, the particular array involved being one somewhat reminiscent of the pre-kill staging or armament sites in the Belen and Folsom assemblages. The environmental components of 45JP9 are distinctive only with relation to the distance to the hunting area which is very far (3 miles), and the fact that it is the only Cody site with a sloping landform.

One other site, 13DR4, is unique to the survey sample in that it is located in the middle of a hunting area, and it is unique to the Cody sample from several standpoints. First, with reference to the surrounding terrain it is the lowest of the Cody sites and thus the furthest from an overview. The artifact assemblage at this site differs primarily in the lack of side scrapers, the higher incidence of spokeshaves, and the predominant hard wear exhibited by the transverse scrapers. In other words, were it not for the aberrant environmental variables, this site would be a candidate for an armament site. Due to the particular constellation of variables it does exhibit, however, it is better to assume that the Cody Complex yields a pattern distinct from other PaleoIndian in the survey area, one for which not enough data exists at present to permit accurate determination or even description.

To summarize the Cody pattern as well as it can be determined from the few sites which exhibit regularity in environmental and lithic components, we can say that it is definitely distinct from the other PaleoIndian sites investigated, and that this distinctness stems primarily from the Cody selection of locations distant from hunting areas and distant (both vertically and horizontally) from the nearest source of water. Cody sites are found in terrain which is in much more sharp relief than the other PaleoIndian sites in the survey. One further distinction is that the Cody sites also reveal the only instance where soft wear scrapers outnumber hard wear scrapers. Given the much higher average distance to water in these sites, this fact is also anomalous with respect to the other PaleoIndian sites.

The Clovis Occupation

Only one site (13JB5) definitely attributable to the Clovis culture was recorded in the survey, and this site yielded a total of 43 artifacts. Obviously this was not sufficient to permit intensive analysis of the lithic technology exhibited by Clovis within the survey region. In order to permit comparative analyses at the general PaleoIndian level, the Clovis sample was augmented by additional data from the Mockingbird site located south of the survey region. Thus, the lithic components as described below are not to be considered representative of the survey area itself, and are presented for comparative purposes only. Whenever statements are made about the Clovis occupation of the survey

248

region, they will be based on the survey material only. Following the
lithic analysis, a brief description will be given of the environmental
variables of the single Clovis site.

A.   Lithic Components:

1.   Projectile Points:

Data on 26 Clovis projectile points were assembled for further
analysis, the results of which are shown in Table 15.[7] Regarding the
material types utilized, the data shown in Table 15 reflect the survey
sample only and the Mockingbird points, which are primarily of jasper,
have been omitted from the analysis of this component. Thus within
the survey area, Clovis points were made primarily from chalcedonies
(43%), with chert and obsidian used equally (21% each).

In terms of the components of production and morphology, evidence of the original facet was present on only 19% of the total sample,
indicating that the original flake blank was both large and relatively
thick. The actual production techniques of Clovis points are not yet
completely known. It is assumed that the flake blank was worked bifacially into a roughly point-shaped preform, which was then fluted.
There is no evidence of the rectanguloid preform and snapped tips
which characterize the Folsom technique. The Clovis fluting technique
was different also in that flutes were struck from a bevelled platform,
rather than a nipple-shaped one. The general lack of emphasis by

_____

[7]Thirteen of these points (50% of the sample) are from the Mockingbird Clovis site.

Table 15: Analysis of Clovis Projectile Points[a]

A. Continuous Variables: (measured in millimeters)

Attribute	Mean	Standard Deviation	Coefficient of Variation	Maximum	Minimum	Range
1. Maximum Width	26.39	2.656	10.06	32.2	22.0	10.2
2. Hafting Width	25.69	2.721	10.59	32.0	21.0	11.0
3. Basal Width	23.92	2.679	11.19	29.2	19.1	10.1
4. Hafting Flute Width	12.29	1.630	13.26	16.5	9.9	6.6
5. Hafting Flute Thickness	4.17	.652	15.63	5.1	3.0	2.1
6. Hafting Thickness	5.21	.851	16.34	7.9	4.1	3.8
7. Maximum Thickness	5.84	1.186	20.32	9.0	4.1	4.9
8. Concavity Depth	3.46	1.256	36.27	7.1	1.5	5.6

9. Hafting index = .203

B. Discrete Variables (percentage occurrence):

	Chalcedony	Chert	Obsidian	Miscellaneous
1. Material type	.43	.21	.21	.15

	Lateral	Concavity	Both	Absent
2. Basal Grinding	.11	.00	.89	.00

	Present	Absent
3. Evidence of Original Blank Facets	.19	.81

[a]N = 26

Clovis on the preparation of both the preform and the striking platform
resulted in shorter, more irregular flutes than are found on Folsom
points.

As Table 15 indicates, the attributes of width are more critical
here than those of thickness, although none of the variables achieve
the very close tolerances exhibited by Folsom and Cody Complex
points. This is evidenced by the relatively high coefficients of variation in the Clovis sample. Concavity depth is the least critical, and
in this case, as in the others discussed previously, this attribute is
a function of the fluting or basal thinning process. The Clovis hafting
index is .203, virtually identical to that of the Belen points. Clovis
points, however, are somewhat larger and thicker.

A very prominent feature of the Clovis bases is the high incidence (89%) of grinding present both laterally and in the basal concavity.
Furthermore, microscopic analysis revealed that in 65% of the cases
this grinding was very heavy. A test of this feature, discussed in the
next chapter, indicates that it may have been significant in terms of
hafting.

Functionally, in addition to service as projectile points, Clovis
points may have been used as knives. There is no evidence of this
from the survey area since few complete points were located. I have
seen a number of Clovis points from Colorado which have been retouched
laterally to facilitate knife function. These were surface finds however,

and thus it is possible the points may have been reworked by later peoples. Unfortunately, Clovis channel flakes are not common enough to permit analysis of function, as was the case in the Folsom assemblage.

In terms of related function, it is not known whether Clovis people employed the spearthrower or not. William Roosa (personal communication) has suggested the use of a thrusting spear only. However some Clovis bone implements which may have served as foreshafts are known, and it is difficult to envision the use of these in conjunction with a thrusting spear alone. I would also suggest that the fluting process itself, which is an alternative to laterally directed percussion thinning, was undertaken for the express purpose of preserving the weight of the point. Whether this should be taken as supporting a projected (with the aid of a spearthrower) missile or a thrust missile can be debated.

The articulation of the Clovis components indicates the need for a relatively heavy, basally thinned point, in which a desired hafting width was consciously sought. I would suggest, as I have previously, that a probable explanation would be that the point bases were being fitted to a bone or antler haft, and that grinding was to facilitate both entry and removal of the point base. I would also consider this a fruitful area of research in more extensive Clovis collections where the contextual attributes of the points under consideration are more accurately known.

2. Transverse Scrapers:

Clovis transverse scrapers were analyzed primarily for comparative purposes in that again the sample had to be augmented by scrapers
from outside the survey area, specifically from the Mockingbird campsite. Based on this sample, the Clovis scraper type percentages
exhibited remarkable similarity to the Cody sample, as indicated by
Table 7. In fact, the two major categories (TU and TB) are identical,
comprising 32% and 40% respectively of the total sample. However,
further analysis reveals that the individual types themselves are quite
different with respect to component attributes, thus no association is
implied by the above similarities.

As shown in Table 8, the Clovis sample is dominated by the
selection of chalcedony (44%), with chert and jasper comprising 31%
and 19%. The latter may be a result of the incorporation of the Mockingbird material into the sample, since jasper was used predominantly
in that area.

In terms of production and morphology, the Clovis TU scraper
is generally larger than the TB type, although it is less divergent.
In other words the TU type is a larger, more parallel-sided scraper,
while the TB is smaller, yet more highly divergent. These characteristics are reflected in the production components of facet angle, in
which the TB type has a much higher angle, and in the number of
dorsal facets, where the TB has a higher incidence of multiple facets.

Neither type exhibits a high percentage of cortex, indicating the lack of use of primary decortication flakes. The only other area of major difference between the two types is that of undercut corner, of which the TU type reveals a much higher incidence.

Regarding artifact function, the TU type tends to be used as a hard wear scraper distally, with a fairly high incidence of bifacial knife wear along the lateral edges. The TB type tends to soft wear distally, while the right lateral wear suggests use of that side as a side scraper.

Reviewing the articulation of these components of the Clovis transverse scrapers, the data indicate that the TU type was primarily a scraper used on hard surfaces such as bone or hard wood, and that the lateral edges were used to cut similar materials. The morphology of this type indicates that it could be hafted easily when necessary. To produce this type of scraper, either a more angular core was utilized, or the more angular parts of the core, and flakes were struck generally parallel to the core ridges. I would suggest that this was one of the primary implements used in the working of bone or very hard wood.

The TB type, on the other hand, was probably a utility scraper selected for use in hide working when necessary. The relatively high divergence suggests it was hand-held, though it could possibly have been hafted for heavy work through the use of lateral notching. Unequal lateral wear indicates the selection of the right lateral edge for scraping

or cutting functions, and thus favors the hand-held use of the implement. Flakes selected as blanks for this scraper type were generally
struck from cores which had been well-worked previously, as indicated by the high incidence of multiple facets on the dorsal surface.

3. Other Artifacts:

Only 14 other implements were recorded in the Clovis site in the
survey area, of which 11 were side scrapers. Thus an analysis of each
of these artifacts is prohibited by lack of sufficient data. Mention
should be made of the relatively high percentage of side scrapers
found in this Clovis site, which is in keeping with evidence from Clovis
sites elsewhere (Irwin and Wormington 1970). Unfortunately the sample
derived here is too small to permit assessment of whether the high
incidence of side scrapers is offset by a lower incidence of another
tool type which would satisfy side-scraping functions. This should
certainly be an area of investigation in future Clovis research, and
further comments on this subject will be offered in the following
chapter.

4. Component Articulation:

If there is one thing that can be concluded from the investigation
of a relatively small, albeit mixed, sample of Clovis materials, it is
that the campsite assemblages investigated here do not reveal the blade
orientation (in the Old World sense) which has been attributed the
Clovis culture in the past (Green 1963). This is not to deny the

validity of such evidence, it is simply to state that a well-developed
blade technology is not revealed in the majority of the transverse and
side scrapers examined from campsites in the Rio Grande area. I
would suggest that if Clovis people did frequently utilize tools derived
from blade blanks rather than flake blanks, that such tools are more
in evidence from kill site situations such as Blackwater Draw, than in
campsites in the Rio Grande area. This certainly would be a fertile
area for future investigations of Clovis assemblages.

B. Environmental Components:

Since only one Clvois site is known from the survey area, no
comments can be made on a Clovis settlement "pattern," except to
note one consistency which occurs in the two Clovis campsites which
I have had the opportunity to visit; 13JB5 and the Mockingbird site.
Both of these sites are situated in an environmental situation somewhat distinct from the other PaleoIndian sites dealt with in the survey
in that both are located between two sources of water. 13JB5 is found
on a very low shelf separating two shallow arroyos. The Mockingbird
site is located on a sandy ridge separating a shallow basin from a
shallow drainageway (Robert Weber, personal communication). In
addition, the site from the survey area which I termed earlier as
"proto-Folsom" (8XK8) was also situated on a low shelf or ridge
separating two shallow arroyos. Thus I would suggest that this basic
pattern be investigated more thoroughly in attempting to carry out
Clovis and other pre-Folsom research elsewhere in North America.

C.   Clovis Settlement Technology:

Again, due to lack of an adequate sample, little can be said about the settlement technology of the Clovis occupation of the survey area. I would like to point out one factor, though, which I consider important to further analysis of Clovis assemblages. I feel that the information regarding lithic technology which has been offered in the past about Clovis has been quite seriously biased toward a kill, rather than camp, situation. As noted previously, the blade orientation simply does not predominate in the campsites investigated here. This, I feel, illustrates the potential dangers inherent in generalizing about a culture as a whole based on data derived from only one aspect of its settlement technology.

Many more Clovis campsites will have to be located and excavated before one can generalize about Clovis lithic and settlement technology and, ultimately, about the origin of Clovis in the New World.

This completes the intracultural analyses of each of the Paleo-Indian cultural manifestations located in the survey area. Rather than summarize the findings at this point, the next chapter will deal entirely with the comparative analysis of this material, and the final chapter will offer a general summary of both the intracultural and intercultural analyses.

CHAPTER VII

Intercultural Analysis

Introduction

This chapter deals primarily with the diachronic comparative
analysis of the processes of culture change revealed by the lithic and
settlement technologies of the various PaleoIndian occupants of the
central Rio Grande valley. It is the explanation of processual change
that has been advanced as the fundamental goal of archeology (Binford
1962). Of necessity, an archeological survey must deal less with explanation and more with the definition of problems leading to eventual
explanation, and diachronic analysis based on survey data is no exception. However, the explanation of specific cultural process will be
undertaken whenever the data and analytic methods permit it.

The survey resulted in the identification of four major Paleo-
Indian cultures which had occupied the area: Clovis, Folsom, Belen,
and Cody Complex. These are felt to represent a chronological
sequence, based on reasoning presented in Chapter 4. Nevertheless,
the objective nature of the systems approach adhered to in this study
does not permit the a priori assumption that these four cultures represent a developmental sequence, except to the extent that they represent four distinct chronological periods in a very generalized Paleo-
Indian tradition.

The following discussion will consist of a comparison of the lithic technologies of the four cultures followed by a comparative analysis of the settlement technologies.

Comparison of Lithic Technologies

For analytic purposes, the lithic implements recovered in the survey will be divided into weaponry, consisting of projectile points and preforms, and utility implements (all other tools analyzed).

Table 16 lists the mean values and coefficients of variation of the continuous variables measured in the projectile point sample used previously. The variables are listed in the order presented for the Clovis sample in Table 15. It will be recalled that this order varied somewhat for each culture, in that it was based on increasing values of the coefficient of variation. The important point is that all cultures emphasized hafting width over hafting thickness in terms of the limits of tolerance required. In other words, in producing PaleoIndian points, the width of the base was a more critical variable (e.g., required closer tolerances), than was its thickness.

In reviewing the data presented in Table 16 from the standpoint of comparing coefficients of variation, the most important thing to note is the general similarity between the Clovis and Belen points, and the distinctiveness of Folsom and Cody, both from each other and from Clovis and Belen. The similarity between Clovis and Belen is revealed in identical rankings of coefficients of variation, in general magnitude

Table 16: Mean Values of Continuous Variables of PaleoIndian
            Projectile Points[a]

Variable	Clovis	Folsom	Belen	Cody
1. Maximum Width:				
mean	26.39	21.51	22.75	18.24
coefficent of variation	(10.06)	(6.93)	(9.66)	(8.19)
2. Hafting Width:				
mean	25.69	20.58	21.59	17.73
coefficient of variation	(10.59)	(6.45)	(10.91)	(7.34)
3. Basal Width:				
mean	23.92	19.42	20.41	17.31
coefficient of variation	(11.19)	(5.79)	(11.70)	(6.84)
4. Hafting Flute Width:				
mean	12.29	13.35	----	----
coefficient of variation	(13.26)	(11.00)	----	----
5. Hafting Flute Thickness:				
mean	4.17	2.43	----	----
coefficient of variation	(15.63)	(18.15)	----	----
7. Maximum Thickness:				
mean	5.84	3.83	5.19	5.72
coefficient of variation	(20.32)	(12.54)	(16.07)	(14.01)
8. Concavity Depth:				
mean	3.46	2.89	1.60	----
coefficient of variation	(36.27)	(40.15)	(66.93)	----
9. Hafting Index:				
mean	.203	.169	.206	.309

[a]All measurements in millimeters.

of the coefficients, in the hafting index, and in the hafting thickness (variable 5 for Clovis, variable 7 for Belen). The main difference between the two is in terms of gross size, the Belen points being somewhat smaller than the Clovis specimens. The other major variation between the two, that of concavity depth, can be explained by the fact that Clovis points were consistently fluted, and concavity depth is in large part a function of this fluting.

It has long been held by American archeologists that Folsom developed from Clovis, largely on the basis of the fact that both point types are fluted. The data in Table 16 would tend more to deny than confirm this hypothesis. Yet one cannot overlook the generic relationships implicit in the fact that these are the only two points in the Plains area which are fluted, even though the actual fluting process differs. I would interpret these data as indicative of the possibility that Clovis may have been a generalized typological base from which a number of later PaleoIndian point types derived, including the generalized lanceolate Plano point type represented here by Belen. The reduction in size could be explained either by an adaptation to a different type of game, or an improvement in the ability to thin points by means of lateral percussion, or both.

Based on the comparative analysis of the data in Table 16, Folsom emerges as a highly specialized thin point, while Cody (Eden in this case) is a highly specialized thick one. Eventually such differences in specialization will undoubtedly be explained in terms of variations in hafting techniques, and hypotheses which might lead toward the solution of this problem will be offered shortly.

It will be noticed in Table 16 that both Folsom and Cody exhibit very low coefficients of variation in basal width, while those of Clovis and Belen are relatively higher. It is important to note that in the case of Folsom and Eden points the desired basal width is attained by the application of pressure retouch, a factor which is lacking in the cases of Clovis and Belen. This suggests that it might be profitable to search for the possibility of some other factor compensating for pressure retouch in the case of the Clovis and Belen points. I had noticed during the recording of the data on the points that some exhibited extremely heavy lateral grinding, while on others the degree of grinding was light enough to be discernible only with a microscope. To test the possibility that there might be a correlation between the degree of lateral grinding and basal width, the data on these two variables for each culture were submitted to statistical tests of association. The results of these tests are presented in Table 17.[1]

---

[1]As noted in Table 17 (and Tables 19 and 22 which follow), the chi-square test of association was used wherever possible. However, the validity of the chi-square test has been questioned for those 2 x 2 tables where the expected frequency of any single cell is less than five (cf. Edwards 1967:333-334). In such cases, the exact probabilities are presented here in addition to the chi-square approximation. The exact probabilities, based on Fisher's exact test, were derived from computations by McGuire and others (1967).

Table 17: Test of Association between Basal Width and Degree of
Lateral Grinding.

Basal Width	Heavy grinding O	Heavy grinding E	Light grinding O	Light grinding E	Total
1. Clovis:					
Above average width	10	7.1	1	3.8	11
Below average width	7	9.8	8	5.1	15
Total	17		9		26

$\chi^2 = 5.596$ d.f. $= 1$ p. $= .024^a$

2. Folsom:					
Above average width	6	7.0	9	7.9	15
Below average width	9	7.9	8	9.0	17
Total	15		17		32

$\chi^2 = 0.559$ d.f. $= 1$ p. $< .70$

3. Belen:					
Above average width	6	3.5	7	9.4	13
Below average width	2	4.4	14	11.5	16
Total	8		21		29

$\chi^2 = 4.249$ d.f. $= 1$ p. $= .055^a$

4. Cody Complex:					
Above average width	7	5.2	4	5.7	11
Below average width	4	5.7	8	6.2	12
Total	11		12		23

$\chi^2 = 2.159$ d.f. $= 1$ p. $= .15^a$

---

[a] Exact probability computed due to low expected frequency.

Two of the tests, those of Clovis and Belen, resulted in values significant at the .024 and .055 levels respectively, while Folsom and Cody showed no significant association between basal width and degree of lateral grinding. The Clovis and Belen samples indicate that points which are above average in width generally exhibit heavy lateral grinding. This strongly suggests that in the case of these two types, heavy lateral grinding was used to attain a desired basal width, in the absence of fine pressure retouch. In the case of Folsom and Cody, width was attained by pressure modification, thus eliminating the necessity to depend on heavy grinding.

The above data, when viewed in conjunction with the systems trajectories of each point type as presented in Chapter 6, permit the formulation of tentative conclusions regarding the functional taxonomy of PaleoIndian projectile points. First with reference to PaleoIndian points in general (Clovis, Folsom, Belen, Cody), it has been shown that hafting width and hafting thickness are critical variables, with the attainment of a desired width being relatively more important than achieving a desired thickness. Lateral grinding is a characteristic of all the point types while basal grinding is not, though it may be frequently present. Finally, compared to projectile points of later cultures, PaleoIndian points are lanceolate in outline, and lack any type of lateral, corner, or basal notching. The chi-square test of basal width and degree of grinding revealed that in the final stage of manufacture the points dealt with here are evidently being adapted to fit something. Due to the fact that basal width is the most critical variable, I have sug-

gested that the point base was being fitted to a foreshaft, probably of

the socket type. Where this final fitting was achieved by pressure

flaking (Folsom, Cody), the variation in basal width is much less than

when the fitting was attained by heavy grinding (Clovis, Belen).

Assuming the point bases were being fitted to a foreshaft, the

latter must have been more difficult or time-consuming to produce than

the points themselves, otherwise concentration would have been on the

foreshaft rather than the point. I would thus conclude that the foreshafts

were of bone, and that a number of points would be pre-fitted to a

given bone foreshaft and then ground to facilitate insertion and re-

moval. The use of bone as foreshaft material would provide the weight

necessary for penetrating force in use on megafauna such as mammoth

and bison. The foreshaft may or may not have been rigidly fixed to a

mainshaft; the important thing to note here is that the foreshaft-mainshaft

combination was evidently considered a fixed unit, while the removable

point was viewed as expendable. Such a system would facilitate what

might be termed "reloading" in a more modern sense. For instance,

if a shot missed the target and the point broke on impact with the ground,

the shaft unit could be recovered, the broken point removed, and a

new, previously fitted point inserted quite rapidly. The preponderance

of broken bases found in the campsites would result from carrying

back broken points, or more likely, would represent those bases which broke flush at the socket and were not extractable in the field. This incidentally might explain the numerous "1/4" bases found in Folsom campsites (i.e., bases which are broken in half vertically). These could result from driving a wedge between the flute and the inside of the foreshaft in an effort to remove the broken base.

It might be instructive at this time to note briefly the difference between the PaleoIndian hafting technique suggested above, and the later Archaic technique which can be documented empirically. Hafted Archaic projectile points, foreshafts, and broken mainshafts have been recovered archeologically, and excellent examples of these can be found in the University of New Mexico Museum of Anthropology. Some were found at a site known as the Correo Snake Pit in the survey area. In Archaic times, the points were generally corner notched (e.g., Pinto Basin, San Jose), and these were fixed rigidly to a wooden foreshaft with a sinew binding. The foreshaft was roughly pointed at the base and inserted into a socketed mainshaft. The important fact is that in this system the point-foreshaft combination was the removable unit, and it was evidently this unit which was replaced in the event of point breakage since it would have been both difficult and time-consuming to rehaft and rebind points in the field.

The critical difference between this method and that postulated above for the PaleoIndian is the Archaic use of a wooden foreshaft which was much easier to manufacture than a bone one. Wooden foreshafts were permitted in that the game taken by Archaic peoples was considerably smaller than that taken by the PaleoIndian, and thus the penetrating power provided by weighting the end of the missile was not necessary. In that wood is easier to shape than bone, a number of foreshafts with points fixed to them could be taken into the field. I feel this hypothesis could be tested independently by measuring hafting width of a number of Archaic points, although I did not have the opportunity to do so. If the thesis is valid, these should exhibit a considerably higher coefficient of variation than do the same PaleoIndian attributes, in that less care would be taken to fit the Archaic point bases to a given foreshaft dimension.

It was mentioned earlier that variations in PaleoIndian projectile point technology might ultimately be explained in terms of differences in hafting techniques. Assuming that the hypothesis of a removable point in a bone foreshaft has validity, I would suggest that differences between various types of PaleoIndian points will obtain primarily from variations in the types of foreshafts to which the points were fitted. Furthermore, foreshaft variation may quite probably be found to correlate with either different types of bones selected as foreshaft blanks, or different sizes (species) of animals utilized. Further investigations along the lines suggested by this analysis might prove quite informative in explaining variation in PaleoIndian projectile point typology.

With reference to the utility implements, the other major category of artifacts comprised by the lithic assemblage, certainly the transverse scraper merits the most intensive analysis. In that the transverse scrapers are by far the most predominant implement type in all of the PaleoIndian assemblages in the survey area, they lend themselves most readily to reliable cross-cultural quantitative analysis. Furthermore, since the scrapers are utility implements rather than weapons, they are probably less susceptible to relatively extensive typological fluctuation through time, and intercultural changes may be more subtly expressed. I feel, however, that if technological change can be isolated from an analysis of the various scraper assemblages, it might accurately reflect the more basic changes in lithic technology which took place during the PaleoIndian period.

Earlier it was noted (Chapter 4) that transverse scrapers were classified into obvious categories based on the presence or absence of lateral modification. Analysis of scrapers from each culture was undertaken in Chapter 6, based on data presented in Tables 7 and 8. In general, only two of the four possible scraper types were predominant in the various survey assemblages: the endscraper which was unmodified laterally (TU type), and the type in which both lateral edges had been modified and reshaped by secondary retouch (TB type). The only exception to this pattern was in the Belen assemblage, where the scrapers which were modified on the right lateral edge only (TR type) were more predominant than those of the TB type.

Reviewing the various analyses presented in Chapter 6, some initial conclusions can be offered regarding PaleoIndian transverse scraper technology as a whole. First, two basic types of flake blanks were generally recognized as suitable for modification into transverse scrapers. One was a flake with a relatively high (acute) dorsal facet angle which most frequently had only two dorsal facets. The other type of flake had a much lower (obtuse) facet angle and quite commonly exhibited more than two (multiple) dorsal facets. A comparative analysis of selected attributes reveals that these two types of blanks were selected for the production of the two distinct types of scrapers which predominate in the assemblages. This is indicated in Table 18, which compares the mean divergence angle and the mean facet angles of the TU and TB scraper types for all cultures recorded in the survey. In this case the attributes of divergence and facet angle were selected in order to determine which of the two primary production variables of the original flake blanks could be considered critical to the manufacture of the predominant types.

As indicated by the data, the mean divergence angles of the TB scrapers are larger than those of the unmodified TU types, indicating simply that the unmodified scrapers were generally less divergent morphologically than were the laterally modified types.[2] The very

---

[2]Though less divergent, the standard deviation in each case is larger for the unmodified types. This indicates that there was an attempt in the process of laterally modifying a scraper blank, to achieve

Table 18: Comparison of Selected Attributes of TU and TB Scraper
Types.

	Attribute	Clovis	Folsom	Belen	Cody
A.	Transverse Unmodified (TU):				
	1. Mean divergence angle	28.75°	30.50°	24.80°	21.25°
	Standard deviation	21.174	19.142	16.550	14.776
	2. Mean facet angle	122°	132°	116°	121°
B.	Transverse Bilateral (TB):[a]				
	1. Mean divergence angle	31.00°	33.32°	39.62°	34.50°
	Standard deviation	10.834	13.051	13.611	13.169
	2. Mean facet angle	139°	144°	138°	143°
C.	Differences Between TU & TB Means:				
	1. Divergence angle	2.25°	2.82°	14.82°	13.25°
	2. Facet angle	17°	12°	22°	22°

[a]Transverse Right Lateral (TR) for Belen.

high standard deviations shown by the TU scrapers indicate that almost certainly the divergence angle of the flake blank was not a critical
variable in the selection of which blanks to leave unmodified and which
to shape laterally.

On the other hand, reference to the data on the mean facet angle
shows it to vary both considerably and consistently between the TU and
TB types in each culture. As indicated in Table 8, this attribute is
the only one of the production variables which exhibits consistent variation in this manner among all the cultures represented. As such, the
mean facet angle may be considered the attribute of primary technological focus in the selection of scraper blanks for further modification.
In short, the angle at the convergence of the dorsal facets is the critical variable in the formulation of PaleoIndian transverse scraper
taxonomy.

Another feature of technological importance indicated by the data
in Table 18 can be seen by examining the exact nature of the variation
in attribute values between the two scraper types. As shown, Clovis
and Folsom exhibit relatively low differences between means, while
Belen and Cody exhibit relatively high differences, both in divergence
angle and facet angle. This suggests that possible variations in techniques of production of the scraper blanks might exist between the two
clustered groups. In order to test this possibility, the most direct

some sort of common divergence angle, although the range of variation
of TB divergence is still quite large.

indicator of production technique--the attribute of orientation of re-
moval--was tested for significance of correlation with the two scraper
types for each culture (Table 19). As shown, the Belen scrapers attain
significance in this test, indicating that the Belen TR scraper type was
purposefully struck to derive a flake morphology which would facilitate
modification of the right lateral edge. Though this test was valid for
most of the scraper assemblages, further analysis revealed that the
Cody data was insufficient to yield an accurate assessment. This was
due to the high percentage of multiple-faceted scrapers from which
it is impossible to determine the attribute of orientation. Thus the
Cody test was determined inadequate.[3]

This feature, viewed in conjunction with the fact that Cody exhibits a wide variation in facet angles between the TU and TB types,
plus the highest incidence of cortex present on the TU scrapers (Table
8) strongly suggests that a variation in production technique exists between the two Cody scraper types under consideration. Since such a
variation is not immediately explicable in terms of the attribute of
orientation, it can be suggested that Cody flintknappers achieved the
TU-TB scraper distinction through techniques somehow distinct from
the other PaleoIndian cultures.

---

[3]In order to insure the significance of the Cody situation, the
association between multiple-faceted and double-faceted scrapers was
tested for Cody as opposed to the rest of the assemblages. The results
of this test indicated that the percentage of Cody multiple-faceted
scrapers was significantly higher than for the rest of the cultures
($\chi^2 = 4.458$, d.f. = 1, p. $< .05$).

Table 19: Association of Flake Removal Orientation and Scraper Type.

Method of Removal	TU Type		TB Type[a]		Total
	O	E	O	E	
1. Clovis:					
Parallel to dorsal ridge	11	11.7	15	14.2	26
Away from dorsal ridge	3	2.2	2	2.7	5
Total	14		17		31

$\chi^2 = 0.559$ d.f = 1 p > .20[b]

2. Folsom:					
Parallel to dorsal ridge	25	24.7	14	14.2	39
Away from dorsal ridge	8	8.2	5	4.7	13
Total	33		19		52

$\chi^2 = 0.031$ d.f. = 1 p. > .20[b]

3. Belen:					
Parallel to dorsal ridge	18	15.1	4	6.8	22
Away from dorsal ridge	4	6.8	6	3.1	10
Total	22		10		32

$\chi^2 = 5.572$ d.f. = 1 p. = .027

4. Cody Complex:					
Parallel to dorsal ridge	9	8.4	10	10.7	19
Away from dorsal ridge	2	2.7	4	3.4	6
Total	11		14		25

$\chi^2 = 0.377$ d.f. = 1 p. > .20[b]

---

[a] TR type in the case of Belen

[b] Based on exact probability table (McGuire, et al. 1967).

Thus an initial analysis of the transverse scraper assemblages reveals not only variations between the scraper types, but also differences between two cultural groups (Clovis-Folsom and Belen-Cody). Since this is somewhat at odds with the data revealed by the projectile point analysis, a more intensive investigation of the technology of scrapers is warranted in order to determine if general trends of variation can be identified and possibly explained.

In order to adequately cope with the extensive potential variation involved in the data as recorded for the scraper assemblages, it was decided that a more inclusive quantitative technique should be employed. Among the techniques available for the analysis of such covariation are factor analysis, cluster analysis, proximity analysis, and multivariate partialing analysis. The merits and disadvantages of each of these techniques will not be discussed here, since they have been extensively reviewed elsewhere (Tugby 1965, Sackett 1966, Johnson 1967, Binford and Binford 1966, Cowgill 1968, Clarke 1968). Due to the specific nature of the data, the manner in which the variables were recorded, the sample size, and the purpose of the analysis (i.e., not the generation of types, but the determination of changes in lithic technology), it was decided that the technique of factor analysis would most adequately satisfy the requisites of this study. In addition to the fact that the use of factor analysis in the field of anthropology has become increasingly popular (Driver 1965), precedent for the particular

application of factor analysis set forth herein was recently afforded
by Benfer's (1967) analysis of attributes of a small sample of stemmed
projectile points from southwest and central Texas.

As noted by Cattell, "factor analysis aims to explain observed
relations among numerous variables in terms of simpler relations"
(1965:190). It was felt that if this set of "simpler relations" (i.e., the
inherent underlying structure of covariance between the artifact attributes) could be manifested in terms of lithic technology, the nature of
the intercultural variation in the latter would become much more
readily apparent.

Most of the factor analyses performed in the past have been
based on "r" coefficients of correlation where the variables are assumed
to be continuous, although Driver and Schuessler (1957) have presented
the technique based on the non-parametric "phi" coefficient, suitable
for use with discrete variables. In the present study of transverse
scrapers, it was decided to utilize the r-coefficient since discrete
characteristics with multiple internal gradations could be set up quite
easily for the scraper assemblages, thus approximating the assumed
continuous variable structure. In addition, available computer programs
for analysis utilized the r-coefficient, and to modify them for phi was a
relatively complex task. The encoding formula utilized was based
on the artifact analysis form shown in Figure 19, modified to maximize

the internal gradations of those characteristics dealing primarily with lithic technology. The names of the 35 variables utilized are given in Figure 24.

A total of 235 transverse scrapers were submitted to analysis, with roughly equal numbers selected from each of the four cultures represented in the survey. Following the analysis of the artifacts, the descriptive characteristics were transferred to a standard data processing form, and then punched on computer cards. Computer facilities used were those of the University of New Mexico's IBM-360, and the main program, termed FACTO, was derived from the IBM-360 Programmer's Manual. In this program, the computed correlation matrix of r-coefficients is factor analyzed by the principle component method in which eigenvalues greater than 1.0 are retained. A factor matrix is computed from the retained eigenvalues and then rotated orthoganally by the varimax method.

Each cultural component (Clovis, Folsom, Belen, Cody) was factor analyzed separately, and then in order to provide a standard of comparison for the interpretation of technological changes, the total assemblage of the four groups combined was factor analyzed as a whole. The latter is termed herein the "collective" factor analysis. The original 35 by 35 correlation matrix was reduced to 12 factors in the case of the collective analysis.

Variable
  No:

Description:

1. Length
2. Width
3. Thickness
4. Working Factor*
5. Distal retouch*
6. Divergence*
7. Distal cross-section
8. Corner angle
9. Presence of striking platform
10. Method of flake detachment
11. Presence of cortex
12. Type of proximal modification
13. Number of dorsal facets
14. Core facet angle*
15. Orientation of flake removal (relative to dorsal facets)*
16. Flake trajectory (ventral curvature)
17. Right lateral modification (shaping)
18. Left lateral modification (shaping)
19. Right lateral retouch (secondary)
20. Left lateral retouch (secondary)
21. Presence of notching (lateral edges)
22. Presence of spur(s)
23. Corner undercutting by retouch
24. Corner sharpness
25. Ventral surface treatment (shaping)
26. Distal micro wear
27. Distal surface wear
28. Distal undercutting
29. Right lateral micro wear*
30. Right lateral macro wear *
31. Right lateral surface wear*
32. Left lateral micro wear*
33. Left lateral macro wear*
34. Left lateral surface wear*
35. Type of lithic material

*See Chapter 5 and Figure 19 for further explanation of these variables.

Figure 24. Variables Utilized in Factor Analysis of Transverse Scrapers.

The data derived from the collective factor analysis is presented in Table 20. The variables comprising the factor matrix have been re-grouped and ranked according to the highest loadings exhibited within each factor in order to portray visually the components of each factor. Only loadings over .200 are shown in the table. Each factor in the collective analysis was given a "name" based on the nature of the component variables as grouped in the collective matrix. A list of the named factors, with both component and related variables is presented in Figure 25.

Prior to examining the results of the factor analysis, it should be reiterated that its purpose was not to verify existing hypotheses, but to suggest general trends in lithic technology which can be subjected to verification through empirical testing at some future date. As pointed out by Cattell (1965:190), factor analysis can yield either a set of classificatory categories or a number of hypothetical variables. Although this dichotomy may be less pronounced in actual practice, perhaps most of the existing analyses in anthropology have emphasized the former. However some, such as Sawyer and Levine (1966), have treated the resultant factors as variables themselves. Implicit in this approach is an emphasis on the structure of the factor matrix itself, and the present analysis attempts to maximize the interpretative potential exhibited by these structural characteristics.

The factor matrix (computer printout) comprises a list of factor loadings of each variable with respect to each factor. Each loading is

Table 20: Factor Matrix--Collective Analysis of all Scraper Assemblages[a]

Variable No.						Factors						
	1	2	3	4	5	6	7	8	9	10	11	12
19.	.756								.259			
31.	.689											
17.	.620								.454			-.414
30.	-.535							.362	-.296	.206		.245
16.	.388			.200								
5.		-.965										
2.		-.912										
4.		-.727	-.404							-.230		
6.	.207	-.593				.261				.304	.313	
22.			.811									
24.			.761									
8.			.543							.520		
14.				-.734								
3.		-.270		.719								
7.	-.271			.593								-.234
32.					-.809							
29.					-.805							
9.						.905						
10.						.901	.746					
35.					.239		-.598	-.312				
27.				-.432			-.445	.295				
13.								.761				
26.											-.412	
28.				.314				-.478				

(continued next page)

Table 20: Continued

Variable No.	1	2	3	4	5	6	7	8	9	10	11	12
						Factors						
20.									.828			
18.	.237								.742			
33.									-.620			-.329
34.								.255	.577			
21.										-.601		
1.		.377	-.216	.239	-.234					-.564	-.275	
23.			.318		-.244					-.338	.233	.290
25.											.725	
15.					-.212	.256						.596
12.	.323									-.389	.292	-.410
11.				.272	.282		.215				.301	.345

a Variables grouped according to factors. Only those loadings over .200 are shown.

Factor No.	Name of Factor	Component Variables	Related Variables
1.	Right lateral treatment	19, 31, 17, 30, 16	12, 7, 18, 6
2.	Morphology (dimensions) of distal end	5, 2, 4, 6	1, 3
3.	Secondary treatment of distal corners	22, 24, 8	4, 23, 1
4.	Nature of scraper blank	14, 3, 7	13, 28, 11, 1, 16
5.	Lateral wear	32, 29	11, 23, 27, 1, 15
6.	Technique of flake removal	9, 10	6, 15
7.	Nature of raw material	35, 27, 13	11
8.	Distal wear	26, 28	16, 27, 13, 34
9.	Left lateral treatment	20, 18, 33, 34	17, 16, 19
10.	Secondary treatment of lateral edges	21, 1, 23	8, 12, 6, 4, 16
11.	Secondary ventral treatment	25	28, 6, 11, 12, 1, 23
12.	Orientation of flake removal	15, 12, 11	30, 33, 23, 16, 7

Factor Groupings for Comparative Analysis:

1. Basic Morphology:

    Factors 1, 2, 9

2. Production Component:

    Factors 4, 6, 7, 12

3. Modification Component:

    Factors 3, 10, 11

4. Function Component:

    Factors 5, 8

Figure 25. Named Factors and Analytic Groups.

a relative expression of common variance and furthermore, as Sawyer and Levine have pointed out, "because the loading is a correlation between variable and factor and because a factor can be regarded as a composite variable, these loadings can be interpreted just like correlations between any two variables" (1966:714). If, therefore, a specific factor can be interpreted as protraying a certain aspect of lithic technology, any changes in the structural relationship within the factor (i.e., alterations in the relative loadings of the variables) will indicate varying emphases in the contribution to total factorial variance on the part of the individual variables, and will thus illuminate variations in lithic technology. It is proposed, then, that any differences in lithic technology which may be present between the cultural components represented in the scraper sample will be reflected in terms of alterations in the structure of the derived factors of each component.

One method of isolating structural alterations is to compare each of the component factor matrices with that derived from the analysis of the four groups as a whole (i.e., the collective matrix). This can be accomplished quite easily by naming the factors in the component matrices and comparing each named factor with the corresponding one in the collective matrix. A quantitative expression of the degree of correspondence can be obtained by calculating the Spearman rank correlation coefficient for each pair of corresponding factors (Judge 1968). A high coefficient would indicate close correspondence between the individual cultural factor and the collective factor and, consequently, little variation in lithic technology with respect to that particular factor. Conversely, a low coefficient would indicate that some type of variation in lithic technology on the part of the culture represented has resulted in a significant structural alteration of the factor components. Further analysis of the factor loadings of each variable should permit the isolation of those variables responsible for the alteration, and the description of the nature of the variation in terms of lithic technology.

In order to facilitate the analysis of the compared factors, the factors were grouped into four major divisions based on similarities in lithic technology. These groupings deal with factors related to the morphology of the artifact, with its techniques of production, with the methods of modification for specific functions, and finally with function itself. A list of these groups, together with the component factors of each, is provided at the bottom of Figure 25.

The results of the comparative analyses of individual versus collective factor structures is presented in Table 21. The data has been arranged in the groups noted above. Each rank correlation coefficient represents the degree of correspondence between the named factor for a given culture, and its counterpart in the collective factor matrix. Theoretically, it would be beneficial to examine in detail the structural variations represented by each coefficient, but this would be extremely time consuming. Therefore, the interpretive portion of this analysis

Table 21: Rank Correlation Coefficients for Comparable Factors[a]

Factor Name	Clovis	Folsom	Belen	Cody
A. Basic Morphology:				
1. Right lateral treatment	.5348	.7592	.6233	.6524
2. Distal morphology	.8321	.8603	.6197	.5796
9. Left lateral treatment	.6201	.8727	.4318	.5327
Mean rank correlation	.6623	.8307	.5582	.5882
B. Production Component:				
4. Nature of scraper blank	.4366	.6554	.4715	.3800
6. Flake removal technique	.6771	.5499	.7440	.6253
7. Nature of raw material	.1972	.4628	.2388	.1065
12. Orientation of removal	.2841	.4852	.3045	.3720
Mean rank correlation	.3987	.5383	.4397	.3709
C. Modification Component:				
3. Secondary distal treatment	.5961	.8085	.3164	.6215
10. Secondary lateral treatment	.4038	.6757	.5332	.1031
11. Secondary ventral treatment	.2101	.4852	.4017	.2160
Mean rank correlation	.4033	.6564	.4171	.3135
D. Function Component:				
5. Lateral wear	.4838	.6199	.1314	.5824
8. Distal wear	.3860	.2037	.1322	.5166
Mean rank correlation	.4349	.4118	.1318	.5495

Cultural Differences in Mean Rank Correlations.[b]

1. Clovis: 1) Morphology, 2) Function, 3) Modification, 4) Production
2. Folsom: 1) Morphology, 2) Modification, 3) Production, 4) Function
3. Belen: 1)Morphology, 2) Production, 3) Modification, 4)Function
4. Cody: 1) Morphology, 2) Function, 3) Production, 4)Modification

[a] Values underlined are significant at greater than the .05 level.

[b] Components listed in order of decreasing correspondence.

will be confined to an examination of those instances of relatively extensive variation from the norm, as indicated by those rank correlation coefficients which are not large enough to achieve significance at the .05 level. For the present sample, this would be those values less than .296 (Edwards 1967:344, Table VI). These values have been underlined in Table 21. In addition, the cultural variations in technological emphasis, based on the values of the mean rank correlations, have been presented at the bottom of the table, in order to facilitate visual interpretation of the data.

In analyzing the results of the comparative factor analyses, it can be seen that all cultures show most correspondence in the factors of basic morphology. This is to be expected since all the implements analyzed were, by definition, transverse scrapers. Regarding the other component groupings, however, there is considerable variation among the cultures. Clovis corresponds to the collective assemblage least closely with respect to the production component. Folsom and Belen correspond least in terms of function, and Cody in modification. These will be briefly analyzed now to determine the source of the variation by referring to the original factor matrices in each case.

1. Clovis:

The Clovis sample shows lowest mean rank correlation values in modification and production components. With regard to the former, it can be seen that the primary source of variation here is in Factor 11

(ventral treatment). A review of the Clovis data reveals that two elements contribute to variation in this factor. First, the attribute of
secondary ventral treatment is much less frequent in the Clovis sample.
Only 19.5% of the Clovis TU and TB scraper types exhibit this trait,
as opposed to the 31.6% in the other PaleoIndian assemblages.
Secondly, where this trait is present in the Clovis sample, it is associated with heavy hard wear on the right lateral edge of the scraper.
Thus, though ventral treatment is relatively unimportant to Clovis
scraper technology, where present it is associated with the side-
scraping functions of the transverse scraper.

Regarding the production component, there are two main sources
of variation; Factor 12 (orientation) and Factor 7 (raw material). With
respect to the orientation factor, inspection of the structure of the
factor matrix reveals that Clovis de-emphasizes variable 11 (cortex)
which is a component variable of Factor 12 in the collective matrix.
Clovis emphasizes instead the variables of lateral retouch (19, 20).
The key to the variation here lies in the high incidence of the technique
of parallel removal orientation for the bilaterally modified (TB)
scrapers. The fact that blanks for both scraper types were removed
in the same fashion is the source of variation with respect to the other
PaleoIndian scrapers.

In reference to Factor 7 (raw material), variation in this case
stems from the preference for jaspers in the Mockingbird Clovis

scrapers and thus cannot be utilized to inform on the survey Clovis material in general. However, the Clovis matrix shows again a de-emphasis of variable 11 (cortex), and this can be considered valid for the survey material, since it is a consistent variation.

In conclusion, Clovis varies from the rest of the PaleoIndian sample primarily in terms of production techniques, and this variation can be traced to two important characteristics; 1) Clovis struck the majority of the scraper blanks by the same method (parallel orientation), regardless of intended type, and 2) there is a lack of use of primary decortication flakes for this purpose. There is further variation in the Clovis assemblage in the modification component, some of which results from the low incidence of ventral modification and some undoubtedly stems from the high incidence of lateral modification of Clovis scrapers. The majority (68%) of Clovis scrapers are modified laterally, and there is a high percentage of hard lateral use of such implements. This indicates the use of the TB type scraper as a side scraper by the Clovis people.

As pointed out previously, the Clovis survey assemblage exhibited the highest percentage of side scrapers, and the percentage is even higher outside the survey area. This fact, together with the data derived from the factor analysis, suggests that Clovis struck flakes from a core in a standardized fashion (parallel removal), and then selected some of these flakes as blanks for side scrapers, and others as blanks

for end scrapers. Due to the lack of primary decortication flakes indicated above, it is quite possible that such flakes were utilized for
side scraper blanks, while those without cortex were employed for
transverse scraper production.[4] Most of the transverse scraper
blanks were modified laterally and frequently used as side scrapers.
As such, it is apparent that in the Clovis case the transverse scraper
had not yet assumed the dominant potition which it occupies in the
later PaleoIndian assemblages. Furthermore, specialized modifications of the transverse scraper such as secondary ventral treatment
were quite rare.

2. Folsom:

As shown in Table 21, the Folsom assemblage shows less correspondence in production and function components. The lowest rank
correlation in the production component is in Factor 7 (raw material),
but since this rank coefficient (.4628) is significant as the .05 level, it
cannot be considered a significant deviation from the norm and will not
be dealt with here.

In terms of the component of function, there is one primary
source of variation in the Folsom case and that is in Factor 8 (distal
wear). Inspection of the Folsom data shows that one reason for this
variation is the relative lack of specialized function associated with
Folsom transverse scrapers. As shown in Table 22 (see below) Folsom
exhibits the lowest values of both chi-square and the phi coefficient

---

[4]I was unable to test this on the Clovis survey sample due to inadequate data on the side scraper production techniques.

in the test of association between scraper types and wear patterns. Further analysis of the Folsom factor matrix indicates that in Factor 8, Folsom generally de-emphasizes production variables in this factor, particularly that dealing with the number of dorsal facets (13). This suggests that production techniques had little to do with ultimate functional employment of transverse scrapers in the Folsom case. There was a slight emphasis in this factor on the secondary modification technique of undercutting a distal corner (variable 23). Further analysis revealed a strong correlation between distal wear and undercut corner on the Folsom TB scraper type, indicating the use of the undercut as a slashing tip on the TB scrapers used in hideworking. There was no evidence of this somewhat specialized modification in the Clovis assemblage.

In summary, the Folsom de-emphasis of production variables associated with the functional factor (Factor 8), plus the lack of functional specialization with respect to the TU and TB types, indicates the multi-purpose nature of the Folsom transverse scrapers. Furthermore, the presence of the slashing tip on soft-wear scrapers shows an awareness of the multi-functional potential of this implement. A review of the production techniques involved indicates a lack of any specific core treatment for scraper blank removal with respect to the TU and TB types. Evidently scraper blanks were selected from random flakes, and almost half (48%) were left unmodified laterally.

Those selected for lateral modification were selected on the basis of facet angle, not on the basis of the number of dorsal facets.

It should be recalled that there is a very strong correspondence between the ratio of material types utilized in Folsom scraper production and the ratio of materials used in projectile point production. This suggests that the scraper blanks were probably by-products of core treatment in preparation for the removal of projectile point blanks. The low incidence of cortex in the Folsom scraper assemblage indicates that primary decortication flakes were not used extensively as scraper blanks, and the disposition of such flakes remains an enigma.

3. Belen:

The Belen sample corresponds less in the components of modification and function. The lowest rank correlation for the modification component is Factor 3, but as in the case of Folsom the value is too high to be considered a significant deviation from the norm.

Regarding the component of function, both Factor 5 and Factor 8 are sources of variation in the Belen case. With reference to Factor 5 (lateral wear), Belen emphasizes variable 13 (dorsal facets) here to the point of ranking it first in terms of variable loadings for this factor. There are two significant elements here: First, Belen generally selected a double-faceted blank for modification into the TR type, which it will be recalled was more dominant than the TB type in the Belen assemblage. Second, the emphasis on dorsal facets is also reflected in the Belen selection of multi-faceted blanks for the TB type scraper. Although the latter type is not too important to the Belen assemblage, it does contribute to the variations in technology.

As noted previously (Chapter 6) the Belen flintknappers struck flakes specifically to produce blanks for the TR type scraper. As revealed by the orientation variable (Table 8) these flakes were struck away from the prominent ridge of the core, later to become the dorsal ridge of the scraper. This technique resulted in an offset triangular blank which was then modified along the right lateral (thin) edge. Generally a single spur was chipped into the modified corner. A comparison of the projectile point and transverse scraper material ratios indicated that point cores were not being dressed in the case of TR scraper production, but probably were in producing TU scraper blanks. This prompts a closer look at the utilization of Belen core material (Factor 7), which also shows significant variation with other PaleoIndian cultures. In this case, Belen emphasizes modification components strongly in this factor. Further investigation revealed a strong correlation between core material (variable 35) and orientation (variable 15) in the Belen correlation matrix, indicating the frequent selection of a specific raw material for the production of the TR scraper type. Reference to the data (Table 8) indicates preference for flint, the only incidence of dominance of this specific material in the total survey assemblage.

With reference to Factor 8 (distal wear), Belen emphasizes variable 14 (core facet angle), ranking it second in factor loadings, while other production variables were relatively de-emphasized. This suggests two things: First, there is a very strong difference in the selection of the flakes for modification (or for retention as unmodified) on the basis of the core facet angle. This is supported by the data in Table 18, there being a mean difference of 22° between the TU and TR types. Second, it indicates the association of this variation with a given function, as shown by the TR scraper type which revealed 77% hard distal wear, the most prominent distinction of wear in the entire scraper sample.

In summary, the variation of the Belen assemblage results primarily from the rather aberrant TR scraper type. In this case, the evidence indicates that specific materials were selected for the production of scraper blanks with a specific morphology. This was achieved through a specialized production technique with a predetermined function in mind. This is the first instance (chronologically) in the survey sample of specialization in scraper production relative to intended function.

The TU scraper in the Belen assemblage does not exhibit this type of specialization. From all appearances, it was a utility scraper serving a variety of needs, and was selected for on the basis of core facet angle. The high incidence of cortex on these scrapers, plus the

correspondence in raw material ratio with that of the projectile points,
indicates they may well have been by-products of core dressing for
point blank production.

4. Cody Complex:

The Cody sample reveals significant variations from the collective sample in both the production and modification components.
Regarding the former, the primary source of variation comes from
Factor 7 (raw material). In the Cody matrix, this factor is a single
variable factor, other variables being de-emphasized considerably,
some even to the extent of marked inverse (negative) factor loadings.
Even variable 11 (cortex) is de-emphasized here, although the Cody
TU scraper types exhibit the highest frequency of cortex in the entire
survey sample. This lack of association with other variables in this
factor indicates little selection on the part of the Cody flintknappers for
specific materials for the various scraper types.

Referring to the modification component, there are two sources
of variation in the Cody data; Factor 11 (ventral treatment), and Factor
10, (lateral treatment). An analysis of secondary ventral treatment
of the Cody scrapers indicates that this trait exists in 40% of the sample, as opposed to 31.6% for the survey sample as a whole. Notable
also in the structure of this particular factor is the de-emphasis by
Cody of those variables dealing with production and primary modification (shaping), and the corresponding emphasis of variables related

to function and specific modification. Further analysis revealed that ventral treatment of the Cody TB scraper type permitted specialized use of the implement as a backed knife. A significantly high correlation between ventral treatment (variable 25) and left lateral macrowear (variable 32) in the correlation matrix of the TB scraper types indicates that most probably the left edge was used as the knife edge (ventrally modified), while the right lateral edge, already retouched, was employed as the blunt edge.

With regard to Factor 10 (secondary lateral treatment), there was a general de-emphasis of the modification variables normally associated with this factor, and an emphasis on the production variable 13 (dorsal facets), to the extent that it was ranked first. The characteristic of notching (variable 21) which is the best measure of the factor in the collective matrix, is reduced here due to the very low incidence of notched TU Cody scrapers and the relatively high incidence of notching in the TB types.

After a considerable amount of analysis of the correlation matrix of the TB type, it was discovered that at least two specialized subtypes exist within the TB category. One is a fairly divergent, proximally modified, notched scraper which generally lacks lateral wear. This was evidently a hafted utility scraper, since no definite correlations with distal wear patterns were obtained. The other subtype was the hand-held hard-wear scraper, specially modified for use as a backed knife, as discussed above.

There is a possibility that a third subtype may also be present in the TB category, perhaps cross-cutting the other two subtypes. This is revealed by a significant correlation in the TB matrix between the absence of spurs and the presence of heavy soft wear distally, indicating that unspurred TB scrapers were generally utilized for hide-softening.

In the TU type of Cody scraper, subtypes are not as immediately apparent, although the correlation matrix indicates a possible separation on the basis of scraper thickness, the thicker ones being correlated with hard wear, and the thinner ones with soft.

In conclusion, the Cody sample emphasizes the specialized functional modification of transverse scrapers, as opposed to primary modification for the attainment of basic morphology. At least two, and possibly three, definite subtypes exist within the TB category. There is a possibility of subtypes within the TU category, which exhibits the highest percentage (69%) of soft wear of any of the survey groups. Apparent in the Cody assemblage, then, is specific secondary modification for relatively specialized function. In fact, it may be that the analytic categories initially set up in this study (laterally modified versus unmodified scrapers) simply do not fit the Cody material, and some other criteria should be used to distinguish the variation. Possibly this might be in terms of one of the production components, since Cody exhibits the lowest mean rank correlation of the total sample in the production component (Table 21). This is hinted at further by the possibility of TU subtypes based on the production variable of thickness. However, an intensive review of the attribute frequencies, the correlation matrix, and the factor analyses did not yield the exact nature of this variation, and thus it cannot be isolated at this time. In general we can only conclude that with Cody we see an increasing variety of functionally specialized scrapers derived through specific secondary modifications, and possibly based on fundamental variations in production techniques.

The results of the factor analysis of the four scraper assemblages can be briefly summarized as follows: It is apparent that Clovis struck flakes in a standardized fashion and selected some for transverse scraper blanks and presumably others for side scraper blanks. Taking into account both the results of the survey analysis and data from elsewhere in the Plains area, it is apparent that the transverse scraper was only beginning to become an important tool in the Clovis lithic assemblage, and furthermore, its use was limited by type to fairly specific functions. Table 22 tests the association between scraper wear and scraper type for all the survey cultures, and it can be seen that although not significant, the chi-square value for Clovis is considerably larger than for the rest of the PaleoIndian cultures represented.

Table 22: Association of Scraper Wear Patterns and Scraper Type.

Type of Wear	TU Type O	TU Type E	TB Type[a] O	TB Type[a] E	Total
1. Clovis:					
Soft distal wear	5	7.5	11	8.4	16
Hard distal wear	11	8.4	7	9.5	18
Total	16		18		34

$\chi^2 = 3.098$ d.f. = 1 p.< .10

2. Folsom:					
Soft distal wear	16	15.3	8	8.6	24
Hard distal wear	23	23.6	14	13.3	37
Total	39		22		61

$\chi^2 = 0.124$ d.f. = 1 p. < .80

3. Belen:					
Soft distal wear	10	8.5	3	4.4	13
Hard distal wear	15	16.4	10	8.5	25
Total	25		13		38

$\chi^2 = 1.092$ d.f. = 1 p. > 20[b]

4. Cody Complex:					
Soft distal wear	11	10.2	12	12.7	23
Hard distal wear	5	5.7	8	7.2	13
Total	16		20		36

$\chi^2 = 0.273$ d.f. = 1 p. < .70

[a]TR type in the case of Belen

[b]Based on exact probability table (McGuire, et al. 1967).

By Folsom times the transverse scraper had assumed a dominant position in the tool kit, if not in terms of functional importance, certainly in terms of implement frequency. Here, however, functional specialization of scraper types was minimized (Table 22) as the multipurpose potential of the implement began to be realized. Folsom scrapers were used for a wide variety of functions, regardless of type.

In the case of Belen, the transverse scraper was definitely the dominant utility implement and the multipurpose potential of it was well understood. In addition, in the Belen assemblage we encounter the initial alteration of production and modification techniques for the manufacture of the TR scraper intended for a rather specialized function, evidently bone and wood working.

Finally, the results of the Cody analysis indicate that while Cody maintained the emphasis on transverse scrapers in the utility tool kit, the diversification of this implement was increased considerably by stressing specific modifications toward functional specialization. The latter was carried to the extent that the typological categories adequate to describe the other PaleoIndian transverse scrapers were not sufficient to account for the variety in the Cody assemblage. Functionally specialized subtypes within the standard categories tend to cancel each other with respect to wear patterns, thus yielding the very low chi-square evident in Table 22.

As mentioned at the outset of the factor analysis, its purpose was to determine if general trends in the lithic technology exist within the transverse scraper assemblages derived from the survey. I feel that the data strongly suggest a generalized model of implement development through time within the PaleoIndian tradition. The model assumes basically that central traits--including technological traits--are adaptive, and that adaptation includes not only adjustments to the environment of the system, but also adjustments to increase efficiency in energy capture (i.e., the reduction of cost to the system while maintaining function). The model can be described as follows:

At any given stage of cultural development, all tools utilized are functionally adaptive, yet some are potentially more efficient than others. (Efficiency here includes the adaptive potential for multipurpose function.) As such tools are produced and utilized, there is of course continual experimentation taking place toward increasing efficiency.

As the adaptive potential for multipurpose function of any specific tool is recognized and explored, that particular implement becomes increasingly prominent in the cultural assemblage, reaching maximum prominence as the full range of multipurpose functions are realized. Serving a wide variety of needs in the technological system, the specific tool in fact becomes generalized. Meanwhile, other implements whose function it is replacing gradually decline in popularity.

Finally, concurrent with, or perhaps as a function of, maximum utilization, further methods are explored which will increase adaptive efficiency of the generalized tool through modification for specialized function. This is achieved initially by simple modifications of the generalized tool. As increased efficiency of specialization is explored, production techniques are gradually altered to facilitate the achievement of specific modifications. This results in the proliferation of implement subtypes, each of which has a given potential for future adaptation. The implement has developed from the generalized to the specific state.

In summary, the model suggests a cyclical reiteration of implement forms from general to specific states. From a generalized tool form a number of specific implements are developed, each of which varies in adaptive potential. As the adaptive potential of one (or more) of these becomes recognized, it in turn becomes the generalized form from which more specific forms are developed, and so on.[5] It is suggested here that this model can be applied to the development of the

---

[5] This model is not new, and can be considered simply the technological analog of the biological model of development from the general to the specific states.

transverse scraper in the PaleoIndian assemblages included in this survey. Again, I am not suggesting a developmental sequence of cultures here, simply the gradual development of a given utility implement within the PaleoIndian tradition as a whole.

In applying the model, it is convenient to arbitrarily divide the PaleoIndian tradition into initial, secondary, and tertiary stages. In the initial stage of development, there was a generalized "scraper" category which included a number of different kinds of implements, among them side scrapers and transverse scrapers. Each of these had its own potential for future adaptation. As indicated by the present analysis, Clovis would be included at the end of the this initial stage.

In the secondary stage, the potential inherent in transverse scraper was evidently found to be most adaptive to PaleoIndian needs and it became the predominant tool in the PaleoIndian tool kit, serving a wide variety of functions. In effect, it became a generalized transverse scraper, fundamentally a multipurpose tool. As a result of the increased use of this implement, modifications were introduced in order to more efficiently derive specific functions, and some specializations began to appear at this time, represented in the survey sample by the Folsom and Belen occupations.

Finally, the tertiary stage of development (represented by Cody) saw the diversification of the transverse scraper and the proliferation of specialized adaptive (functional) categories, thus completing the development in the PaleoIndian tradition of the transverse scraper from the general to the specific states. It can be postualted that the development did not stop there, but continued into the Archaic period. One of the tertiary stage transverse scraper types (possibly the distally rounded, unspurred hideworking scraper mentioned in the Cody sample) evidently held most adaptive potential for the Archaic needs, and it was retained in the tool kit. Further investigation along these lines might indicate that this tool in turn developed into a generalized multi-purpose Archaic tool from which later specialized types developed.

This model of tool development is presented here as having been suggested by the factor analysis of PaleoIndian transverse scrapers and is offered not as fact but as a working hypothesis which could be tested in the future as more data on PaleoIndian lithic technology are acquired. As further support for the model, an initial test will be presented here, based on the implement frequencies given in Table 2. Those frequencies were calculated on the basis of each culture's tool assemblage as a whole. For a more accurate test of the present model, it is necessary to separate the utility implements from the weapons, as shown in Table 23. This separation results in a "pure" represen-tation of utility implement variation through time in the PaleoIndian tradition, not influenced by variation in weaponry. Unfortunately, most of the Clovis data must be declared invalid (with the possible ex-ception of transverse and side scrapers) since one cannot generalize on the basis of such a small sample from one site.

302

Table 23: PaleoIndian Utility Implement Frequencies.

	Type	Clovis %	Folsom %	Belen %	Cody %	Total %
A.	**General Utility Tools:**					
	1. Transverse Scrapers	56.3	54.4	66.5	66.7	58.9
	2. Side Scrapers	34.4	14.1	14.8	10.9	14.4
	3. Knives	00.0	8.0	3.8	8.0	6.7
	4. Gravers	6.3	14.0	7.7	5.8	11.1
	5. Utility Flakes	00.0	6.0	2.4	2.8	4.5
B.	**Specialized Tools:**					
	1. Chisel Gravers	00.0	1.4	1.4	0.7	1.2
	2. Drills	3.1	0.4	00.0	2.2	0.6
	3. Spokeshaves	00.0	1.8	3.3	3.0	2.2
C.	Percentage of Utility Implements in Total Assemblage:					
	Percentage	74.4	69.8	84.7	82.2	74.7
	Number	32	566	209	138	945

The eight types of utility implements recovered by the survey have been further categorized into two basic groups, based on relative specialty of function. The first group, termed "general utility", includes transverse and side scrapers, knives, gravers, and utility flakes. The second group, "special tools", includes chisel gravers and drills (probably serving the same function), and spokeshaves.

A number of definite trends are shown by the data in Table 23. First of all, there is a general increase in the percentage of transverse scrapers through time, and this is accompanied by a general decrease in the frequency of other utility tools, with the exception of knives. This conforms generally to the expectations of the model, as the transverse scraper gains prominence in the tool assemblages. Furthermore, as the transverse scraper increasingly assumes the function of other utility tools and the latter decline in frequency, it can be expected that the specialized tool frequencies will become relatively more pronounced. This trend also is indicated in general terms in Table 23. The most aberrant feature of this test is the case of the Belen knives, which decrease markedly in frequency relative to Folsom and Cody. This is at present inexplicable, but it might be suggested that the use of the specialized Belen TR scraper may supplant somewhat the necessity for the separate manufacture of knives. This should be investigated in the future.

This test is by no means conclusive since the sample is relatively small and the Clovis data cannot be considered representative. It does indicate, though, that the model may be supported in the future following more extensive testing. I think that at even this inconclusive state it reveals an important consideration with respect to PaleoIndian lithic technology. This study has shown that there is considerable variation through time in the utility implement technology of the PaleoIndian tradition, as well as in the weaponry technology. Much of this variation has gone unnoticed in past studies of PaleoIndian assemblages, and where noticed, there has been a tendency to explain such variation with reference to changing subsistence patterns (Wendorf and Hester 1962:168-69). Although the latter is certainly a possibility, I do not feel that it is the only avenue of explanation. Much of the variation in the utility implement technology in the survey sample can be explained with reference to variations in transverse scraper technology as the adaptive potential of this implement was recognized and it became increasingly efficient functionally. I feel that documented variation of this type, if not offering the most reasonable explanation available, at least affords us one which cannot be discounted lightly.

Comparison of Settlement Technologies

Prior to discussing the variations in settlement technology per se, a brief summation of the PaleoIndian occupation of the survey area will be presented. A total of 59 PaleoIndian occupational loci were recorded in the survey. Of these, all but six could be assigned to one of the four cultures analyzed (Clovis, Folsom, Belen, Cody Complex). The six remaining consisted of five mixed or unclassifiable assemblages, and one possible pre-Folsom site (Table 1).

Those loci which yielded less than 2% of the total sample of a given culture were arbitrarily labeled "localities" rather than sites. Based on this criterion, 23 of the loci recorded were localities, leaving 30 sites which were subjected to intensive lithic and environmental analysis.

Regarding the question of the cultural significance of the Paleo-Indian localities, there is really no way to accurately determine their true nature until each can be tested through excavation, or at the minimum, continually rechecked for evidence of further deflation which might reveal more artifacts. The one exception to this is the single Clovis locality, which was found on the top of a very high and sharply defined mesa overlooking the central San Jose-Rio Puerco drainage area. This locality was undoubtedly a Clovis lookout station.

It was suggested previously that the PaleoIndian localities in general are loci of very limited cultural activity, the nature of which cannot be determined due to inadequate tool samples. Table 24 presents data on the comparison of the sites versus the localities with reference to their frequency of occurrence in each culture, and the

Table 24: Comparative Data: PaleoIndian Sites vs. Localities.[a]

A. Ratio of Number of Sites to Localities per Culture:

Culture	Sites		Localities		Total
	N	%	N	%	N
1. Folsom	15	51.8	14	48.2	29
2. Belen	9	69.1	4	30.8	13
3. Cody Complex	5	55.7	4	44.3	9
4. Total PaleoIndian	29	56.9	22	43.1	51

B. Comparison of Point-Scraper Ratio: Sites vs. Localities:

Culture	Projectile Points		Transverse Scrapers		Total
	N	%	N	%	N
1. Folsom					
Sites	117	27.6	308	72.4	425
Localities	18	45.0	22	55.0	40
2. Belen					
Sites	29	17.3	139	82.7	168
Localities	4	15.4	22	84.6	26
3. Cody Complex					
Sites	25	21.4	92	78.6	117
Localities	8	47.1	9	52.9	17

[a]Clovis omitted due to insufficient data.

projectile point-transverse scraper ratios. Clovis has been omitted from the table due to insufficient data.

Comparing the percentages of localities to the total occupational loci of each culture, it can be seen that Folsom and Cody are quite similar in this respect. Folsom localities comprise 48.2% of the total Folsom occupation, while 44.3% of the Cody loci are localities. Belen, however, has a much higher ratio of sites. Only 30.8% of the Belen loci are localities.

Section B of Table 24 compares the ratio of projectile points to transverse scrapers for the localities of each culture, and also gives the site ratios as a standard of comparison. Here again, the Folsom and Cody localities appear quite similar, both revealing a higher percentage of projectile points in the localities than in the sites. Belen, on the other hand, inverses this ratio, and shows a decrease in the percentage of points relative to the site frequency, although the decrease is minor. Thus although the comparison of sites and localities from these two standpoints does not reveal the cultural significance of the localities, it does point to the distinctiveness of the Belen localities, and it suggests that these may eventually prove to be functionally distinct from the other PaleoIndian localities. However, a review of the environmental data recorded for the Belen localities revealed nothing distinctive about them. One possible answer to this problem may be that the Belen localities are potential sites which have not yet deflated sufficiently to produce a significant artifact yield, while the majority

of the other PaleoIndian localities do in fact represent areas of limited

activity.

In reference to the total extent of PaleoIndian occupation of the

central Rio Grande valley, it was noted previously that in comparison

with PaleoIndian sites elsewhere in North America, this region pro-

duced a relatively low artifact yield per site. This fact itself suggests

the hypothesis that the occupation of the survey region by PaleoIndian

groups was simply not as extensive as elsewhere. Such an hypothesis

is supported by other data which can be discussed here briefly.

Extensive analysis of lithic technology and raw material utiliza-

tion of the excavated material at the Rio Rancho site led Dawson to

conclude that it was probably occupied by 3-5 small bands of hunters

for only a few weeks at a time (Dawson and Judge 1969:159-60).[6] Using

the implement frequencies from this excavated site as a guide, we

can estimate a maximum of 12 bands operating from Folsom base camps

in the survey area, each for only a few weeks at a time. This estimate

is based on 5 bands at 9CM3, 5 bands at 13GX5, and 2 bands at 12OA3.

Assuming one band at each of the other Folsom sites, we can add

another 12 bands, again for only a few weeks at a time. Thus the total

Folsom occupation of the area can be estimated at a maximum of 24

---

[6]It should be noted that in terms of artifact abundance, the Rio
Rancho site (9CM3) is the most prolific site dealt with in the survey
analysis.

bands. In all probability, the number of distinct bands was less than this, since the same band may have occupied more than one site, or the same site more than one time. This may compensate somewhat for the possibility that not all Folsom sites in the area were located by the survey.

In order to assess this occupation more accurately, an index of the intensity of band occupation can be calculated simply by multiplying the number of bands estimated, by the maximum time each could occupy a site (3 weeks, based on the Rio Rancho estimate). We can thus state that the total Folsom occupation of the sites located in the area can be represented as 72 "band-weeks". Presumably, the other PaleoIndian cultures would be in rough proportion to the Folsom estimate, as indicated by the site and artifact frequencies (Tables 1 and 2). This should not be taken as a final assessment, but instead as the most accurate extimate based on the data available. It is presented here only to permit comparison with data from outside the survey area.

Using this same index of occupation, the 7000 artifacts from the excavated portion of the Lindenmeier site would represent a total of 630 "band-weeks" of occupation. This is not to imply that this is an accurate figure for the Lindenmeier site either, since it may represent an entirely different type of settlement technology. It is offered solely as a basis of comparison. The magnitude of the differences involved-- 72 band-weeks for the entire survey area versus 630 band-weeks for the excavated portion of a single site in northern Colorado--more than

compensates for whatever errors might have been incurred in estima-

ting occupational intensity in either area.

Further support for the hypothesis of less extensive occupation

in the survey area is lent by environmental data derived from the sur-

vey itself. This is indicated by the relatively high frequency of suitable

site locations encountered which were found to be devoid of PaleoIndian

cultural evidence. These areas abound in playas, are broad and open,

and are all adjacent to either major or minor hunting areas. Although

surveyed, no evidence of sites or localities were found in these areas.

Furthermore, a number of locations outside the survey region offering

excellent potential for PaleoIndian site evidence were checked out and

no evidence was found. These locations were between Bernalillo and

Santa Fe. Although this may possibly be classified as negative evi-

dence, one would assume that if the occupation of the survey region

by the PaleoIndian groups were at all intensive, such areas exhibiting

excellent site potential would almost certainly have been occupied at

one time or another.

In conclusion, although a relatively large number of campsites

representing four major PaleoIndian cultural groups were located in

the survey region, the available evidence does not indicate that the

area was occupied as intensively as elsewhere on the Great Plains.

If the band-week estimates are at all accurate, it can be suggested

that the occupation of the region by these groups was of short duration,
possibly seasonal. It should also be noted at this point that the survey
region is characterized by restricted access, which might have resulted in a relatively rapid depletion of the local game population.
Thus in addition to possible seasonal occupation, the region may have
been avoided periodically due to lack of sufficient game.

With reference to the comparison of the various settlement technologies exhibited by the four PaleoIndian cultures, some of the environmental variables were found to be common to all. This permits the
definition here of a very generalized PaleoIndian settlement pattern.
All sites, for instance, were accessible to a source of water which
in some instances would have provided an attraction for game and water-
fowl in addition to satisfying the basic needs of drinking, hide-soaking,
etc. Futhermore, all the sites were within a relatively short travel
time of what has been termed herein a "hunting area"; a broad, open
area relatively unobstructed by sharp topographical relief, which
could have supported a large game population. Finally, all the sites
were found either at or near a location termed an "overview", that is,
a point relatively higher than the surrounding terrain which offered
a clear view of the hunting area. Thus the environmental variables
common to all the PaleoIndian sites were a water source, proximity
to a hunting area and an overview.

Some of the environmental conditions were not deemed essential by all PaleoIndian cultures for selection of campsite locations, and thus are not considered essential to the construction of a generalized settlement pattern. Among these were soil type, which seemed to make little difference in site selection, although it varied considerably from sandy clay to sharply fragmented lava. Another variable recorded, that of a potential game trap area in the vicinity, also did not seem to be an essential variable in site selection. Nor were the playas essential, except to one particular culture (Folsom). Finally, the particular direction from the site to the various environmental variables seemed of little importance except in a limited number of circumstances as, for instance, in the case of the Folsom orientation to the hunting area.

Thus of the many possible environmental requisites for the establishment of campsites, the PaleoIndian occupants of the survey area selected three which they considered essential as minimal requirements: water, overview, and hunting area. Of these, the necessity for water would certainly have been expected, but the overview-hunting area combination is to my knowledge unreported elsewhere. It is possible that this combination may have special reference only to the survey region, but it might prove beneficial to search for this pattern in other regions also.

The intensive analysis of each culture represented in the survey revealed a number of variations on this basic settlement pattern.

With the exception of Clovis, the settlement technology of each culture was expressed in a distinctive constellation of environmental variables, though all were maintained within the range of variation of the basic pattern. Again, we cannot generalize about Clovis settlement technology on the basis of a single site, so it will be omitted from the comparative analysis. The basic settlement technologies of Folsom, Belen, and Cody will be briefly reviewed prior to discussing the general trends in variation. The review is based on data provided in Tables 4 and 5, and the relevant analyses in Chapter 6.

1. Folsom:

The distinctiveness of the Folsom site pattern is based on the close proximity to water (both vertical and horizontal distance included), and the important role which the playa plays as a source of water. Folsom sites are, on the average, somewhat more distant from the overview than the Belen sites, and about the same distance as the Cody sites. With reference to the hunting area, the Folsom sites are on the average closer to this feature, which is generally of the major variety. There was also a strong tendency to locate the Folsom sites on the northern ends of these major hunting areas.

2. Belen:

The Belen sites are generally further from water than the Folsom sites, but most distinctive in the Belen pattern is the concern with the overview component. Belen exhibits the highest percentage of sites located at overviews, and the closest mean distance for those sites not at the overview. A unique feature here is a consistently flat landform selected for site location. Even those sites not on ridge tops were located on flat shelves on the ridge slopes. With reference to the hunting area, the Belen sites are slightly further away than Folsom, and somewhat more laterally located. Sites located near minor hunting areas outnumbered those near the major ones, indicating an increasing tendency to utilize the former.

3. Cody Complex:

Significant in the Cody pattern is the association with much more sharp topographical relief than that found in the other PaleoIndian patterns. This is most accurately reflected by the average distances to water, which were the highest of all cultures, and the distance to the hunting area, which was the furthest in the sample. Also in the case of Cody there is a strong de-emphasis of the playa as an environmental component. Most of the nearest sources of water were streams. The data on the overview variable are quite similar to that of Folsom, but this apparent similarity is conditioned considerably by the distinctive topography resulting from the increased distance to water and the hunting area in the case of the Cody sites.

Viewing the above settlement configurations as a temporal progression within the PaleoIndian tradition, several general trends emerge with respect to the water/hunting/overview pattern. First, there is a general progression from an emphasis on select locales with specific

relationships to a major hunting area (Folsom), to an increased distance from the hunting area with less concern for specific relationships
to it (Cody). Second, there is a general increase through time in the
distance to the nearest source of water, and the playa also becomes increasingly less important. Finally, there is a general increase in the
relative height of the sites, and an accompanying emphasis on the proximity to an overview situation.

These general trends defined by the variations in settlement technologies in the survey area should not be considered valid for generalization about the PaleoIndian tradition as a whole, since they are related
specifically to the environmental conditions present in the central Rio
Grande valley. However, some explanations can be offered about the
variations present here which may have bearing on the site situations
encountered elsewhere.

I would suggest that the key to the explanation of the intercultural
variation in settlement technology lies in the critical environmental
component of water. I am not referring to water here in the sense of
that required to satisfy immediate human needs. Humans can survive
at locations quite distant from water, as the numerous Archaic sites
in the area exemplify. However animals, specifically large gregarious
game animals, cannot get along well without a constant supply of water.
For instance under modern conditions, herbivores such as cattle cannot
survive in the grazing areas of the survey region without artificial

water supplies. The latter are found in the form of windmills, earth tanks, and in some cases, hauling water with tank trucks.

Assuming that in early PaleoIndian times environmental conditions were such that the playas were good sources of water, these same hunting areas could have supported numerous animals dependent upon the playas for water supply. The advent of such conditions would explain the Folsom ability to be quite selective in choosing those environmental variables most conducive to human encampment and game capture. By Cody times, however, the moisture situation might well have deteriorated to the extent that playas were no longer adequate sources of water for the animal population. The animals would in turn seek out areas located more closely to streams, rivers, and springs which would serve as reliable water sources. By the same token, human groups during Cody times would seek out areas near the game supply for their campsite locations. In fact, of the five Cody Complex sites, only one is located near a playa, and this is the aberrant 13DR4, unique in a number of other respects. All other Cody sites are near permenent sources of water which are still running today.

Belen sites might well represent an intermediate position. Playas evidently still contained water during Belen times, though perhaps only intermittently. The total impression one gets from analyzing the Belen settlement technology is one of an adaptation quite similar to that of Folsom, but with a less abundant supply of game. This situation might well obtain from a decrease in the amount of moisture, which would affect floral coverage, water availability, and ultimately the megafaunal population.

Although there is considerable debate over the nature and extent of the altithermal period (Antevs 1962, Martin 1963), there is little doubt that in general, post-glacial climatic conditions were somewhat drier than those of the terminal Wisconsin period. It is suggested here that the gradual change toward increasing dryness may explain much of the variation in PaleoIndian settlement technology within the survey area.

Finally it should be noted that subcultural variation in PaleoIndian settlement technology does exist and is documented in the cases of Folsom and Belen. More adequate data for Clovis and Cody would undoubtedly permit the recognition of intracultural variation in these cases also. For Folsom and Belen, base camps, armament camps, and processing camps have been defined on the basis of variations in activities performed as evidenced by specific articulations of select environmental and lithic components.

Both Folsom and Belen appear similar with respect to this subcultural settlement variation. Undoubtedly distinctions exist, but these are not immediately apparent at this very early stage in the attempt to understand PaleoIndian settlement technology. For both cultures, base camps indicate multiple activity, while the other two

represent activities of a more limited nature. Armament camps
are concerned primarily with the production of weaponry and are located in strategic overview situations. Processing camps emphasize
the activities of hide-working and weapon refurnishing, and are located
closer to sources of water.

It might be well to point out at this time the nature of some of
the problems confronting an investigation into the difference between
the Folsom and Belen subcultural settlement patterns. For instance,
the test of association between scraper wear and distance to water
(Tables 10 and 12) revealed a much higher chi-square value in the case
of the Belen data. Does this variation indicate a difference in settlement technology, or can it be explained on the basis of a general trend
toward increasing specialization of scraper function? The answers to
such questions will have to await the attainment of much more data on
both PaleoIndian settlement and lithic technology.

CHAPTER VIII

Summary and Conclusions

Summary

It was stated at the outset of this study that the specific respons-
ibility of the survey archeologist is the elucidation of archeological
problems. Minimally, this involves the fulfillment of three main
objectives: First, there must be an accurate description of the number
and types of sites represented in the survey region. Second the
data collected by the survey must be analyzed to the fullest extent
possible, and conclusions relevant to the explanation of cultural process must be drawn from this analysis. Finally, the survey archeologist is responsible for the delineation of major hypotheses applicable
to the orientation of further archeological research in the survey area,
or elsewhere that similar cultural manifestations might be encountered.

It is felt that the best method to achieve these goals is the investigation of what is here termed the "settlement technology" of the
cultures under analysis. Settlement technology, viewed analytically
as a subsystem of a cultural system, is considered the primary vehicle
of articulation between the total cultural system and its environment.
This is not a new view in anthropology, in fact the subsystem of
settlement technology is closely akin to what Steward (1955:37) termed

the "core" elements of a culture. Here it is felt that this subsystem is so basic to the dynamics of cultural process, that its intensive analysis will afford the most efficient method of interpreting the results of a regional survey.

The weakest point in survey archeology is the lack of adequate control over many of the contextual attributes of the data collected. Given this incumbrance, and the necessity to accurately define those archeological problems offering most promise of solution through further research, it is imperative that the survey archeologist utilize efficient analytic techniques. For this reason, the analytic survey model proposed herein has concentrated on the investigation of the settlement technologies of the archeological cultures represented. To support this, the various collection methods and analytic techniques employed were oriented toward a thorough recording and interpretation of the lithic and environmental components. The problem was approached through the formulation of a procedural model utilizing the theoretical and interpretative framework afforded by general systems theory.

Actual survey methodology involved the location of PaleoIndian sites, the collection of surface lithic material, the recording of the diverse environmental variables, and the intensive analysis of the recorded data. Sites were located by the application of a technique termed "site pattern recognition" to the interpretation of aerial photographs of the survey region. In addition, in order to compensate for biases inherent in this method of locating sites, a randomly selected sample portion of the region was surveyed intensively for further evidence of PaleoIndian sites.

Analytic techniques consisted of intensive analysis of the data at the intracultural level, followed by a comparative analysis of the similarities and differences exhibited between cultures. The procedural model employed for this analysis involved the successive application of several analytic steps at increasingly higher systemic levels. At each component level of analysis, the relevant variables were defined, their articulation examined, and those variables critical to the definition of a functional taxonomy isolated. This resulted in the most efficient method of realizing the maximum interpretative potential of the data, necessarily limited to surface collections and observations.

The region surveyed in this study is the central Rio Grande valley, approximately 3000 square miles in extent. In this area manifestations of 59 PaleoIndian occupational loci were recorded by the survey. Of these, 30 sites were considered productive enough in terms of lithic material to permit further analysis of a more intensive nature. PaleoIndian cultures represented by these sites included Clovis, Folsom, Belen, and Cody Complex. All of these except Belen are well-defined elsewhere in the Plains area. The Belen manifestation is

322

tentatively accepted here as a new type, primarily for purposes of analysis. It is most closely related to the Plainview/Midland/Milnesand subdivision of the generalized Plano category. Temporally, Belen was initially felt to have occupied a position between Folsom and Cody within the survey area. The results of the intensive analysis tend to confirm this estimate, although no absolute determination of the exact chronological position of Belen was possible with the data available.

A total of 1486 artifacts from the 30 sites were submitted to various types of analyses, both qualitative and quantitative. One implement category, that of the transverse scrapers, was factor analyzed to permit a cross-cultural assessment of changes in lithic technology. In addition, recorded data on 18 attributes relevant to the environmental component were analyzed to determine the essential features in the subsystem of settlement technology for each culture. The major results of this study can now be summarized:

No evidence of Sandia campsites were revealed by the survey, although Sandia cave lies immediately east of the survey area. No explanation of this anomaly is apparent at this time, and the existing Sandia data remain an enigma which begs clarification through further study.

The earliest cultural evidence from the region itself was that of Clovis. One Clovis site and one locality were found, indicating either

a very small Clovis occupation, or perhaps a site pattern on the part
of Clovis which has not yet been fully recognized.

The next culture to occupy the valley was Folsom, which yielded
by far the highest number of sites. Fifteen Folsom sites and 14 Folsom localities were recorded in the survey. Another site, labeled here
"proto- Folsom" was the only Folsom-like site which did not correspond closely to the "classic" Folsom typology common to the Plains
area. It was suggested that this proto- Folsom site might be included
in a widespread Clovis- Folsom transitional stage which may well
have originated in eastern North America.

Following Folsom in the survey area were Belen and Cody Complex cultures, and all indications point to the chronological separation
of these two. Nine Belen sites and four localities were located, making
it second in total number of sites. A total of five Cody Complex sites
and four localities were found, all of which were of the Eden variety.

In terms of site frequency then, the order of cultural manifestations from most to least numerous is Folsom, Belen, Cody, and Clovis.
It was suggested that this order represents in gross terms the intensity
of occupation of the central Rio Grande valley by each of the listed
cultures.

The lithic material derived from the surface collections of each
of the 30 sites was analyzed intensively in terms of two separate categories; weaponry (including preforms and projectile points), and

utility implements (all other tools). This intensive analysis involved the treatment of each implement or weapon category as a component of the subsystem of lithic technology, and its analysis in terms of the inessential, essential, and key variables responsible for its functional placement in the lithic subsystem. Only the projectile points and transverse scrapers provided sufficient data to permit quantified analysis, but the other implements were discussed with respect to their relationship to these two key components.

The results of the analysis of weaponry revealed a number of considerations not previously noted in PaleoIndian studies. First, the projectile point analysis showed that for all cultures, the width of the base of the point was a more critical attribute than the thickness of the base. This was determined by examining the ranges of variation exhibited by various attributes of the projectile point bases, as measured by the coefficient of variation of each. Of all the attributes examined, that of the depth of the basal concavity was the least critical, i.e., it exhibited the most variation.

Further analysis was conducted to determine the manner in which the critical variable of basal or hafting width was achieved by each culture. It was found that the Clovis and Belen samples manifested heavy lateral abrasion of those bases which were above average in width. Folsom and Eden did not exhibit a significant correlation in this respect, thus it was concluded that the fine pressure retouch exhibited by the latter two types compensated for the heavy grinding on the part of Clovis and Belen in achieving the acceptable range of variation in basal width.

This analysis led to the formulation of an hypothesis regarding the hafting techniques utilized by PaleoIndian groups. This will be explained here, and then reiterated later as an hypothesis suitable for future testing in other PaleoIndian studies. Basically, the critical attribute of basal or hafting width is seen as indicating that these points were being produced and modified to fit into something, presumably a socket type foreshaft. The latter would have been made of bone, or some other material more difficult to shape than stone. Thus the points were being fitted to the foreshaft, rather than vice versa. It was suggested that this indicates a PaleoIndian weapon system quite distinct from that known to have been used in the Archaic period. In the latter system, the notched point was rigidly fixed to a wooden foreshaft by sinew binding, and this combined unit was easily removable from the main shaft socket. If a point were broken, a new foreshaft with an affixed point was inserted in the mainshaft.

On the other hand, the evidence for the PaleoIndian system suggests that the point itself was considered the removable unit, and that grinding of the lateral edges was to facilitate the easy insertion and removal of the point bases into the bone foreshaft. The latter may or may not have been rigidly fixed to the main shaft; the significant thing is that the points were removable, and in the event of breakage, a new point was simply inserted into the foreshaft. This permitted the use of a heavy bone foreshaft which was probably necessary to achieve sufficient penetration power for use on big game. Had the point been rigidly fixed to the foreshaft as in the Archaic system, numerous fore-shaft-point units would have to have been carried with the hunter. Due to the amount of work involved in shaping bone, this system would have been quite inefficient. It was permitted in Archaic times only by the use of a wooden, rather than bone, foreshaft, presumably as a result of an adaptation to smaller game.

Verification of this hypothesis would explain a number of enigmas in PaleoIndian weaponry; among them, the reason for lack of notching of PaleoIndian points, the function of the lateral grinding, and the increased length of such points relative to those of later cultures. It also strongly suggests that within the generalized PaleoIndian tradition, variations in projectile point typology will eventually become explicable in terms of variations in the types of foreshafts utilized. Differences either in the kind of bone selected, or in the species of animal used, or both, might account for variation in this latter dimension. The one exception to this may well be the Folsom situation, which herein is seen as a highly specialized adaptation oriented toward the most effi-cient utilization of lithic source material.

Analysis of the utility implements focused primarily on the transverse scrapers (endscrapers), since these were by far the most abundant of all artifacts recovered in the survey. Other implements comprising the PaleoIndian tool kits were side scrapers, knives, gravers, chisel gravers, drills, spokeshaves, and utility flakes. The latter category (utility flake) was offered as a new PaleoIndian tool type which serves the multipurpose functions of basic graving, scraping, and cutting needs. All utility tools were examined microscopically to determine wear patterns, and on this basis it was suggested that the chisel graver, a specialized implement found in PaleoIndian assemblages, may frequently have been utilized as the functional equivalent of a drill. All the other tools exhibited wear patterns expected by their classification.

With reference to the transverse scrapers, these were divided into four analytic categories based on the degree of lateral modification: unmodified (TU), left or right modified (TL, TR), and bilaterally modified (TB). These analytic types seemed to work well for all PaleoIndian cultures with the possible exception of Cody. The TU and TB types were the most frequently used in all assemblages, except for Belen where the TR was substituted for the TB type. Selection was made for the production of these scraper types on the basis of core (dorsal) facet angle, which was determined to be the key variable in transverse scraper modification. Those flakes exhibiting a low angle (high profile) were generally left unmodified, while those of a high angle (low profile) were usually modified along one or both of the lateral edges.

With respect to these basic categories of transverse scrapers, it was found that considerable variation occurred between the cultures examined. The frequency of occurrence of the TU and TB types varied considerably, as did the wear patterns associated with each of these types. In addition, no consistent pattern could be determined regarding the association of these scraper types with the production of projectile points in terms of raw material utilization. Such variation is as yet unexplained, but presumably can be clarified through further analysis of more complete PaleoIndian lithic assemblages.

However, the degree of variation exhibited by the transverse scrapers did prompt further investigation at the intercultural level. A sample of 235 scrapers from all cultures was submitted to a computerized factor analysis in order to define the nature of the diachronic variation in utility tool technology, and if possible isolate the variables primarily responsible for such change. The results of this analysis suggested that much of the intercultural variation in transverse scraper technology could be explained in terms of a generalized model of utility implement development through time. In other words, though some of the variation undoubtedly resulted from specific response to variations in the lithic subsystem environment, much of it could be attributed to internal adjustments within the utility implement subsytem as the adaptive potential of the transverse scraper was recognized and exploited by the various PaleoIndian groups.

Made explicit, the implement development model recognizes a progression from a generalized to a specialized state in terms of artifact function, analogous to similar developments in biological or cultural evolution. In the survey case, Clovis is seen to exhibit a generalized "scraper" category, comprising both side and transverse scrapers. Each of these categories was relatively specialized functionally for Clovis, as indicated by the transverse scraper wear patterns. By Folsom times, however, the adaptive potential of the transverse scraper as a multipurpose implement had been recognized and it was treated as a generalized category in itself. Following this, we see evidence of the gradual specialization of the transverse scraper in the Belen assemblage. By Cody times, production techniques were being altered to produce functionally specialized transverse scrapers. This is offered as an explanation for the lack of correspondence of the previously acceptable analytic types to the Cody scraper assemblage.

It is felt that this model of implement development might be useful in helping explain variations in lithic technology which occur at the macro-temporal scale. Its value lies chiefly in the realm of utility implements, since these reflect change much more subtly than do the artifacts associated with weaponry.

The analysis of the environmental data collected on the 30 sites
resulted in the formulation of a generalized PaleoIndian settlement
pattern for the survey area. This pattern involves the articulation of
three major environmental components: a "hunting area" or broad,
open area of minimal topographical relief which was capable of
supporting large numbers of herbivorous animals; a source of water
for both the game and the human elements, frequently occurring in the
form of a playa; and an "overview," or ridge near the site, from which
an unobstructed view of the hunting area was afforded. These three
components--water/overview/hunting--were found to be the key variables in the general PaleoIndian settlement pattern. It should be
pointed out that with the exception of the hunting feature, Wendorf and
Hester (1962:166) recognized a roughly similar pattern in the Llano
Estacado. This pattern was generally confirmed and further refined
by the present study.

Analysis of the two most numerous cultural manifestations
(Folsom and Belen) indicated the existence of subcultural variation in
settlement technology. Three basic variations on the general theme
were encountered and defined as base camps, armament sites, and
processing sites.[1] Wilmsen (1967:151) has distinguished between

[1]Since subcultural variation in settlement pattern is previously
unreported in the PaleoIndian literature, I offer this terminology on a
tentative basis only, pending the acceptance of terms which more suit-
ably describe the activities represented and thus more accurately define these settlement types.

"limited activity locations" and "multiple activity locations" at the inter-cultural level in the PaleoIndian stage. This distinction is followed herein at the subcultural level and is buttressed considerably by con-sistency in the patterning of environmental and lithic components at each of the settlement types. I have termed as "base camps" those multiple activity locations which in the survey sample yield evidence of either extended occupation or a wide variety of activities. Loci of more limited activity were defined either as "armament sites," which were evidently associated with preparations for a hunt, or "processing sites," which involved post-hunt hide preparation and weapon renewal. The key variables involved in the differentiation between the two types of limited activity loci are 1) type of scraper wear (hard, soft), 2) the mean distance to the overview, and 3) the mean distance to the nearest source of water. A chi-square test of association among these variables reached significant levels in both of the cultures tested; soft scraper wear was associated with proximity to water, and hard scraper wear with proximity to an overview. Unfortunately, neither the Clovis nor the Cody Complex manifestations in the survey area yielded sufficient data to permit the assessment of subcultural variation in either of their respective settlement technologies.

Campbell (1968:18) has pointed out that based on observations of modern Eskimos, the settlement patterns of early hunting groups may be far more complex than those discernible from the archeological

data. This is undoubtedly true, yet I feel that by paying closer attention to the interpretative potential afforded by the limited data which is
available, we will at least be able to approach an understanding of this
admittedly complex situation. For instance, even though significant
distinctions exist with respect to environment and technological levels,
I feel there may be broad parallels between Campbell's Type I settlements and the base camps defined herein, between his Type III settlements (hunting/fishing camps) and the armament sites, and finally
between the processing sites and his non-food collecting (Type IV)
settlements (cf. Campbell 1968:15-19).

In addition to the subcultural distinctions existing for Folsom and
Belen, further variations in settlement technology were found when
a comparative analysis at the intercultural level was undertaken.
Basically, the analysis of the variation exhibited by the general patterns
of Folsom, Belen, and Cody reflects a settlement adaptation on the
part of each to a faunal water source. As the post-glacial period of
dessication gradually progressed, the herbivorous fauna evidently
became less reliant upon playas as permanent sources of water, and
were forced to depend increasingly on streams, rivers, and springs.
This is manifest culturally by the Folsom selection of locations near
playas and the major hunting areas early in the period, and much later
by Cody's selection of site locations near streams and springs. Belen
occupies an intermediate position in this respect, possibly exploiting

the playas as intermitten water sources only. Unfortunately, we cannot generalize about Clovis, represented by a single site, but it should be pointed out that the environmental variables exhibited by this Clovis site do conform to the situation which would be expected in pre-Folsom times.

Conclusions

The goals of this survey were first to explain cultural process to the extent permitted by the data, and secondly to offer hypotheses relevant to problem orientation of future analysis or research. The general conclusions offered below are based on explanations resulting from analyses presented in the foregoing chapters. These will be followed by a statement of the major hypotheses formulated for future testing.

Intensive analysis of the systems trajectories responsible for the production of Clovis and Folsom points revealed two distinct techniques in the preparation of the preform for fluting and the ensuing removal of thinning flutes. Further comparative analysis of other projectile point attributes indicated that Clovis shares a number of similarities with the Belen projectile point type. When the distinction in fluting between Clovis and Folsom is given adequate consideration, and when all other attribute values are compared, it is apparent that Clovis may well be as close typologically to Belen as it is to Folsom.

This leads to the view subscribed to here that Clovis may well represent a very generalized base from which a number of lanceolate projectile point types developed--not just Folsom alone. Furthermore, there is just as much, if not more, difference between Belen and Cody as there is between Folsom and Clovis, yet the former are generally lumped into a single generalized Plano tradition, while the latter two are separated. This is simply inconsistent, and I would suggest that an alternative view might be more logical: Clovis served as a general base for a lanceolate point tradition which emphasized rather thin points in relation to basal width. Among the later points in this tradition are those such as Plainview, Midland, Milnesand, and Belen, presently considered part of the Plano tradition. Folsom represents a related but highly specialized form within this Clovis-based tradition. On the other hand, the very distinctive Cody material might well represent the developed stage of a different tradition which emphasized thick point bases in relation to width. Earlier types within this tradition might include the Alberta, Hell Gap, and Agate Basin types, and ultimately leaf-shaped points from the Pacific Northwest (cf. Bryan 1965:50).

Regardless of the final placement of these various types within the proper traditions, it has been suggested here that the most rational approach to solving the typological problems of the PaleoIndian stage is through a system based primarily on hafting techniques, as shown by the analysis of the critical variables of projectile points presented in this study. Furthermore, the results of the analysis of associated utility implements tend to confirm this, at least with respect to those PaleoIndian cultures represented in the survey area.

Although generalizations are frequently made on the basis of projectile point typology, I do not believe we have yet arrived at the degree of sophistication in PaleoIndian studies that we can afford to make statements such as the following: . . . "we know for certain that the Folsom Fluted point developed from the Clovis form, a development which occurred in a relatively circumscribed area of eastern New Mexico, eastern Colorado, eastern Wyoming, and the immediately adjoining territories of bordering states" (Willey 1966:42). Much more work is necessary before the places of origin of any of the PaleoIndian point types can be pinpointed with such accuracy.

Fundamentally, the question of PaleoIndian cultural development is not one of determining whether Clovis or some other archeological manifestation is the earlier in terms of an absolute chronology. The problem most significant to students of cultural process is whether the PaleoIndian big-game hunting tradition, as manifest by the "classic" early Plains cultures, is basically a New World development or an Old World development. Ultimately, of course, all PaleoIndian cultures have roots in the Old World, but it remains to be seen how much of this distinctive tradition can be attributed to indigenous development.

Resolution of this problem need not await the acquisition of more data. By careful analysis of the available material we can determine the processes of change which took place with respect to known variables. With such information we can more informatively construct hypotheses relevant to the origin of the PaleoIndian, and test these with respect to the data available on earlier cultures in both North America and Northeastern Asia. In this manner, the problem of PaleoIndian indigenous development will eventually be resolved.

With regard to settlement technology, the fundamental hypotheses stated at the outset of this study were verified empirically. Variations in PaleoIndian settlement technology do exist, both at the subcultural and intercultural levels. A considerable amount of change through time was demonstrated in the general settlement pattern, and this was explained as primarily a function of an adaptation to a faunal water source, which varied with changing climatic conditions. This suggests that we must review carefully, and perhaps modify, such statements as that by Wendorf and Hester who conclude that during the period under consideration, "the types of sites, site situations, hunting techniques, butchering techniques, and most of the tool inventory of the Paleo-hunters remained constant" (1962:169).

The foregoing study has dealt in some depth with the concept of technology as the primary intervening variable between a cultural system and its environment. Yet I feel one of the conclusions must be that it is misleading to discuss technology in general without close regard for the details of the actual technologies involved. Utility implement technology, while related to weapon technology, may also vary somewhat independently with respect to internal change in the subsystem itself, as suggested herein by the model of implement development. Thus, though variation in the faunal water source may well be the primary environmental stress causing change in the PaleoIndian settlement subsystem, we must be cautious in attempts to derive all change (including that of utility tools) from this source. In short, the technology of a culture is no less complex than any of the other subsystems which comprise it.

In order to satisfy the second goal toward which the present study was directed, the following hypotheses are offered as a guide for future problem-oriented research either within the survey area, or in other regions where similar PaleoIndian manifestations occur:

1. "Major variations in PaleoIndian projectile point typology are primarily explicable with reference to differences in hafting techniques."

This hypothesis assumes the validity of the use of a bone foreshaft in combination with a removable projectile point in the PaleoIndian weapon system. It can be most reliably tested

through careful analysis of bones which are consistently found

to be missing in the kill sites of the various PaleoIndian cultures,

and/or further analysis of the metric attributes of projectile

points derived from a much broader geographical base.

2.   "A considerable part of the variation observed in the utility

      implement types and frequencies between various Paleo-

      Indian cultures can be explained with reference to the

      development of the transverse scraper from a generalized

      to a specialized implement. "

This can be tested through the utilization of more sophisti-

cated analyses of the function of all implements, and more

intensive analysis of transverse scrapers based on a broader,

more inclusive sample which would include data from kill sites

as well as campsites.

3.   "Subcultural variations in settlement technology can be ex-

      plained with reference to the selection of different arrays

      of environmental components for the differential per-

      formance of cultural activities. "

This was shown to have validity within the survey area, but

needs to be tested elsewhere to determine whether the particu-

lar patterns exhibited here are peculiar to, and thus a function

of, the central Rio Grande geomorphology.

4. "Within the central Rio Grande valley, the PaleoIndian
    multiple activity locations (base camps) are directly re-
    lated to the sites of limited activity (armament and
    processing sites), indicating synchronic occupation of
    these loci by individual social units."

The verification or rejection of this hypothesis is crucial
to the ultimate understanding of the demographic and social nature
of the PaleoIndian occupation of the survey area. It can be
tested only by actual excavation of selected sites with special
attention paid to the derivation of accurate contextual attributes
of the lithic material, followed by extensive analysis of these
data with the intent of verifying site relationships as suggested
in the present study. At the moment, there is no reliable evidence which would indicate whether this hypothesis will eventually
be accepted or rejected.

5. "The primary source of variation in intercultural change
    of PaleoIndian settlement technology derives from an
    adaptation to a faunal water source which changed con-
    siderably as a result of climatic variation during the
    PaleoIndian period."

This hypothesis is acceptable with respect to the central Rio Grande valley, but it must be tested elsewhere to insure that it is not simply a function of the specific ecological situation peculiar to the survey area.

The resolution of these hypotheses is felt to be extremely relevant to understanding the nature of the PaleoIndian occupation of the central Rio Grande valley much more thoroughly than is possible through the survey analysis alone. Ultimately, they bear directly on a more adequate understanding of the PaleoIndian tradition in general, as manifest throughout North America. It is hoped that the presentation of these hypotheses, as well as the information derived from the present study, will facilitate the task of those interested in more intensive work in the PaleoIndian field in the future.

LITERATURE CITED

Agogino, George A.
1961   A New Point Type from Hell Gap Valley, Eastern Wyoming. American Antiquity 26:588-560.

Agogino, G. A. and W. D. Frankforter
1960   A Paleo-Indian Bison Kill in Northwestern Iowa. American Antiquity 25:414-415.

Agogino, G. A. and F. C. Hibben
1958   Central New Mexico Paleo-Indian Cultures. American Antiquity 23:422-425.

Agogino, G. A. and I. Rovner
1964   Palaeo-Indian Traditions: A Current Evaluation. Archaeology 17:237-243.

Anell, Bengt
1969   Running down and driving of game in North America. Studia Enthographica Upsaliensia XXX. Lund: Berlingska Boktryckeriet.

Antevs, Ernst
1949   Geology of the Clovis Sites. In "Ancient Man in North America," by H. M. Wormington. Denver Museum of Natural History, Popular Series 4:185-192.

1962   Late Quaternary Climates in Arizona. American Antiquity 28:193-198.

Baker, Ele M.
1968   Belen: A Paleo-projectile Point Type from the Middle Rio Grande Basin. Paper read at the 33rd. Annual Meeting, Society for American Archeology. Santa Fe, New Mexico.

Benfer, Robert A.
1967   A Design for the Study of Archeological Characteristics. American Anthropologist 69:719-730.

Binford, Lewis R.
1962   Archeology as Anthropology. American Antiquity 28:217-225.

Binford, Lewis R.
1964   A Consideration of Archeological Research Design. American Antiquity 29:425-441.

1967   Comment. In "Major Aspects of the Interrelationship of
Archeology and Ethnology, " by K. C. Chang. Current
Anthropology 8:234-235.

Binford, L. R. and S. R. Binford
1966   A Preliminary Analysis of Functional Variability in the
Mousterian of Levallois Facies. American Anthropologist
68:238-295.

Binford, Sally R.
1968   Ethnographic Data and Understanding the Pleistocene. In
Man the Hunter. R. B. Lee and I. DeVore, eds. Chicago:
Aldine.

Binford, Sally R. and L. R. Binford, eds.
1968   New Perspectives in Archeology. Chicago: Aldine.

Bliss, Wesley L.
1948   Preservation of the Kuaua Mural Paintings. American
Antiquity 13:218-222.

Bordes, Francois
1952   Stratigraphie du loess et evolution des industries Paleo-
lithique dans l'ouest du Bassin de Paris. L'Anthropologie
56:405-452.

Bryan, Alan L.
1965   Paleo-American Prehistory. Occasional Papers of the
Idaho State University Museum, No. 16.

Buckley, Walter, ed.
1968   Modern Systems Research for the Behavioural Scientist.
Chicago: Aldine.

Campbell, John M.
1968   Territoriality Among Ancient Hunters: Interpretations
from Ethnography and Nature. In Anthropological Archeology in the Americas. Washington, D. C.: The Anthropological Society of Washington.

Cattell, Raymond B.
1965 Factor Analysis: An Introduction to the Essentials (Parts 1 and 2). Biometrics 21.

Clarke, David L.
1968 Analytical Archaeology. London: Methuen.

Clisby, Kathryn H. and P. B. Sears
1956 San Augustine Plains--Pleistocene Climatic Changes. Science 124:537-539.

Cohen, Yehudi A.
1968 Culture as Adaptation. In Man in Adaptation: The Cultural Present. Y. A. Cohen, ed. Chicago: Aldine.

Cowgill, George L.
1968 Archeological Applications of Factor, Cluster, and Proximity Analysis. American Antiquity 33:367-375.

Crabtree, Don E.
1966 A Stoneworker's Approach to Analyzing and Replicating the Lindenmeier Folsom. Tebiwa 9:3-39.

Crabtree, D. E. and B. R. Butler
1964 Notes on Experiments in Flint Knapping: 1, Heat Treatment of Silica Minerals. Tebiwa 7:1-6.

Crabtree, D. E. and E. L. Davis
1968 Experimental Manufacture of Wooden Implements with Tools of Flaked Stone. Science. 159:426-428.

Dawson, Jerry
1967 The Rio Rancho Folsom site. Paper read at the 32nd Annual Meeting, The Society for American Archeology. Ann Arbor, Michigan.

Dawson, Jerry and W. J. Judge
1969 Paleo-Indian Sites and Topography in the Middle Rio Grande Valley of New Mexico. Plains Anthropologist 14:149-163.

Dick, Herbert W.
1943 Alluvial Sites of Central New Mexico. New Mexico Anthropologist 25:19-22.

Driver, Harold E.
  1965   Survey of Numerical Classification in Anthropology. In
          The Use of Computers in Anthropology. Dell Hymes, ed.
          The Hague: Mouton and Co.

Driver, H.E. and K.F. Schuessler
  1957   Factor Analysis of Ethnographic Data. American Anthro-
          pologist 59:655-663.

Edwards, Allen L.
  1967   Statistical Methods. (2nd. Edition) New York: Holt,
          Rinehart and Winston.

Fisher, Reginald D.
  1930   The Archeological Survey of the Pueblo Plateau. University
          of New Mexico Bulletin, Archeology Series 1.

Fitting, J.E., J. DeVisscher, and E.J. Wahla
  1966   The Paleo-Indian Occupation of the Holcombe Beach.
          Anthropological Papers, Museum of Anthropology, Uni-
          versity of Michigan, No. 27.

Flannery, Kent V.
  1968   Archeological Systems Theory and Early Mesoamerica.
          In Anthropological Archeology in the Americas. Washington,
          D.C.: The Anthropological Society of Washington.

Freeman, Leslie G., Jr.
  1968   A Theoretical Framework for Interpreting Archeological
          Materials. In Man the Hunter. R.B. Lee and I. DeVore,
          eds. Chicago: Aldine.

Frisbie, Theodore R.
  1967   The Excavation and Interpretation of the Artificial Leg
          Basket-Maker III - Pueblo I Sites near Corrales, New
          Mexico. Unpublished M.A. Thesis, University of New
          Mexico.

Frison, George C.
  1967   The Piney Creek Sites, Wyoming. University of Wyoming
          Publications 33:1-92.

Green, F.E.
  1961   Geologic Environment of Pollen Bearing Sediments. In
          Paleoecology of the Llano Estacado. F. Wendorf, ed.
          Santa Fe: Museum of New Mexico Press.

Green, F.E.
1963   The Clovis Blades: An Important Addition to the Llano
        Complex. American Antiquity 29:145-165.

Hall, A.D. and R.E. Fagen
1968   Definition of System. In Modern Systems Research for
        the Behavioral Scientist. W. Buckley, ed. Chicago: Aldine.

Harris, A.H. and J.S. Findley
1964   Pleistocene-Recent Fauna of the Isleta Cave, Bernalillo
        County, New Mexico. American Journal of Science 262:
        114-120.

Haynes, C. Vance, Jr.
1964   Fluted Projectile Points: Their Age and Dispersion.
        Science 145:1408-1413.

1966   Geochronology of late Quaternary Alluvium. Interim
        Research Report, Geochronology Laboratories, University
        of Arizona, No. 10.

Haynes, C.V. and G.A. Agogino
1960   Geological Significance of a New Radiocarbon Date from
        the Lindenmeier Site. Denver Museum of Natural History
        Proceedings, No. 9.

Heizer, R.F. and J.A. Graham
1967   A Guide to Field Methods in Archeology. Palo Alto: The
        National Press.

Hibben, Frank C.
1937   Association of Man with Pleistocene Mammals in the
        Sandia Mountains, New Mexico. American Antiquity 2:
        260-263.

1941   Evidences of Early Occupation in Sandia Cave, New Mexico,
        and Other Sites in the Sandia-Manzano Region. Washington,
        D.C.: Smithsonian Miscellaneous Collections 99:1-44.

1943   Discoveries in Sandia Cave and Early Horizons in the
        Southwest. Proceedings of the American Philosophical
        Society 86:247-254.

1951a   Sites of the Paleo-Indian in the Middle Rio Grande Valley.
        American Antiquity 17:41-46.

Hibben, Frank C.

    1951b   A Survey of the Sites of the Paleo-Indian in the Middle Rio
                Grande Valley, New Mexico. Texas Journal of Science
                3:362-367.

    1955   Specimens from Sandia Cave and Their Possible Signifi-
                cance. Science 122:688-689.

    1966   A Possible Pyramidal Structure and Other Mexican Influ-
                ences at Pottery Mound, New Mexico. American Antiquity
                31:522-529.

Hole, Frank and R.F. Heizer

    1969   An Introduction to Prehistoric Archeology. (2nd. Edition)
                New York: Holt, Rinehart, and Winston.

Honea, Kenneth

    1965   A Morphology of Scrapers and Their Methods of Production.
                Southwestern Lore 31:25-40.

    1969   The Rio Grande Complex and the Northern Plains. Plains
                Anthropologist 14:57-70.

Humphrey, Robert L.

    1966   The Prehistory of the Utakok River Region, Arctic Alaska.
                Current Anthropology 7:586-588.

Irwin, Henry T.

    1968   The Itama: Early Late-Pleistocene Inhabitants of the Plains
                of the United States and Canada and the American Southwest.
                PhD. Dissertation, Harvard University.

Irwin, Henry T. and H.M. Wormington

    1970   Paleo-Indian Tool Types in the Great Plains. American
                Antiquity 35:24-34.

Irwin-Williams, Cynthia

    1967   Picosa: The Elementary Southwestern Culture. American
                Antiquity 32:441-457.

Jelinek, Arthur J.

    1962   The Use of the Cumulative Graph in Temproal Ordering.
                American Antiquity 28:241-243.

Jelinek, Arthur J.
1966   Some Distinctive Flakes and Flake Tools from the Llano
        Estacado. Papers of the Michigan Academy of Science,
        Arts, and Letters 51:399-405.

Johnson, LeRoy Jr.
1967   Toward a Statistical Overview of the Archaic Cultures of
        Central and Southwestern Texas. Texas Memorial Museum,
        Bulletin No. 12, Austin.

Judge, W. James
1968   A Quantitative Analysis of PaleoIndian Endscrapers. Paper
        read at the 33rd. Annual Meetings, The Society for Amer-
        ican Archeology. Santa Fe, New Mexico.

1970   Systems Analysis and the Folsom-Midland Question. South-
        western Journal of Anthropology, In Press.

King, J.E.
1964   Modern Pollen Rain and Fossil Profiles, Sandia Mountains,
        New Mexico, M.S. Thesis, University of New Mexico.

Kottlowski, F.E.
1967   Rocks that Shape the Enchanting Landscape. In Mosaic of
        New Mexico's Scenery, Rocks, and History. P.W. Chris-
        tiansen and F.E. Kottlowski, eds. Socorro: New Mexico
        Bureau of Mines and Mineral Resources.

Kottlowski, F.E., M.E. Cooley, and R.V. Ruhe
1965   Quaternary Geology of the Southwest. In The Quaternary
        of the United States. H.E. Wright, J R. and D.G. Frey,
        eds. Princeton: Princeton University Press.

Leopold, Luna B.
1951   Pleistocene Climate in New Mexico. American Journal
        of Science 249:152-168.

Luhrs, Dorothy L.
1937   Observations on the Rio Puerco of the East. El Palacio
        42:126-134.

MacDonald, George F.
1968   Debert: a Palaeo-Indian Site in Central Nova Scotia.
        Anthropology Papers, National Museum of Canada, No. 16.

Martin, Paul S.
    1963   The Last 10,000 Years. Tucson: University of Arizona
           Press.

Martin, P.S. and P.J. Mehringer, Jr.
    1965   Pleistocene Pollen Analysis and Biogeography of the
           Southwest. In The Quaternary of the United States. H.E.
           Wright and D.G. Frey, eds. Princeton: Princeton Uni-
           versity Press.

Martin, P.S. and H.E. Wright
    1967   Pleistocene Extinctions: The Search for a Cause. Yale
           University Press.

Mason, Ronald J.
    1958   Late Pleistocene Geochronology and the Paleo-Indian Pene-
           tration Into the Lower Michigan Peninsula. Anthropological
           Papers, Museum of Anthropology, University of Michigan,
           No. 11.

    1962   The Paleo-Indian Tradition in Eastern North America.
           Current Anthropology 3:227-278.

Mason, R.J. and Carol Irwin
    1960   An Eden-Scottsbluff Burial in Northeastern Wisconsin.
           American Antiquity 26:43-57.

McGuire, J.U., Lehman, R.P., and A.L. Heath
    1967   Tables of Exact Probabilities for 2 x 2 Contingency Tests.
           Agricultural Research Service, Bulletin ARS 20-15. U.S.
           Government Printing Office.

Miller, James G.
    1965   Living Systems: Basic Concepts. Behavioral Science
           10:193-237.

Plog, Fred T
    1968   Archeological Surveys: A New Perspective. M.A. Thesis,
           University of Chicago.

Prufer, Olaf H.
    1962   Survey of Ohio Fluted Points, No. 8. Cleveland: Cleve-
           land Museum of Natural History.

    1963   Survey of Ohio Fluted Points, No. 9. Cleveland: Cleve-
           land Museum of Natural History.

Prufer, Olaf H. and R. S. Baby
    1963   Paleo-Indians of Ohio. Columbus: The Ohio Historical
            Society.

Reinhart, Theodore R.
    1968   Late Archaic Cultures of the Middle Rio Grande Valley,
            New Mexico. PhD. Dissertation. University of New
            Mexico.

Richmond, Gerald M.
    1965   Glaciation of the Rocky Mountains. In The Quaternary of
            the United States. H. E. Wright and D. G. Frey, eds.
            Princeton: Princeton University Press.

Roberts, Frank H. H. Jr.
    1935   A Folsom Complex, Preliminary Report on Investigations
            at the Lindenmeier Site in Northern Colorado. Smithsonian
            Miscellaneous Collections 94(4).

    1936   Additional Information on the Folsom Complex: Report on
            the Second Season's Investigations at the Lindenmeier Site
            in Northern Colorado. Smithsonian Miscellaneous Collec-
            tions 95 (10).

    1937   New Developments in the Problem of the Folsom Complex:
            Explorations and Fieldwork at the Smithsonian in 1936.
            Smithsonian Publications, No. 3407:69-74.

Roosa, William B.
    1956a Preliminary Report on the Luch Site. El Palacio 63:36-49.

    1956b The Lucy Site in Central New Mexico. American Antiquity
            21:310.

    1968   Data on Early Man Sites in Central New Mexico and Michi-
            gan. PhD. Dissertation, University of Michigan.

Ross, Ashby, W.
    1963   An Introduction to Cybernetics. London: Chapman and
            Hall.

Rovner, I. and G. A. Agogino
    1967   An Analysis of Fluted and Unfluted Folsom Points from
            the Blackwater Draw. The Masterkey 41:131-137.

350

Ruppe, Reynold J.
　1966　The Archeological Survey: A Defense. American Antiquity
　　　　31:313-333.

Sackett, James R.
　1966　Quantitative Analysis of Upper Paleolithic Stone Tools.
　　　　American Anthropologist 68:356-394.

Sahlins, M.R. and E.R. Service, eds.
　1960　Evolution and Culture. Ann Arbor: University of Michigan
　　　　Press.

Sawyer, Jack and R.A. Levine
　1966　Cultural Dimensions: A Factor Analysis of the World
　　　　Ethnographic Sample. American Anthropologist 28:356-394.

Sellards, E.H.
　1952　Early Man in America: A Study in Prehistory. Austin:
　　　　University of Texas Press.

　1955　Fossil Bison and Associated Artifacts from Milnesand, New
　　　　Mexico. American Antiquity 20:336-344.

Semenov, S.A.
　1964　Prehistoric Technology. New York: Barnes and Noble.

Spaulding, Albert C
　1953　Statistical Techniques for the Discovery of Artifact Types.
　　　　American Antiquity 18:305-331.

　1960　Statistical Description and Comparison of Artifact Assem-
　　　　blages. In The Application of Quantitative Methods in
　　　　Archeology. R.F. Heizer and S.F. Cook, eds. Viking
　　　　Fund Publications in Anthropology 28:60-83.

Steward, Julian
　1955　Theory of Culture Change. Urbana: University of Illinois
　　　　Press.

Streuver, Stuart
　1968　Problems, Methods and Organization: A Disparity in the
　　　　Growth of Archeology. In Anthropological Archeology in
　　　　the Americas. Washington, D.C.: The Anthropological
　　　　Society of Washington.

Tugby, Donald J.
1965   Archeological Objectives and Statistical Methods: A
        Frontier in Archeology. American Antiquity 31:1-16.

Warnica, James M.
1966   New Discoveries at the Clovis Site. American Antiquity
        31:345-357.

Warnica, James M. and T. Williamson
1968   The Milnesand Site--Revisited. American Antiquity 33:
        16-24.

Weber, Robert H.
1967   Before Coronado. In Mosaic of New Mexico's Scenery,
        Rocks, and History. P. W. Christiansen and F. E.
        Kottlowski, eds. Socorro: New Mexico Bureau of Mines
        and Mineral Resources.

Weber, Robert H. and G. A. Agogino
1968   Mockingbird Gap Paleo-Indian Site: Excavations in 1967.
        Paper read at the 33rd. Annual Meeting, The Society for
        American Archeology. Santa Fe. New Mexico.

Wendorf, Fred
1961   A General Introduction to the Ecology of the Llano Estacado.
        In Paleoecology of the Llano Estacado. F. Wendorf, ed.
        Santa Fe: Museum of New Mexico Press.

Wendorf, F., A. D. Krieger, C. C. Albritton, and T. D. Stewart
1955   The Midland Discovery. Austin: University of Texas Press.

Wheat, Joe Ben
1967   A Paleo-Indian Bison Kill. Scientific American 216:44-62.

White, Anta M.
1963   Analytic Description of the Chipped-Stone Industry from
        Snyders Site, Calhoun County, Illinois. In "Miscellaneous
        Studies in Typology and Classification," A. M. White, et.
        al. Anthropological Papers, Museum of Anthropology,
        University of Michigan, No. 19.

White, A M., L. R. Binford, and M L. Papworth
1963   Miscellaneous Studies in Typology and Classification.
        Anthropological Papers, Museum of Anthropology, Uni-
        versity of Michigan, No. 19.

White, Leslie A.
    1959   The Evolution of Culture. New York: McGraw-Hill.

Weiner, N.
    1948   Cybernetics. New York: John Wiley and Sons.

Willey, Gordon R.
    1966   An Introduction to American Archeology, Volume 1: North
           and Middle America. Englewood Cliffs: Prentice-Hall.

Wilmsen, Edwin N.
    1967   Lithic Analysis and Cultural Inference: A Paleo-Indian
           Case. PhD. Dissertation, University of Arizona.

Wormington, H. Marie
    1957   Ancient Man in North America. (4th Edition) Denver
           Museum of Natural History, Popular Series 4.

Wormington, H.M. and R.G. Forbis
    1965   An Introduction to the Archeology of Alberta, Canada.
           Denver Museum of Natural History, Proceedings, No. 11.

Wright, H.E. Jr.
    1946   Tertiary and Quaternary Geology of the Lower Rio Puerco
           Area, New Mexico. Geological Society of America,
           Bulletin 57:383-456.

INDEX

Abo Canyon, 29
Activities: female-associated, 207, 209; male-associated, 205-08 passim
Agate, 143. See also Chalcedony, Rio Grande
Agogino, George A., 78; and Frankforter, 76, 77; Haynes and, 66; and Hibben, 43; and Rovner, 66; Rovner and, 172
Alamo Muerto site, 44
Albuquerque, N.M., 25, 29, 44
Albuquerque Gravel Pit site, 36
Analysis: collective, 275-77; factor, 295; intercultural, 257-318 passim; techniques for, 273, 274
Anasazi, 25
Anasazi Origins Project, 44, 78
Animals, game, 315. See also individual species
Antelope, 40
Antevs, Ernst, 39, 317
Antler haft, 251
Archaic: cultures, 56, 57, 81, 145; period, 9, 25, 41, 77, 265, 301; sites, 43, 62, 315
Archeological survey, defined, 8-9
Archeology: fundamental goal of, 23; specific goals, summarized, 337-39
Archeology, survey. See Survey archeology; Archeological survey
Arctic, the, 82
Arizona, 47, 75
Arrowheads, 81
Arroyo. See Trap area
Arroyo Cuervo Region, 44
Artifacts: analyses of, 322; Belen, 210-24; Bone, 156; Clovis, 222, 247; Cody Complex, 242-43; Folsom, 164, 188-90, 198, 222; functional components, 151-60;

morphological components, 149-51; PaleoIndian, 43, 65, 138; production of, 145-49. See also Primary technology; Secondary technology
Artificial Leg sites, 25
Ashby, Ross, 11 n2
Asia, northeastern cultures, 336
Assemblages: Archaic, 57, Basketmaker II, 57; Belen, 71, 96, 97, 211-22 passim, 228, 242, 246; Clovis, 242, 254-55, 256; Cody Complex, 235-43 passim; Folsom, 89, 96, 97, 100, 103, 104, 112-15 passim, 166, 188-89, 192, 204, 227, 242, 246; Lindenmeier, 103; lithic, 91, 146; PaleoIndian, 56, 89, 106-08 passim, 143-45 passim, 189
Atlatl hook, 84
Avifauna, 40

Baby, R. S., 6
Bajada, occupation, 42, 145
Baker, Ele M., 43, 45, 48, 51 n2, 54, 69, 176, 214, 216
Basalt, 57, 144, 235
Basecamps, 207, 209, 210, 317-18, 330-31; Belen, 234; Folsom, 199-201 passim; as multiple activity locations, 205
Basketmaker, 62. See also Assemblages
Bear, 35
Belen occupation, 69, 71, 115; comparative analysis, 257-318 passim; cultural analysis of, 210-35; dated, 72; summary of, 333-39 passim. See also Projectile points, individual sites
Belen sites, 69, 80, 212, 217, 224-26 passim; armament, 230-33 passim; processing, 230-33 passim

Survey archeology: defined, 7; limitations of, 9, 320; objectives, 319; procedural model, 320-21
Survey method, 8, 19-23 passim; primary purpose, 7; secondary purpose, 7. See also Site pattern recognition; Survey archeology; Survey model
Survey model, 161; analytic techniques, 137-42

Tahoka Pluvial, 39
Taxon, functional, defined, 138
Taxonomies: analytic, 140; folk, 141; functional, 140, 141
Techniques, survey, 5
Technology, blade, 255
Technology, tertiary, 153-56
Technology, working definition, 2. See also Lithic technology; Settlement technology
Tertiary Age: deposits, 31; geomorphology during, 30
Texas, 274
Tijeras Canyon site, 29, 142
Tool assemblage: Archaic, 301; Cody Complex, 240-42 passim; Folsom, 158, 176, 191, 198, 201, 203-04, 208; PaleoIndian, 93, 115-20 passim, 243
Tools: as indication of mobility, 192-93; multipurpose, 209; tips, burned, 112-15
Trajectory, defined, 12
Transverse scrapers, 112, 140, 152, 153, 155, 204, 243, 246, 267-304 passim, 324, 327-29 passim; Belen, 217-23 passim; classifications, 93; Clovis, 252-55 passim; Cody Complex, 240-42; defined, 91; Folsom, 77, 154, 159-60, 178-88, 190, 191, 197-98, 203, 217; function, 93; morphology, 92; PaleoIndian, 91
Trap area, as environmental component, 127-29, 136, 193-97 passim, 255-27 passim, 245, 312-15 passim
Tugby, Donald J., 159; on quanti-

tative technique, 273
Typology, 138-39

United States Geological Survey, maps by, 54
University of New Mexico, 35; computing center, 159; Department of Anthropology, 43, 159; excavations by 42, 44. See also Maxwell Museum of Anthropology
U.S.G.S. See United States Geological Survey
Utility flakes, 108-110, 189, 190, 191, 327; construction of, 110; functions, 110
Utility implements, 242, 253, 324, 337; analysis of, 327-29 passim

Variables. See components
Vernon, Frank, 43
Volcanoes, Pleistocene, 30
Vulcanism, 30

Warnica, James M., and Williamson, 69, 215
Water, as environmental component, 120-25, 193-97 passim, 203, 205, 226, 228, 311-15 passim
Weapon assemblage, 85; production, 205, 233; renewal, 204, 209, 234, 318
Weaponry, 156, 323, 329; analysis of, 324
Wear patterns, 328. See also Hard-wear; Soft-wear
Weber, Robert H., 39, 45, 75, 143 n1, 160, 255
Weiner, N., 11 n2
Wendorf, Fred, 32, 40; and Hester, 34, 36, 37, 43 n2, 48, 66, 75, 103, 240, 243, 304, 330; quoted, 336
Wheat, Joe Ben, 84, 128
White, Anita M., 151; Binford and Papworth, 112
White, Leslie A., 2
Willey, Gordon R., 335
Williamson, T., Warnica and, 69, 215

Wilmsen, Edwin N., 65, 98, 154, 205; on limited and multiple activity locations, 330-31
Wisconsin (state), 77
Wisconsin, Age, 31-32, 33, 37, 38. See also Glaciation
Wisconsin, ice sheet: See Ice sheet, Wisconsin
Wisconsin maximum. See Tahoka Pluvial

Wolf, 36
Womsley, 43
Woods, 145; silicified, 57
Wood shaping, 221
Wormington, H. Marie, 56, 65, 71, 74, 138, 157, 174, 238; Irwin and, 81, 93, 96, 101, 103, 107, 108, 254
Wright, H. E., Martin and, 40-41
Wyoming, 34, 335